Exploring Postc⟨
Biblical Critic⟨

Exploring Postcolonial Biblical Criticism

History, Method, Practice

R. S. Sugirtharajah

WILEY-BLACKWELL

A John Wiley & Sons, Ltd., Publication

This edition first published 2012
© 2012 R. S. Sugirtharajah, with the exception of Chapter 3 © 2012 Blackwell Publishing Ltd.

Blackwell Publishing was acquired by John Wiley & Sons in February 2007. Blackwell's publishing program has been merged with Wiley's global Scientific, Technical, and Medical business to form Wiley-Blackwell.

Registered Office
John Wiley & Sons Ltd, The Atrium, Southern Gate, Chichester, West Sussex, PO19 8SQ, United Kingdom

Editorial Offices
350 Main Street, Malden, MA 02148-5020, USA
9600 Garsington Road, Oxford, OX4 2DQ, UK
The Atrium, Southern Gate, Chichester, West Sussex, PO19 8SQ, UK

For details of our global editorial offices, for customer services, and for information about how to apply for permission to reuse the copyright material in this book please see our website at www.wiley.com/wiley-blackwell.

The right of R. S. Sugirtharajah to be identified as the author of this work has been asserted in accordance with the UK Copyright, Designs and Patents Act 1988.

Library of Congress Cataloging-in-Publication Data
Sugirtharajah, R. S. (Rasiah S.)
  Exploring postcolonial biblical criticism : history, method, practice / R.S. Sugirtharajah.
    p. cm.
  Includes bibliographical references (p.   ) and indexes.
  ISBN 978-1-4051-5856-5 (hardcover : alk. paper) – ISBN 978-1-4051-5857-2 (pbk.: alk. paper)
1. Bible–Postcolonial criticism. I. Title.
  BS521.86.S84 2012
  220.601–dc22

                                                                    2010044404

A catalogue record for this book is available from the British Library.

This book is published in the following electronic formats: ePDFs 9781444396638; Wiley Online Library 9781444396652; ePub 9781444396645
Set in 10.5 on 13.5 pt Palatino by Toppan Best-set Premedia Limited
Printed in Singapore by Ho Printing Singapore Pte Ltd
1   2012

Contents

Contents

vi

Acknowledgments

I am very grateful to Rebecca Harkin for commissioning this book and for her patience, her understanding and especially her enthusiasm for this project. Like my previous books, this too has benefited from Dan O'Connor's wisdom and guidance, but more importantly from his forcing me to rethink and rewrite. I owe huge thanks to Ralph Broadbent for providing an important chapter in this volume. My heartfelt thanks also to Lorraine Smith for her support and encouragement. Finally, my thanks to my wife Sharada, without whom none of my writing projects would have been possible. All that I can say about her is to repeat the words of the unknown Oriental sage: "Many women have done excellently, but you surpass them all."

Introduction

I tried to tell myself that the answers were irrelevant, that the questions had to be asked differently.[1]

When I was a student, biblical studies was a mild and a minor discipline. It meandered along with its own business which nobody outside the discipline took any notice of. Occasionally there were minor disputes, such as the Matthean priority which questioned the traditional conjecture that Mark was the first gospel, or the doubting of the authenticity of the resurrection narratives. In between these disputes, it was simply a case of academics recycling the nineteenth-century historical questions or of biblical scholars reverentially quoting each other's work. But this cozy world was succeeded by a state of upheaval and confusion in the 1980s. This was caused by reading practices informed by Marxism, feminism, and African-American and Third World interpretation. These new methods energized biblical studies. The proliferation of methods

Exploring Postcolonial Biblical Criticism: History, Method, Practice, First Edition.
R. S. Sugirtharajah.
© 2012 R. S. Sugirtharajah, with the exception of Chapter 3 © 2012 Blackwell Publishing Ltd.
Published 2012 by Blackwell Publishing Ltd.

and the pluralization of voices resulted in the emergence of a semi-autonomous subfield of studies within the larger rubric of biblical studies.

One of the new reading practices which made a difference was postcolonial criticism. For those of us who were from the former colonies and taught by missionary scholars, and who were tired of interacting with Western agendas, the arrival of postcolonial criticism came as an act of emancipation from the tyranny of Western biblical scholarship. These Western reading strategies grew out of nineteenth-century Europe's rationalism and pietism and were not of the remotest interest to us in any of our hermeneutical quests. Before the advent of postcolonialism, some of us were like the character in M.J. Vasanji's novel *No New Land*, going through "battle by battle" and reliving "all their battles" and "spiritual struggles." Postcolonial criticism enabled us for the first time to frame our own questions rather than battling with somebody else's. It provided us with a new set of conceptual tools to investigate the text and interpretation. This volume is the story of how a critical theory which emerged in the secular humanities departments entered the arena of biblical studies.

Postcolonial biblical criticism is basically about posing its question differently to the biblical narratives and to the manner in which they have been interpreted. It approaches texts with the same kind of questions as any other critical practice: "What is a text?"; "Who produced it?"; "How is its meaning determined?"; "How is it circulated?"; "Who interprets it?"; "Who are the beneficiaries of the interpretation?"; "What were the circumstances of the production?"; "Does a text have any message?"; "If so, what sort?" Like historical criticism, postcolonialism is committed to a close and critical reading of the text. But there are crucial differences. While both mainstream biblical criticism and postcolonialism pay attention to the context of the text, one concentrates more on the history, theology, and religious world of the text, the other on the politics, culture, and economics of the colonial milieu out of which the texts emerged. One is about revealing the kingdom of god and its implications for the world, and the other is about unveiling biblical and modern empires and their impact. One focuses on justification by faith for individuals, the other on the freedom of subjected nations; one uplifts the prophetic writings which are largely against other cultures, the other prefers the Book of Proverbs, an amalgam of international wisdom sayings. When mainstream biblical critics pose their questions to the text, they are driven by Reformation and Enlightenment agendas. When those who are not shaped exclusively by Western cultural norms employ postcolonialism, their approach is not necessarily motivated by a European ecclesiastical or intellectual agenda. Essentially, postcolonial biblical criticism is about exploring who is entitled to tell stories and who has the authority to interpret them.

My aim is not to resolve tensions, arguments, and disputes surrounding postcolonial theory, or to frame its ideas, issues, and concepts in a more sophisticated way. That task is well beyond the scope of this volume. My objective ultimately lies not only in critiquing both ancient and modern colonialism, but also in spelling out what kinds of hermeneutical approaches are possible, and how to be vigilant when politicians and commentators speak of a new imperium and scholars revert to Oriental practices in their writings. The hope of the volume is not simply to identify, describe, and analyze marks of colonialism in scholarly discourse, but to understand the past in order to assess the present and be alert.

About the Contents of the Volume

The first chapter, "Postcolonialism: Hermeneutical Journey through a Contentious Discourse," is an attempt at providing a brief history of the emergence of postcolonialism. In addition to this, the chapter narrates the main concerns and preoccupations of postcolonialism and its innovative contribution to reading practices such as contrapuntal reading. This chapter not only traces and records more recent forms of colonialism but also considers how postcolonial theory itself has moved on since its inception. The chapter ends with highlighting the theory's flaws and achievements.

The major focus of the second chapter, "The Late Arrival of the 'Post': Postcolonialism and Biblical Studies," is the mapping of the historical factors which paved the way for the advent of postcolonialism in biblical studies. It sets out the major marks of postcolonial biblical criticism and its major thrusts. This chapter also addresses the awkward question of the colonizing tendencies enshrined in the Bible and the complicated story of the unsavory association between biblical studies and colonialism.

Chapter 3, "Postcolonial Biblical Studies in Action: Origins and Trajectories," surveys some of the leading biblical scholars who work in the area of postcolonialism, their working practices, and the important texts that emerged during the period. It also examines the context and the contents of empire studies, especially in the US, and the interaction between postcolonialism and feminism. This chapter is written by Ralph Broadbent.

Chapter 4, "Enduring Orientalism: Biblical Studies and the Repackaging of Colonial Practice," has two related aims. One is to argue that biblical studies should be placed within the parameters of Oriental studies. The contention of the chapter is that the geographical focus, the culture, and the texts that biblical studies deal with make the discipline an ideal candidate to be part of Oriental studies. Second, the chapter provides examples of how current biblical studies, especially popular books written for mass audiences by those who practice social-scientific criticism, regurgitate some of the discredited and questionable characteristics of Orientalism in their exegetical and commentarial practices.

Chapter 5, "Postcolonial Moments: Decentering of the Bible and Christianity," recounts the two important postcolonial moments that happened during the halcyon days of colonialism: the publication of *The Sacred Books of the East* in 1879 and the Parliament of Religions held in Chicago in 1893. Both had deep implications for Christian theology and biblical interpretation. The chapter highlights how the publication of the religious texts of the East challenged the unique beliefs of the Bible. It also recalls how the delegates from the East used the occasion of the Parliament to blame and shame the West for its moral failures. The strategy they used

4

involved the very Orientalism constructed by the West. The chapter also discusses the differences between the resistance that happened during the colonial period and the oppositional stance of the current postcolonialism.

Chapter 6, "The Empire Exegetes Back: Postcolonial Reading Practices," provides examples of how to read the biblical texts from a postcolonial perspective. The first example utilizes the contrapuntal method, a method which has come to be associated with postcolonialism as its own distinguished contribution, to read the birth narratives of two masters – the Buddha and Jesus. The second example makes use of Edward Said's "late style" to understand the writing of two of the most interesting and complicated New Testament authors – Paul and John. Late style, a method that Edward Said proposed near the end of his life, was about comprehending the dramatic changes one finds in the late works of writers, or in artists when they arrive at a position which is completely different from the one they held earlier in their career. The third example is about the rhetoric of representation, and as a case study it looks at the Parable of the Rich Man and Lazarus and investigates how the rich and the poor are represented in the parable and the ideological biases which undergird the subsequent interpretations of the parable.

The Afterword, "Postcolonial Biblical Criticism: The Unfinished Journey," brings the volume to a close by asking whether postcolonialism will have any future or just fade away like other critical practices. The contention of this chapter is that postcolonial critical practices will have a role to play as long as a culture thinks of itself as superior to others; as long as markets are there to be exploited; as long as sacred texts sanction conquest; and as long as people assume that they are chosen to carry out god's special task. The chapter also provides some markers for the next step in postcolonial biblical criticism.

The merit of the volume lies not only in its registering of the faults and failures of imperialists and missionaries, but also in recording the hermeneutical habits of nationalists who pressed into action some of the classical patterns of Orientalism and turned these into a convenient weapon to meet various hermeneutical and political needs. Sometimes they appropriated that very Orientalist message in order to recover their identity and repair their culture, battered by colonial and missionary onslaughts. At other times they were simply imitating the standard rhetoric of Orientalism as a suitable way to get approval and recognition from the West.

Readers who are used to inclusive language may find some of the quotations from the nineteenth- and twentieth-century writers offensive. I have left them as they are to indicate the type of thinking that prevailed at that time.

Let me end with a quotation from Crispin Salvador, a character in Miguel Syjuco's novel *Illustrado*. It comes out of a Filipino context, so substitute Filipino with Indian or Chinese or Nigerian. Similarly, instead of Tagalog, insert Sankrit or Mandarin or Swahili. Salvador's words could act as a warning against, a manifesto for, or a caricature of postcolonial criticism and those who engage with it:

> What is Filipino writing? Living on the margins, a bygone era, a loss, exile, poor-me angst, postcolonial identity theft. Tagalog words intermittently scattered around for local color, exotically italicized. Run-on sentences and facsimiles of Magical Realism, hiding behind the disclaimer that we Pinoys were doing it before the South Americans.[2]

Notes

1. Shashi Tharoor, *The Great Indian Novel* (New Delhi: Penguin, 1989), p. 379.
2. Miguel Syjuco, *Ilustrado* (New York: Farrar, Straus and Giroux, 2010), p. 207.

1

Postcolonialism
Hermeneutical Journey through a Contentious Discourse

Too much theory and not enough literature. What do I know about "terror" and the "colonial encounter"?[1]

I came to theory because I was hurting ... Most importantly, I wanted to make the hurt go away. I saw in theory then a location for healing.[2]

The British government's Home Office has recently produced a booklet *Life in the United Kingdom* – a booklet which is essential reading for those who wish to apply for British citizenship. Let me quote a passage from the booklet to illustrate how the prospective candidates are informed about the British empire:

> However for many indigenous peoples in Africa, the Indian sub-continent, and elsewhere, the British Empire often brought more regular, acceptable and impartial systems of law and order than many had experienced under their own rulers, or under alien rulers

Exploring Postcolonial Biblical Criticism: History, Method, Practice, First Edition.
R. S. Sugirtharajah.
© 2012 R. S. Sugirtharajah, with the exception of Chapter 3 © 2012 Blackwell Publishing Ltd.
Published 2012 by Blackwell Publishing Ltd.

other than European. The spread of the English language helped unite disparate tribal areas that gradually came to see themselves as nations. Public health, peace and access to education, can mean more to ordinary people than precisely who are their rulers.[3]

What this supposedly peaceful and progressive colonial history fails to disclose to the soon-to-be British citizens is the other face of imperialism – the atrocities committed by the empire. Apart from calling the Atlantic slave trade an "evil," the Home Office's version of colonial history is silent about the unsavory aspects of the empire.

There are four tyrannical "isms" which have played a dominant role in recent history: fascism, communism, racism, and colonialism. In the vanquisher's version of history, two of these "isms" – fascism and communism – are projected as heinous crimes. Since it was the West which had a major role in bringing down the cruel regimes and ending the atrocities of Hitler and Stalin, fascism and communism are seen as inhuman and unparalleled in human history. To this, the crimes of other despots – China's Mao, Cambodia's Pol Pot, North Korea's Kim Il-sung, and Ethiopia's Mengistu – are also added. But when it comes to colonialism, there is a willful amnesia and a moral blindness. For most of the last century, many countries in Africa, Asia, and the Caribbean were under the governance of Western nations which never fail to remind others of their proud liberal and democratic credentials. But the atrocities of colonialism are not given equal attention to those of Nazism and communism. There are works on Nazism which record the evil committed by those who pursued this ideology. Then there is the highly acclaimed *Black Book of Communism: Crimes, Terror, Repression* by a group of European academics which tries to catalogue the murders, tortures, extrajudicial killings, deportations, and artificial famines faced by those under communist rule. The report of the Truth and Reconciliation Commission deals with the question of apartheid in South Africa. There has, however, been no similar comprehensive documentation or condemnation of the colonial record except for sporadic disapproval of slavery. The question which the late Edward Said posed is still a valid one: "We allow justly that the Holocaust has permanently altered the consciousness of our time: why do we not accord the same epistemological mutation in what colonialism has done, and what Orientalism continues to do?"[4]

To revert to the Home Office's booklet, this citizenship exam is likely to be taken not only by those who were part of the former British colonies but also by those who were affected by British imperial adventures in China, Afghanistan, Iraq, and Somalia. The booklet maintains a total silence about the British imperial buccaneering in these regions: the Opium Wars caused by the British attempt to force the drug on China; the three Afghan Wars where the British were trying to impose their authority and will; the British occupation of Mesopotamia (Iraq) from 1918 to 1958 and the brutal suppression of several national uprisings; and the violent restraint of the Dervish uprising in Somalia. In the colonies themselves, in Kenya for example, the Mau Mau uprising resulted in thousands of detainees dying as a result of starvation, torture, exhaustion, and disease in the "British gulags" organized well before Guantanamo Bay and Abu Ghraib. Then there are examples of the British gassing the Kurds, and the massacre of the Malaysian communists by the Scots Guards. Besides these political atrocities, there were disasters created entirely by willful political and commercial decisions. For example, millions died in the famine in India between 1876 and 1908, which Mike Davis calls a "Victorian holocaust" – a misfortune caused not by the weather but by a mixture of British insensitivity and free-market ideology. These misdeeds were not exclusive to the British empire. In the early 1900s, nearly 10 million Congolese died because of the forced labor and mass murder by the Belgian government, while during the 1960s, when Algerians fought for their independence, nearly a million of them died at the hands of French forces.

The Home Office's booklet and current commentators, politicians, historians, and theologians talk about the benefits that came in the wake of modern colonialism, such as the railways, the rule of law, and education. But they conveniently forget the tyranny, torture, poverty, desolation of lands, and destruction of cultures that accompanied the empire. If you look at places like Sudan, Iraq, Afghanistan, Kashmir, Palestine, and Sri Lanka, where conflict is raging, a close scrutiny will reveal that the cause of the conflicts goes back to colonial administrative mismanagement and policies. These are stains on the seductive story of the British empire's civilizing mission which its sympathizers would prefer to overlook. The current advocates of humanitarian intervention conveniently write out these colonial atrocities.

Also omitted from the Home Office's booklet are any references to the "native" resistance to the empire except for a brief passing comment about the growth of "liberation or self-government movements" in India in the 1930s. The booklet also notes that the British did not try to impose Christianity on India, which prompts the comment that "the English tolerance of different national cultures in the United Kingdom itself may have influenced the character of their imperial rule in India."[5]

The litany of British imperial misdemeanors is recalled not to apportion blame or to induce guilt feelings, but as a reminder that along with all well-meaning measures like health, education, transport, law and order, and parliamentary democracy, there were also brutality and intolerance. The purpose of this rehearsal is not to impose and judge an earlier generation by contemporary values but to recognize that the past is problematic and that it cannot be reduced to one tidy version. To phrase it differently, the empire is not a straightforward story of success, as the apologists want to portray it, but a complicated ensemble of atrocity and generosity.

I started with the Home Office document to demonstrate how totalizing forms of knowledge production are at work, and the need for a critical revision. Postcolonial criticism offers such a rereading. Its utility lies in its ability to question both the idea of colonialism as a structure of economic exploitation and profit, and the idea of colonialism as a structure of systematic gathering of reliable knowledge about the colonized.

Postcolonialism: A Compendious History

This book is mainly aimed at readers who are interested in postcolonial biblical criticism. Before we look at that, a brief note about the status of postcolonialism as a field of inquiry. Its arrival, its historical reach (where does colonialism start? Columbus's voyage?), its geographical scope (should one include settler colonies like Australia?), and the range of responses varying from antagonism to appreciation that the term "postcolonial" has invoked, have been competently documented in various anthologies and therefore there is no need for me to repeat them here.[6] What I propose to do in the rest of the chapter is to recall some key events and issues related to postcolonialism which have relevance to biblical studies. Postcolonial critical approaches first made their mark in the humanities, especially in English literature departments in the 1980s and mainly on British and American campuses, and made an impact which was contentious, to say the least. Postcolonial theory developed from a variety of sources, critical traditions, and historical experiences such as anti-colonial resistance writings, Marxism, feminism, psychoanalysis, and poststructuralism.

It is worth remembering that postcolonialism did not begin its career in the academy. Before postcolonialism became a potent scholarly discourse in the Western academies, there was a variety of anti-colonial practices which were later incorporated into the discourse as connected to and consonant with what is now known as postcolonial criticism. It had a lengthy, heterogeneous, and complicated history before it made its mark nearly two decades after the end of formal colonialism. The critique of colonialism was initiated by two sets of people – activists and creative writers – who participated in anti-colonial struggles and reflected on them. The current theory owes an intellectual debt to theorist-activists, such as Frantz Fanon, Aimé Césaire, Albert Memmi, and C.L.R. James, whose resistant writings and strategies were energized by colonial racism and Marxist thinking. Novelists like Chinua Achebe, Wole Soyinka, and Ngũgĩ wa Thiong'o in their writings explored colonial prejudices concerning African peoples and the cultural havoc caused by the introduction of Christianity to the continent. To this initial list of novelists, which was confined to Commonwealth countries under British control, other theoreticians and creative people were added when postcolonialism was expanded to include the Spanish, the Portuguese,[7] the French,[8] and the current superpower, the USA.[9] Robert Young, in his near-encyclopedic history of postcolonialism, has found historical and theoretical significance in Irish, Algerian, negritude, and pan-African liberation movements which were absent in the earlier literature.[10]

The text which is often credited with the inauguration of postcolonialism is Edward Said's *Orientalism*. This book produced a cluster of disciplinary approaches, and among them were postcolonialism and colonial discourse analysis. It is worth remembering that Edward Said, in his lifelong pursuit of the study of literature, rarely used postcolonialism as a mode of inquiry. In an interview he called it a "misnomer." Abstract theories did not enthuse him. In the same interview, he said that he "was always trying to gear [his] writing not towards a theoretical constituency but towards a political."[11] For a systematic analysis, his preferred term was "secular criticism." What he was dismissive of was the vacuous and notably tedious and at times unreadable stuff which passed for high theory and not the sort of postcolonial political and cultural concerns that he championed in his life. To the writings of Edward Said, one could add the works of Homi Bhabha[12] and Gayatri Spivak[13] who were in a way responsible for providing a theoretical and much less readable framework.

Any critical theory which has "post" as its prefix is not easy to pin down, and its definition remains unsettled. Postcolonialism is no exception. Postcolonialism, as a term, has both historical and theoretical nuances. In one sense, as an expression, it marks the formal decline of Western territorial empires. On the other, as a theory, it has several functions: (a) it examines and explains especially social, cultural, and political conditions such as nationality, ethnicity, race, and gender both before and after colonialism; (b) it interrogates the often one-sided history of nations, cultures, and peoples; and (c) it engages in a critical revision of how the "other" is represented.

Postcolonialism is largely an intellectual and political pursuit and has unashamedly a committed stance. Unlike other theoretical categories, it is not too preoccupied with detachment and neutrality. It emerged from both indigenous and diasporic contexts. Its critical stance is a creative adoption of the practical insights gleaned from those involved in anti-colonial and neo-colonial struggles and the theoretical tools and perspectives gained from a wide variety of disciplines. This includes a combination of clashing and contradictory voices from literary theory, philology, psychology, anthropology, political science, and feminist studies, with a view to exposing the collusive nature of Western historiography and its hidden support for imperialism. It is an attempt to explore the often one-sided, exploitative, and collusive nature of academic scholarship.

Right from its inception, postcolonialism has functioned as a political indicator and a literary critical tool. One of the least troublesome ways to describe postcolonialism is to recall the words of John McLeod. For him, it is an exploration of "the inseparable relationship between history and culture in the primary context of colonialism and its consequences."[14] To put it at its simplest: it is about the impact created by Western colonization on individuals, communities, and cultures. As with all theoretical practices, the purpose and serviceability of postcolonialism have changed over the years. In the initial stages Homi Bhabha, one of the triumvirate who were at the forefront in shaping the theory, wrote that the aim of postcolonialism was to

> intervene in those ideological discourses of modernity that attempt to give a hegemonic "normality" to the uneven development and the differential, often disadvantaged, histories of nations, races, communities, peoples. They formulate their critical revisions around issues of cultural difference, social authority and political discrimination in order to reveal the antagonistic and ambivalent movements within the "rationalizations" of modernity.[15]

A later definition brings out the larger agenda of postcolonialism which embraces political ideals of transnational social justice and its praxiological nature. Robert Young, who played a critical role in clarifying the field and even came up with a new term, "triconti-nentalism," perceived postcolonialism as a theoretical and political position which not only "attacks the status quo of hegemonic economic imperialism, and the history of colonialism and imperialism, but also signals an active engagement with positive political positions and new forms of political identity in the same way as Marxism or feminism."[16] The Marxism which Young refers to is the non-Western form which was developed to scrutinize the historical forms of imperialism, and similarly the feminism referred to by him includes the aims and practices of Third World feminism. Like most scholarly analysis, postcolonialism is about interrogating texts with certain kinds of question – in this case, those which come with colonial and neo-colonial history and experience. It is about disputing and confronting the after-effects of imperial and the new effects of neo-imperial control.

Concerns and Preoccupations

Postcolonialism is a cluster of disparate writings, and it would be helpful to herd together some of its key interrelated activities and themes which have evolved over the years and energized the field:

1   Investigating the social, cultural, and political impact of colonialism on individuals and indigenous cultures.
2   Reopening different genres of colonial archive in the form of historical documentation, novels, travel writings, and translations which both colluded with and confronted imperial interests in the building and maintaining of the empire. This involves revisiting the literary productions, rereading and reinterpreting them, and exposing the revisions or reinforcements of colonial or national history.

3 Recovering the resistance of the subjugated. This looks not only at the dynamics of colonial domination but also at the capacity of the colonized to resist, either openly or covertly.

4 Identifying postcolonial conditions caused by a set of historical, political, and cultural contingencies – migration, diaspora, refugees, internally displaced persons, and hyphenated identities. It studies the process and effects of cultural displacement on individuals and communities and the ways in which the displaced have defined and defended themselves.

5 Decentering universal and transhistorical values of Western categories of knowledge. It questions the three mainstays of the Enlightenment: objectivity, rationalism, and universalism.

6 Transgressing the contrastive way of thinking. The binary categorizations include colonizer/colonized, center/margins, modern/traditional, and static/progressive. It queries the presences of such dualistic thinking, and applies deconstructive techniques to show that though the histories and orientations of colonized and colonizer are distinct, they overlap and intersect. It encourages productive crossings between the two.

7 Interrogating colonial and contemporary practices of representation of the "other" and the power relations that lie behind the production of such knowledge.

8 Placing women in patriarchal culture, and especially the "double colonization" faced by women who were colonized by both imperial and patriarchal ideologies.

9 Examining the interdependency of race and class and the variety of ways racism was exercised.

10 Scrutinizing debates about multiculturalism and the intermingling of races and religions and their connections to the colonial past.

11 Studying the lingering legacies of colonialism extended and incarnated in the forms of neo-colonialism such as globalization, free-market and multinational firms, and the media.

12 Decentering of dominant forms of knowledge which envisioned the world from a single privileged point of view which simultaneously elevated the cultures of the colonizer – religions, arts,

dances, rituals, history, geography – and undermined those of the colonized.

13 Questioning the privilege accorded to the written over the oral literature of peoples.

14 Paying attention to the nationalist movements for their failure to fulfill and deliver their promises after decolonization, and especially the way they overlooked the needs of dalits, women, and indigenous people.

To these one could add other concerns, notably the environmental crisis and the development policies of international agencies. The current ecological devastation of lands, forests, and rivers is partly rooted in colonial despoliation.

To sum up, postcolonialism is essentially an interventionary tool. Its argumentative and contestatory nature makes the practice defy boundaries and disciplines.

Changing Faces of A Discourse

Colonial discourse analysis began with several theorists who studied colonialism in the Arab world, such as Albert Memmi in Tunisia, Frantz Fanon in Algeria, and Edward Said. Since then it has seen several changes.

First, the way of doing postcolonialism has changed. In the initial stages, following Said, Spivak, and Bhabha, postcolonialism was based on, in Spivak's phrase, a "South Asian model"[17] and was seen as an anglophone affair limited to the imperial adventures of the British. Now, postcolonial studies has widened its scope to include not only the other old European empires like the Spanish, Portuguese, Dutch, Belgian, and French, and Eastern ones like the Japanese, but also the newer empires like that of the United States of America. To this one could add the Soviet empire as well, demonstrating that not all colonialism was from the far right. As Spivak points out, with such a changed and widened focus of attention, the old model derived from South Asia, which was basically "'India' plus the

16

Sartrian 'Fanon' will not serve ... We are dealing with heterogeneity on a different scale and related to imperialism on another model."[18] This also means that the earlier texts of Fanon, Memmi, and Cabral, which supplied exemplary theoretical underpinning in their time, may not have as much purchase as they did with the old colonialism. To meet the different demands of the decolonization process which started soon after the Second World War, and was soon to be caught up in the Cold War and the new imperialism in the form of globalization, new texts are required. One such, which accommodates the new political geography and neo-colonial context, especially in Asia, is Kuan-Hsing Chen's *Asia as Method*.[19] In this volume, Chen takes into account Japanese military occupation, US imperialism after the Second World War, and the emergence of China as both territorial and economic superpower.

Second, the nature of colonialism has changed. The old territorial colonialism has given way to new forms under the heading of neo-colonialism. Unlike the old empires, where one knew the boundaries and identified their power structure, now it is difficult to specify the parameters. The new empire has no territorial center of power or clearly delineated boundaries. As Hardt and Negri put it, it is "a *decentered* and *deterritorializing* apparatus of rule that progressively incorporates the entire global realm within its open, expanding frontiers ... The distinct national colors of the imperial map of the world have merged and blended in the imperial global rainbow."[20] In this barrierless world it is not the traditional nation-states that wield power but the transnationals, which have become the "fundamental motor of the economic and political transformation of postcolonial countries and subordinated regions."[21]

One such borderless empire is environmental colonialism. Just as the old colonialists tried to redeem the savages for the Christian Church, the new conservationists try to save the natural resources not so much for the local people as for the multinationals. With the professedly altruistic motive of preserving the tropical rainforests, Western corporations are buying them up as resources. The lands in which the indigenous peoples lived for long ages have been declared idyllic and turned into wildlife sanctuaries, and local people are forbidden to hunt, cut trees, and quarry stone. The eviction of the aborigines of Palawan Island in the Philippines, and the bushmen in Botswana, in order to create national parks are egregious examples of this type of green colonialism.[22] Physical occupation may be a thing of the past but there is still the desire to extend sovereign rights in a place like Antarctica where the seabed is rich in gas, oil, and minerals.

Colonialist tactics, too, have become much more nuanced. The old colonialists preached Christianity as a way of saving souls, whereas the current neo-colonialists spread the virtues of democracy and human rights in order to prepare countries for a liberalized market economy. According to *The Guardian* columnist Simon Jenkins, democracy has become the new Christianity.[23] The word "mission" has been replaced with the word "intervention." The former British foreign secretary, David Miliband, called for a moral intervention as the West's new mission to encourage democracy through "soft or hard power."[24] The old colonizers saw themselves as masters and used brute force to achieve their goals, but the new colonizers, no less violent, project themselves as liberators, or, to use the words of Reinhold Niebuhr, "tutors of mankind in its pilgrimage to perfection."[25]

Third, there is a remarkable change in the geopolitical landscape. In the north, with the collapse of the Soviet bloc, the old ways of drawing boundaries determined by the Cold War are no longer politically tenable. In the south, the emerging markets have altered the old classification of developing and underdeveloped world. The emergence of China, India, and Brazil as new economic forces on the world stage has unsettled the traditional Western hold on the economy. Rapid globalization and the free-market economy have called into question what is local and indigenous. But the structuring of the world is not as rigid as it used to be. The old stringent oppositional division of colonizer/colonized, East/West, oppressor/oppressed, and First World/Third World has slowly lost its ideological purchase. The world has become more unipolar and more singular, and as such it is now much more nuanced and interrelated.

Fourth, a critical practice which started as a political frame of reference and a tool for literary analysis has moved beyond its general theorizing to a specific, deeper, and more practical phase of engagement. Some of the recent literature offers evidence of engagement of postcolonialism with particular subjects, thus bringing to the fore a variety of fields which are underrepresented in the various earlier anthologies and compilations. To name a few: legal studies, disability,[26] development,[27] international terrorism,[28] environmentalism,[29] film, tourism, popular music, dance,[30] and the history of book production.[31] These studies extend the central debates and concerns of the theory beyond its rich theoretical manifestations. More importantly, these engagements have not only answered the earlier accusation that postcolonialism was pure theory and very much slanted towards high literature, culture, and philosophy, but also introduced popular cultural forms such as music, films, and sport.

Interestingly, a theoretical practice which has its roots in humanistic tradition has now become a serviceable tool providing challenging reflections on religions. There are books using postcolonial insights to study Hinduism,[32] Buddhism,[33] Islam,[34] the Bible,[35] and Christian theology.[36] These books not only demonstrate how ideologies of empire shaped the construction of the Eastern religions but also show how the religions themselves offered a form of resistance to colonial rule.

Meanwhile, postcolonialism has embraced a wide variety of disciplinary fields which have not usually been open to postcolonial inquiry. It has now expanded to include all forms of oppression and subjugation ranging from disability studies to queer studies. It has moved back in time to embrace subjects such as classics[37] and medieval studies which at first glance might not have been seen as having any postcolonial interest. As Barbara Goff, the editor of *Classics and Colonialism*, put it, "it is no longer appropriate to account for e.g. British Romanticism without an acknowledgment of the emergence of the British empire."[38]

Perceptive readers will have noticed the absence of feminism from the above list. Postcolonialism and feminism evolved more or less at the same time, sharing remarkable theoretical and political resemblances but rarely interconnecting. In recent years there has been not only notable interest in each other's concerns but also mutual critiquing. Postcolonialism has exposed the racial and gender bias of Western feminism, while feminism has uncovered patriarchal tendencies in postcolonialism. For a succinct debate surrounding these two theoretical practices, and for extracts from leading feminist practitioners, see Ashcroft, Griffiths, and Tiffin.[39]

Fifth, the nature of the postcolonial condition has perceptively changed. In the early stages, it was as seen as a newly acquired territorial freedom enjoyed by former colonized countries soon after the physical departure of Western countries. Then, with forced and voluntary migration, diasporic status became a new postcolonial status. The resultant border-crossing anguishes such as yearning for home and recovering the cultural soul were treated as new forms of the postcolonial condition. While this predicament of dislocation reified the plight and distresses of the metropolitans, the material conditions of the rural poor were altered by state development policies, agrarian capitalism, and technological changes in food production in the rural economy, which, in Akhil Gupta's view, have led to a condition of postcoloniality for the rural poor and peasants.[40] The definition of postcoloniality was thrown into further confusion with the recent wars in Iraq, Iran, Sri Lanka, and the Balkans, which resulted in a great number of internally displaced people forced to live in detention centers and welfare camps in their own countries.

Sixth, the narratives which postcolonialism dealt with in its initial stages have given way to newer grand narratives. The earlier anti-colonial writers and activists were wrestling with European expansionism, Enlightenment values, and neo-liberalism. The new metanarratives are "war on terror," "ethnic cleansing," "environmental catastrophe," and religious fundamentalisms. The earlier grand narratives resulted in destruction and annihilation of the benighted people, whereas the new ones speak about the redemption and salvation carried out on behalf of the hapless victims.

Seventh, there is a move to go beyond the narrow and restricted confines of theoretical parameters and the academic environment and to see a connection between scholarly commitment and active involvement. Three books which embody this new mood are Akhil Gupta's *Postcolonial Developments*, Robert Young's *A Very Short Introduction to Postcolonialism*, and Simon Featherstone's *Postcolonial Cultures*. Gupta's book, which comes out of a field study of farmers in Alipur, India, challenges a monolithic understanding of the post-colonial condition, and also explores how postcolonial theory was put to use to represent or conceptualize poor people's resistance and social transformation. Young examines the theory not in an abstract fashion from the top down but evidentially from below, and rearticulates the theory within the history of practice. He uses examples like Algerian Rai music, book burning, veiling of women, postcolonial feminism, the plight of dispossessed people, and environmental movements, to name a few, and seeks to place the components of postcolonialism within the history, culture, and politics of ordinary people. Similarly, Simon Featherstone provides in-depth case studies of the indigenes' and the invaders' perceptions of the land in the colonial geographies.[41] What these books have done is to restore social and political agency to the heart of the theory and write back to those critics who accuse postcolonialists of being speculative and lacking popular engagement and political practice.

Lastly, the utility and the application of postcolonial criticism have changed. When it emerged, its perspectives were seen as "the colonial testimony of Third World countries and the discourses of 'minorities' within the geopolitical divisions of East and West, North and South,"[42] but now it is not confined exclusively to that group. Its approaches, positions, and traits are extended to any group who face discriminatory practices. To borrow the words of Paul Gilroy, addressed primarily to the descendants of African slavery, the insights gained from the anti-colonial and anti-racist resistance "will belong to anybody who is prepared to use them. This history of suffering, rebellion, and dissidence is not our intellectual property, and we are not defenders of cultural and experiential copyright."[43]

Discursive Interjections

There are two innovations championed by Edward Said which are relevant to biblical studies. One is the contrapuntal method. It is a mode of reading that tries to deal with the often fractious and awkward nature of the relationship between the texts of the colonizer and the colonized. It was an idea that Said borrowed from the world of classical music. For Said, reading contrapuntally is a means of examining the cultural documentation of the West with "a simultaneous awareness both of the metropolitan history that is narrated and of those other histories against which (and together with which) the dominating discourse acts."[44] Thus, as in contrapuntal music, Said points out, "various themes play off one another, with only a provisional privilege" granted to each narration.[45] In transforming this musical technique into a critical practice, Said provides a means of interrogating those texts and moments which slip and spill into each other's discourse. This could mean thinking through and interpreting not only texts but also incompatible experiences such as "coronation rituals in England and the Indian durbars of the late nineteenth century."[46] Articulating together the works of the margins with those of the mainstream, the marginal texts are treated no longer as interesting and informative ethnographic samples valuable only to a few experts but as a challenging and resisting alternative. Such an act of reading brings these texts out of the neglected and minor status to which they were unfairly consigned for all kinds of political and cultural reasons and positions them in a global setting. The contrapuntal method worked out by Said is a useful tool for biblical studies. For how it works in biblical studies, see Chapter 6.

The second critical practice advocated by Said which has relevance to biblical studies is the restoration of philological studies. He persistently reminds us in his writing that all leading Orientalists like William Jones and Max Müller were linguistic experts involved in the classification of languages and the study of comparative grammar. For Said, philology has two interrelated functions. One is the traditional business of the patient tracing of the original meaning of words, placing them in their cultural and political contexts and recording their reception histories. Added to this is the stigmatization added to words. As Said put it, "a true philological reading is active; it involves getting inside the process of language already going on in words and making it disclose what may be hidden or incomplete or masked or distorted in any text we may have before us."[47] How a meaning is attached to a word is complex and shrouded in cultural, religious, and political mystery. Philological investigation is important not only for unravelling the meaning of ancient texts but also for deciphering how words are used in contemporary public discourse. For instance, naming those who are in a position of vulnerability is a sensitive matter. Descriptions like "illegal immigrants," "economic migrants," and "Islamic terrorists" are all loaded terms which have negative connotations and tend to polarize debate. Similarly, there are other politically driven language constructions which prevent any constructive debate. The language used by the populist Western media during the first Iraq War could serve to illustrate the point. "Our" (i.e., Western) troops are "professional," "confident," "loyal," "resolute," and "brave," whereas "their" (i.e., Iraqi) troops are "brainwashed," "desperate," "blindly obedient," "ruthless," and "fanatical."[48] Said provides examples from American political discourse where language was used as an instrument of polemics – for instance, expressions such as "threat to our way of life" and "axis of evil" – or to camouflage the actual reality. Such phrases, in Said's view, "need laborious dismantling, unpacking, documentation, and refutation or confirmation."[49] The task of the biblical exegete is to make "demystification and questioning" central to his or her enterprise.

The historical-critical method employed by biblical studies largely depends on the study of words. But the work of biblical scholars is principally confined to dry and technical details and is written as if the study of words has no contemporary or ethical consequences. Most of their work is driven by religious motive and confessional interest, and as such there is a failure to note the varied colonial contexts which provided the language for biblical texts. Philological commitment is not simply a matter of poring over ancient manuscripts and fixing the literal meaning of words, but also involves a combative mode of humanistic resistance which should shield one from political misinformation. As Said put it, philological investigation should become a technique of trouble.

Misperceptions, Flaws, Accomplishments

Let me bring this chapter to a close by referring to some hermeneutical issues and concerns that are related to postcolonial criticism. First, it is vital to point out that not all resistance is postcolonial. The investment bank managers who resist tax on their bonuses, the members of the Countryside Alliance in the United Kingdom who protest to protect their privileges, or the fairly well-to-do members of the Tea Party movement in the USA who demand fiscal restraints, lower taxes, and smaller governments, are not only simplifying issues but also making a mockery of the oppositional stance of the economically and politically disadvantaged. These are prosperous and well-connected people and are a million miles away from the angry voices of the grassroots. Narrowing it down to mere protest and resistance could be construed as an act in bad taste. The principal trait which sets apart and distinguishes postcolonial resistance is resentment against the uneven cultural equation and distorted representation.

Postcolonial studies tends to be obsessed with diaspora, migrancy, border crossing. Important though these are, they have only a limited purchase. Although there are massive movements of population, the vast majority of the displaced people in Asia and Africa continue to stay in their own countries and are not diasporic migrants. The obsession with diaspora further fuels the popular criticism that postcolonialism has taken identity issues more seriously than the conduct of the International Monetary Fund, and is animated more by the concerns of the market than by those of marginality. Missing from its literature are terms like capitalism, casteism, land rights, and class struggle. The critical categories popularized by postcolonialism – "mimicry" and "hybridity" – have now almost become clichés. Hybridity is preoccupied with metropolitan issues only; it overlooks the internal cross-fertilization that takes place within vernacular and regional traditions. Hybridity is seen as one-way traffic. It has to do with immigrants fusing creatively the cultures they left behind and the cultures of their new home. But this cultural blending has not been matched by any sort of reciprocal synthesis at the political level on the part of metropolitan masters. Most European governments want the immigrants to absorb and integrate into Western ways of life. The vote against the building of new minarets in Switzerland and the proposed banning of the burqa in public places in France are notable examples of how unilateral is the cultural exchange. What hybridity does is to display and articulate the mesmeric effect of globalization. In doing so, it has forgotten the initial and primary tasks of postcolonialism – "writing back" and "listening again." In the world of the diasporan, postcolonialism is seen no longer as recovering distorted and defamed histories and injustices, but as reframing and recovering the cultural soul in the widening global market.

There is still an understandable but needless fixation with the West. An imaginary and invented West has performed a variety of functions in the postcolonial discourse. As Chen has put it, the West "has been an opposing entity, a system of reference, an object from which to learn, a point of measurement, a goal to catch up with, an intimate enemy, and sometimes an alibi for serious discussion and action." To rephrase it, the West became the model, content, and form for knowledge production. The task now is not to offer even a stringent ideological critique of the West but to discover ways to transcend this obsession. Eschewing the earlier attempts to dismantle the West either by regionalizing or provincializing it so that it became another contextual entity, or by resorting to indigenous resources to counter it, Chen proposes shifting the point of reference towards Asia. His contention is that Asia's historical experiences and practices can be seen as an alternative perspective and can offer a method which can bring out a different understanding of world history. Asia becomes an anchoring point and "societies in Asia can become each other's points of reference, so that the understanding of the self may be transformed, and subjectivity rebuilt."[50] Such a shift is undertaken not with a view to opposing the West or to essentializing Asia but with the aim of loosening and diluting our fascination with the West, which can lead to a productive new critical work. This method of continental self-reference could act as a potential model for Africa, Latin America, and Oceania as well.

Postcolonialism is also guilty of constructing its own canon and privileging certain texts and championing certain theoreticians. It needs to seek and uncover other voices which lie outside Western universities and publishing houses. I shall come back to this issue in the final chapter of this book. Postcolonialism certainly has its fair share of minor accomplishments. It is seen as both a liberatory and a constructive project. As an emancipatory venture, it provided visibility and an entry point into the Western academic discourse. At a time when there is a loss of faith in history, what postcolonialism does is to retell the story of the indigenous subjects of past colonialism and the victims of current neo-imperial policies, not with the intention of idealizing and glorifying them but to make it clear that the narrative is complicated and disputed. The aim is to treat the native narrative as diverse and contested. The idea is not to coopt this history in the service of some fashionable theory but to understand it and treat it with respect. Negatively, as a frame of reference, postcolonialism has flattened all cultural and national differences.

The most frequently asked question about postcolonialism is: does it change anything? It is not an easy question to answer. To be frank, no one knows. The question also has an air of self-importance. Postcolonial criticism has helped us to frame the question slightly differently and does not necessarily encourage us to come up with neat answers. It has served to underline very vividly that colonialism is an ongoing predicament. Postcolonialism teaches that there is no going back to a time when tradition, or identity, or civilization might be recuperated as a whole. What it does is to give us the confidence to question the pieties of the powerful. It has brought home the unpalatable truth that whatever earnestness and sincerity past generations brought to their work, their behavior, actions, and thoughts often now look erroneous and scandalous. It has made scholars conscious of the type of knowledge they produce and disseminate. It has provided us with a healthier understanding of the way the dominant hermeneutics operates. It has helped to encourage a new kind of dealing with the "other" and has tried to move beyond the standard contrastive way of thinking that both the master and the nationalist narratives want us to be locked into – Occident and Orient, the pure indigene and the contaminated invader. In its modest way, it has helped us to unlearn the subtle ways the dominant discourse operates and to relearn how to confront and reshape it. To twist the words of Raymond Williams for our immediate purpose, wherever the mainstream commentators started from, with the arrival of postcolonialism they have been forced to listen to others who started from a different position.[51]

Notes

1   Shiromi Pinto, *Trussed* (London: Serpent Tail, 2006), p. 18.
2   bell hooks, *Teaching to Transgress: Education as the Practice of Freedom* (New York: Routledge, 1994), p. 59.
3   *Life in the United Kingdom: A Journey to Citizenship* (Norwich: Stationery Office, 2004), p. 32.
4   Edward W. Said, *Orientalism* (London: Penguin, 2003), pp. xvi–xvii.
5   *Life in the United Kingdom*, p. 32.
6   Ato Quayson, *Postcolonialism: Theory, Practice or Process?* (Cambridge: Polity, 2000); Nicholas Harrison, *Postcolonial Criticism: History, Theory and the Work of Fiction* (Cambridge: Polity, 2003); Justin D. Edwards, *Postcolonial Literature: A Reader's Guide to Essential Criticism* (Basingstoke: Palgrave Macmillan, 2008); John McLeod, ed., *The Routledge Companion to Postcolonial Studies* (London: Routledge, 2007); Ania Loomba, Suvir Kaul, and Matti Bunzl, eds, *Postcolonial Studies and Beyond* (Durham, NC: Duke University Press, 2005).

7   Clair Taylor, "The Spanish and Portuguese Empires," in *The Routledge Companion to Postcolonial Studies*, pp. 46–58.

8   Charles Forsdick, "The French Empire," in *The Routledge Companion to Postcolonial Studies*, pp. 32–45.

9   Richard C. King, ed., *Post-Colonial America* (Urbana, IL: University of Illinois Press, 2000).

10 Robert J.C. Young, *Postcolonialism: An Historical Introduction* (Oxford: Blackwell, 2001).

11 Edward W. Said, "Edward Said in Conversation with Neeladri Bhattachrya, Suvir Kaul and Ania Loomba," *Interventions* 1, 1 (1998), 81–96 (p. 92).

12 Homi K. Bhabha, *The Location of Culture* (London: Routledge, 1994).

13 Gayatri Chakravorty Spivak, *In the Other Worlds: Essays in Cultural Politics* (New York: Routledge, 1988); *The Postcolonial Critic: Interviews, Strategies, Dialogues*, ed. Sarah Harasym (New York: Routledge, 1990); *A Critique of Postcolonial Reason: Toward a History of the Vanishing Past* (Cambridge: Harvard University Press, 1999).

14 John McLeod, "Introduction," in *The Routledge Companion to Postcolonial Studies*, p. 8.

15 Bhabha, *The Location of Culture*, p. 171.

16 Young, *Postcolonialism*, p. 58.

17 Gayatri Chakravorty Spivak, *Other Asias* (Malden, MA: Blackwell, 2008), p. 251.

18 Gayatri Chakravorty Spivak, *Death of a Discipline* (New York: Columbia University Press, 2003), p. 85.

19 Kuan-Hsing Chen, *Asia as Method: Toward Deimperialization* (Durham, NC: Duke University Press, 2010).

20 Michael Hardt and Antonio Negri, *Empire* (Cambridge: Harvard University Press, 2000), pp. xii–xiii.

21 Hardt and Negri, *Empire*, p. 246.

22 John Vidal, "The Great Green Land Grab," *The Guardian G2* (February 13, 2008), 6–9.

23 Simon Jenkins, "Democracy Is Ill Served by Its Self-Appointed Guardians," *The Guardian* (March 5, 2008), 35.

24 Patrick Wintour, "Miliband: UK Has Moral Duty to Intervene," *The Guardian* (February 12, 2008), 1.

25 Reinhold Niebuhr, *The Irony of American History*, with a new introduction by Andrew J. Bacevich (Chicago: Chicago University Press, 2008), p. 71.

26 Theo Goldberg and Ato Quayson, eds, *Relocating Post Colonialism* (Oxford: Blackwell, 2002), pp. 217–269.

27 Akhil Gupta, *Postcolonial Developments: Agriculture in the Making of India* (Durham, NC: Duke University Press, 1998).

28 Elleke Boehmer and Stephen Morton, eds, *Terror and the Postcolonial* (Oxford: Wiley-Blackwell, 2010).

29 Helen Tiffin and Graham Huggan, *Postcolonial Ecocriticism: Literature, Animals, Environment* (London: Routledge, 2010).

30 Simon Featherstone, *Postcolonial Cultures* (Edinburgh: Edinburgh University Press, 2005), pp. 33–131.

31 Robert Fraser, *Book History through Postcolonial Eyes: Re-Writing the Script* (London: Routledge, 2008).

32 Richard King, *Orientalism and Religion: Postcolonial Theory, India and "The Mystic East"* (London: Routledge, 1999).

33 Donald S. Lopez Jr, ed. *Curators of the Buddha: The Study of Buddhism under Colonialism* (Chicago: Chicago University Press, 1995).

34 Anouar Majid, *Unveiling Traditions: Postcolonial Islam in a Polycentric World* (Durham, NC: Duke University Press, 2000).

35 R.S. Sugirtharajah, *Postcolonial Criticism and Biblical Interpretation* (Oxford: Oxford University Press, 2002); Musa W. Dube, *Postcolonial Feminist Interpretation of the Bible* (St Louis, MO: Chalice, 2000); Fernando F. Segovia, *Decolonizing the Biblical Studies: A View from the Margins* (Maryknoll, NY: Orbis, 2000).

36 Catherine Keller, Michael Nausner, and Mayra Rivera, *Postcolonial Theologies: Divinity and Empire* (St Louis, MO: Chalice, 2004).

37 Barbara Goff, ed., *Classics and Colonialism* (London: Duckworth, 2005).

38 Barbara Goff, "Introduction," in *Classics and Colonialism*, p. 4.

39 Bill Ashcroft, Gareth Griffiths, and Helen Tiffin, *The Post-Colonial Studies Reader*, 2nd edn (London: Routledge, 2006), pp. 232–259.

40 Gupta, *Postcolonial Developments*, p. 338.

41 Featherstone, *Postcolonial Cultures*, pp. 201–231.

42 Bhabha, *The Location of Culture*, p. 171.

43 Paul Gilroy, *After Empire: Melancholia or Convivial Culture?* (Abingdon: Routledge, 2004), p. 61.

44 Edward W. Said, *Culture and Imperialism* (London: Chatto & Windus, 1993), p. 59.

45 Said, *Culture and Imperialism*, p. 59.

46 Said, *Culture and Imperialism*, p. 36.

47 Edward W. Said, *Humanism and Democratic Criticism* (New York: Columbia University Press, 2004), p. 59.
48 "Mad Dogs and Englishmen," *The Guardian* (January 23, 1991), 23.
49 Said, *Humanism and Democratic Criticism*, p. 74.
50 Chen, *Asia as Method*, p. 212.
51 Raymond Williams, *Culture and Society* (London: Hogarth, 1993), pp. 337–338.

2

The Late Arrival of the "Post"
Postcolonialism and Biblical Studies

Colonizing is a Bible thing.[1]

... and that history has to be told by a voice that is non-Western.[2]

This chapter has uncomplicated aspirations. Its chief aim is to
provide historical pointers to anticipations of postcolonial criticism
in biblical studies, and to examine the various ways in which biblical scholarship came to deploy some postcolonial critical principles
in its discourse. In addition to this, it has supplementary ambitions.
One is to demonstrate that the Bible is not merely a simple spiritual
text but has the capacity to foster both spiritual and territorial conquest; and the other is to investigate the complicated story of biblical studies and its close connection with colonialism. The chapter
ends with some critical reflections.

Colonizing Tendencies

The Christian Bible, for all its sophisticated theological ideals
like tolerance and compassion, contains equally repressive and

Exploring Postcolonial Biblical Criticism: History, Method, Practice, First Edition.
R. S. Sugirtharajah.
© 2012 R. S. Sugirtharajah, with the exception of Chapter 3 © 2012 Blackwell Publishing Ltd.
Published 2012 by Blackwell Publishing Ltd.

predatory elements which provide textual ammunition for spiritual and physical conquest. It provides confidence and justification for invading the lands of other peoples and bringing non-Christians into the Christian fold. To rephrase the epigraph, conquest is a Bible thing. The Bible records examples of occupation and invasion. A well-known case is the conquest of Canaan by Israel, a land which did not belong to her. This has provided a cue for modern colonizers who project themselves as a latter-day Israel, and a charter for conquering other peoples' lands. A classic example of biblical texts put to this sort of use was Oliver Cromwell's campaign in Ireland in 1649. In the words of the late Robert Carroll, himself an Irishman: "In the massacres of the Irish towns of Drogheda and Wexford, Cromwell played the biblical Joshua against the Irish as imagined Canaanites. Cromwell invited the Irish towns to surrender and annihilated the occupants when they refused to give themselves up to the invading English forces."[3] The biblical accounts of Joshua's mass murder of the Canaanites and the destruction of their towns provided Cromwell with legitimation and validation for his military strategy of extirpation of the native Irish.

Enshrined in the pages of the Bible is the notion that the heathen should hear the gospel as a sign of the end of the world. Many early colonial pioneers such as Christopher Columbus and Bartolomé de las Casas made use of this biblical idea as a way of justification for conquering other peoples' lands. The popular version has it that Christopher Columbus's travels were motivated by the quest for wealth. That is only partially true. He was equally spurred on by the twin eschatological goals of the time – the recovery of Jerusalem and the conversion of the heathen. Both these tasks, seen as signs of the end of the world, Christians were expected to fulfill before Christ returned. Between his third and fourth voyages, Columbus, with the help of Gasper Gorricio, a Carthusian monk, compiled a book of prophecies which was to be presented to Ferdinand and Isabella, the Spanish king and queen. The volume was a collection of more than 200 prophecies, largely drawn from Isaiah and the writings of early and medieval theologians, which lent support to missions to convert the island of Indies (modern-day West Indies) and all the peoples and nations, and to the recovery of the holy city and Mount Zion. The selection of New Testament passages, although minimal in Columbus's compilation, reiterates the same idea: that the leading message of the Bible is to carry out the prophetic vocation of spreading the good news to the heathen, who are patiently awaiting their deliverance. As Columbus put it: "I have already said that for the voyage to the Indies neither intelligence nor mathematics nor world maps were of any use to me; it was the fulfillment of Isaiah's prophecy."[4] To make sure that his reliance on Isaiah is impeccable, Columbus brings in the authority of early Church scholars such as St Jerome and St Augustine who "highly praised" Isaiah, who was "revered by all." In Columbus's view, Isaiah was "not just a prophet but an evangelist" who "put all his efforts into describing the future and calling all people to our holy Catholic Faith."[5] Columbus was unequivocal about where he got his inspiration:

> I am not relying on my lifetime of navigation and the discussions that I have had with many people from many lands and religions, or on the many disciplines and texts that I spoke of previously. I base what I say only on holy and sacred Scripture, and the prophetic statements of certain holy persons who through divine revelation have spoken on this subject.[6]

Richard Hakluyt, an English chaplain, was another who was motivated by the biblical injunction to preach the gospel before the end time. In his *Discourse of Western Planting*, a tract written to convince Elizabeth I to colonize North America, he reiterated the task of the monarch to evangelize the heathen, as well as the benefits of acquiring foreign territories. He was irritated by the success of the Roman Catholics in the Americas and wanted the Protestants headed by the English Church to play a similar role in the conversion of the heathen. He used the Pauline verse from Romans which speaks about the necessity to preach the gospel to those people who have had no opportunity to hear it: "And how are they to believe in him of whom they have never heard? And how are they to hear without a preacher? And how can men preach unless they are sent?"[7] He also reminded the monarch that the queens and kings of England as "defenders of the faith" had the responsibility of not only supporting and upholding the faith of Christ but also expanding and advancing its cause. Hakluyt also made use of the Acts passage where the Macedonians ask Paul to come over and help them, as a sign that distant countries were eagerly expecting the British to help them. This task, in Hakluyt's view, was the "principal and chief" of all other commandments.

Another factor that fueled the idea of colonialism was the biblical notion of a chosen race elected to do the will of god. Missionary literature is full of citations underlining the special cause for which Europe and America were chosen. George Smith (1833–1919), who worked in India not as a missionary but as an educator, wrote that

> in working out this process the Christians of the United States of America are allied and cooperate with those of the British empire on almost equal terms. We together, 100 millions strong, in Europe and America with the same origin, the same history, the same tongue, the same literature, the same faith, and therefore the same Christ-commanded duty and assured hope, are set over or over against the 300 millions of India in the providence of God.[8]

According to Smith, just as the Turanians were succeeded by the Semitic people, so now it was the turn of the Aryans or Indo-Europeans to play their part in god's plan. Providence had been preparing "the English speaking peoples of the West to fit them for the mightiest work in their history, the Christianising of India and the dark races."[9] This kind of thinking – that the West was the chosen instrument of god – was not confined to the colonizer but was also prevalent even among the colonized. "Natives" internalized the notion that the invader was a chosen vessel of god who had come to enlighten them. Such a view was expressed by Keshub Chunder Sen:

> When India lay sunk in the mire of idolatry and superstition, when Mahometan oppression and misrule had almost extinguished the last spark of hope in the native Indian mind, when Hinduism, once a

pure system of monotheism, had degenerated into a most horrid and abominable system of idolatry and polytheism, when the priests were exceedingly powerful, and were revelling in their triumphs over down-trodden humanity, the Lord in His mercy sent out the British nation to rescue India.[10]

He went on to claim: "Undoubtedly it is mainly owing to British energy and British enterprise, and the exertions of that paternal Government under whose care Providence, in its inscrutable mercy has placed my country [*sic*]."[11] For Sen, the British were god's "instruments" doing god's work.[12]

Allied to this was the notion that the superior people were called upon to improve the lot of the inferior ones. James Emerson Tennent, the colonial secretary of Ceylon, made the extraordinary claim that unlike the Jewish apostles, the first preachers of the gospel who were from a lower culture than Romans and Greeks, the contemporary evangelizers were people of better quality. He observed that "the modern missionary, on the contrary, goes forth from the most enlightened regions to illuminate the most benighted. This superiority implies a duty, distinct, though identified with the main object of his mission; and whenever the mission has been successful civilization has become more or less synonymous with Christianity."[13]

Another mark of colonizing rhetoric has to do with denigrating and shaming the culture, history, and faith of the conquered. What Tennent wrote about Ceylon is equally applicable to other non-Western cultures: "Their country presents no vestiges of art, and their literature no achievements of mind" and their voluminous historical narratives "chronicle few events except the vicissitudes of their national superstition" and the labor spent on irrigating paddy lands.[14] Ram Mohun Roy, whose attitude to the presence of the British was enigmatic, observed how various invaders had depicted a negative image of their vanquished enemy. The Mughals were "highly inimical to the religious exercises of Hindoos"; the generals of Genghis Khan, who themselves did not believe in the existence of god and "were like wild beasts in their manners" when invading the western part of Hindustan, "universally mocked at the profusion of God and of futurity expressed to them by the natives of India." The Greeks and the Romans, who were idolaters and immoral in their behavior, "used to laugh at the religion and conduct of their Jewish subjects, who were devoted to the belief of one God." The English missionaries were no exception. Being the conquerors of India, the missionaries "revue and mock at the religion of its natives." Roy's conclusion was that it seemed almost natural that "when one nation succeeds in conquering another, the former, though their religion may be ridiculous, laugh at and despise the religion and manners of those that are fallen into their power."[15]

The depiction of "degradation" helps the colonizer to introduce human progress in the form of Christian vision, and, more to the point, play god. The Dominican friar Duarte Nunes wrote:

> It would be a service to God to destroy these Hindu temples, just in this island of Goa, and to replace them by churches with saints. Anyone who wishes to live in this island should become a Christian, and in that case may retain his lands and houses just as he has them at present; but if he is unwilling, let him leave the islands ... It may be that these people will not become good Christians, but their children will be ... and so God will be served, and also your highness, by becoming the cause of salvation to so many lost Souls.[16]

The denial of any significance to any existing culture and the declaration that the land was waste resonates with the biblical creation: "the earth was a vast waste, the darkness covered the deep." The new colonizer-heroes played god and were seen as creators of the new world just as god had once made the old world.

The most significant mark of colonizing rhetoric is the projection of a male monotheistic god. The biblical vision of a single-god framework has provided the impetus for many empires, ancient and modern, including the recent US imperium which was justified and reinforced by monotheistic and messianic ambitions. Faced with the bewildering array of gods and goddesses, missionaries laboring in the mission fields came up with two kinds of biblical monotheism – hard and soft. The harder version introduced into

36

theological discourse notions of true and false religion, and the idea of the chosen and the unelected people. The logic of hard monotheism forces one to choose between the one and the many. The religious intolerance intrinsic to a "hard" monotheistic vision had devastating effects on religions in those colonies where religious aspirations were expressed within a polytheistic framework and where numerous gods and goddesses were venerated. The softer version of monotheism that missionaries resorted to was a way of gradually wooing the people without bludgeoning them with the harsher characteristics of a monotheistic god. In this version, the biblical monotheistic god was projected, not as undermining the local deities or eliminating them, but as a rallying point for national unity. The idea was to exalt the biblical god as a unifier of people rather than as an eradicator of polytheistic affiliations. At a time when Indians and Sri Lankans were agitating for national liberation, the biblical god was presented as a god who united disparate people. Henry Lapham, who worked as a Baptist missionary in Sri Lanka, observed that polytheism leads to national and political disintegration.[17] In his view, what was keeping Indians apart and "baffling their laudable aspiration for unity is the prevalence of polytheism in their midst."[18] His answer was one god who unites all people. In order to achieve his hermeneutical strategy, Lapham reread Hebrew scriptures to support the promotion of national integration. The Deuteronomic injunction to set up a central place of worship and disallow scattered shrines, and the opposition to calf-worship at Bethel and other places, were presented not as resistance to idolatry but as "destructive of national unity."[19] His message was that national consolidation should not be hindered by the worship of many different gods. He advanced the notion of "one God above and over all," and that god for him was none other than Jehovah in his holy temple before whom "all the earth ... [should] keep silence." The hermeneutical strategy might be different but the aim was the same. The local messy, divergent, and incompatible deities are replaced with one neat theistic principle which holds together disparate people. It is a classic colonial case of displacement and incorporation.

Indians, too, dabbled with the monotheistic ideal. Their object was slightly different from that of the missionaries. Faced with the missionary defamation of their faith as riddled with polytheism, reformers like Keshub Chunder Sen made great efforts to provide scriptural endorsement for the idea of a single supreme deity: "That God whom the mind of man cannot duly conceive but who conceiveth the every thought of the human mind, is to be regarded as the true God; those finite objects which are worshipped by the people are not the true God."[20] Another reason for turning to a single personal god was an Enlightenment-induced shame and guilt. Sen speaks of the Monotheistic Association of India which had brought under its wing nearly 6000 educated young Indians who professed allegiance to one god because it was an "insult to their understanding and a scandal to their conscience to bow before stone, wood or clay."[21] This was in contrast to the missionaries, who claimed universal reach for a Christian god who was "observable everywhere, even in the histories of individuals and countries that serve diverse gods."[22] Despite the universalistic vision of the *Upanishads*, Hindu reformers were not pressing for the Hindu Brahman presiding over the destiny of the world.

Biblical monotheism enforced choice. Non-biblical religions are portrayed as the pagan "other" of Christianity, propagating superstitious cults rather than a legitimate belief system. More pertinently, monotheistic ideals fail people who are part of a polytheistic world and are self-consciously pluralistic and constantly juggle multiple identities. Adherence to a monotheistic god meant erasing the various gods and goddesses of Asia, or uniting them under a god who originated in Semitic thought and was appropriated and reshaped by Christian theologians.

Finally, the biblical attitude to the empire is a complicated one. On the one hand, empire is seen as god's instrument of liberation, but on the other, it is depicted as the object of god's opprobrium. The Christian Old Testament narrates the story of how Cyrus, the Persian king, became the vassal of god in releasing the enslaved Jews; and at the same time the same scripture condemns another empire, the Assyrian, for its unlimited ambition and arrogance. Both the endorsement and the censure of empire are seen as fulfilling theological purposes. Similarly, in the New Testament, which is set in the Roman colonial context, there is no clear picture about the empire. Jesus and his followers lived under an oppressive empire but there was no evidence of Jesus openly challenging Roman power. His often quoted "render unto Caesar" is too enigmatical to decipher. The New Testament letters are not helpful either and offer conflicting messages. In the letter to the Romans, Paul writes that one should obey civil authorities; however, the writer of the Epistle to the Ephesians tells his readers that our struggle is not against individuals but against leaders, authorities, and structures (Eph. 6.12).

Biblical Studies and Colonial Connections

The two most notable interpretative achievements of the nineteenth century happened at the high noon of modern colonialism. One was the search for the historical Jesus, and the other was textual criticism which went under the name of higher and lower criticism. The European search for the historical Jesus is now seen as tainted with and distorted by ethnic and nationalistic considerations. A recent collection of essays, *Jesus beyond Nationalism*, has shown that these were studies undertaken at a time when European societies were beleaguered by a crisis of identity. Central to this crisis were ideas of nation, nationality, and ethnicity, which sharpened these searchers' portrayals of Jesus. The vast corpus that went under the name of historical Jesus scholarship, as the editors of this volume in their introduction put it, tends to "represent, voice, or support hegemonic cultural assumptions about the nature and role of identity."[23] These assumptions include the idea of empire and colonialism. Departing from intricate and often convoluted doctrinal and ecclesiastical Christological formulations, these studies come up with an exemplary figure of an imagined Jesus who was compromised by the cultural, national, and racial needs of the time.

The other noteworthy feat of the nineteenth century was higher criticism, which provided tools to distinguish between authentic and inauthentic aspects of biblical texts. It became a deadly ally in the cause of spreading Christianity. The tool was put to use effectively this time to discredit the religious texts of Hindus and Buddhists. Missionaries who were raised on the literal truth and revelatory nature of the Bible, when confronted with a wide variety of Hindu and Buddhist texts, used these tools to demolish their authenticity and historicity. The inspiration was provided by John Colenso (1814–1883, an English missionary bishop working in southern Africa) who applied this method successfully to the Pentateuch to demonstrate three arguments. The first was that the events and accounts recorded there were "historically untrue." The second was that some of the precepts prescribed by Mosaic and Levitical codes in the Pentateuch were morally repugnant. Colenso was horrified by laws such as that which allowed the master to go unpunished if the slave whom he had beaten survived for a day or two, because the slave was his property; and that which prescribed stoning a man to death for gathering sticks on the Sabbath. The third was that biblical miracles were rationally unsustainable. Colenso could not bring himself to accept some of the miraculous events of the Bible such as the standing still of the sun and the moon, and the dividing of the waters of the Red Sea.

Confronted with a variety of Hindu and Buddhist texts, the missionaries – most of whom were evangelicals – found that "in reference to the religions of India there is an advantage to be gained from the publications of [Colenso's work]."[24] What spurred them on was not the results that Colenso arrived at, which were uncomfortable to the conservatives, but his method of analysis, which led to the dismissal of the historical and spiritual claims made for scriptural texts. Spencer Hardy (1814–1868), a Methodist missionary working in Ceylon (now Sri Lanka), who was engaged in the comparative study of Buddhist texts, was the first to spot the usefulness of Colenso's work: "The method that bishop Colenso employs, unsuccessfully, in his attack upon the Pentateuch of Moses; we may employ, successfully, in exposing the 'unhistorical' character of the

Pitaka of Buddha."[25] Just as Colenso found contradictions and conflicting accounts in the Pentateuch, Hardy relentlessly searched the Pali texts in order to highlight the discrepancies and contradictions within the Buddhist writings. What Colenso achieved in seven volumes, in demolishing the literary status of the first five books of the Bible, Hardy did in a single slim volume. His *The Sacred Books of the Buddhists Compared with History and Modern Science* effectively debunked the historical and religious claims of Buddhism. He found the different dates of the Buddha's birth in various sources historically confusing. Similarly, the geographical and astronomical information provided by these authoritative texts proved to be "false, unfounded, and unreal, by the demonstrations of science"[26] and the ethics of Buddhism and the morality of its followers were reprehensible. After his textual demolition, Hardy was able to claim very proudly: "I have proved that Buddhism is not a revelation of truth, that its founder was an erring and imperfect teacher, and ignorant of many things that are now universally known; and the claim to exercise of omniscience made for him by his followers is an imposition and pretence."[27]

But not all were engaged in such debunking exercises. Rhys Davids (1843–1922), who began his life as a government servant and later became a leading scholar of Buddhism, employed modern criticism in order to get behind the labyrinth of Buddhist records to ascertain whether there existed an "older system hidden under a later one."[28] He found historical criticism pertinent because it worked on the premise of natural progression. But Davids was honest enough to admit that, far from being an exemplar of neutrality, modern criticism was largely based on "personal impressions, whose validity is very much open to dispute."[29]

To sum up this section: two of the most important achievements of biblical studies occurred at the height of colonialism and both proved to be useful accomplices. One helped to bolster a Jesus befitting national aspiration, and the other was helpful in perpetuating Christian triumphalism. The unrelenting claim by interpreters that their work was objective and neutral now seems to be a false assertion. As the nineteenth-century search for the historical Jesus demonstrated, biblical scholarship was entrenched in the wider national and international political trends of the time.

The Factors That Facilitated the Arrival of Postcolonial Biblical Criticism

Postcolonial biblical criticism first made its appearance in the 1990s, and gradually became a major player in shaping the discipline. Although postcolonial criticism originated in the humanities, its arrival in biblical studies was facilitated by a number of factors. The momentum was provided by those in various humanities departments engaged in the recuperation of the history of the colonized and the colonizer in the aftermath of colonialism. Such an approach challenged the way the texts and knowledge were produced and interpreted. The Christian Bible and biblical interpretation were natural candidates for such an examination on two counts: (a) most of the biblical narratives came out of various ancient colonial contexts and colonial tendencies were embedded in them; and (b) the Christian Bible and biblical interpretation played a pivotal role in modern colonialism.

The changing landscape of humanities departments in the 1980s had its repercussions in biblical studies. This was the time when humanities departments were shaken by the arrival of ideological and cultural critique. Progressive critical forces such as feminism, Marxism, and ethnic studies were making unsettling inquiries into the position of women and the significance of class and race, and in the process were threatening the complacent world of the humanities. This was also the decade when the autonomy of a single academic discipline gave way to an era of interdisciplinary engagement. Academics also lost some of their aura as specialists and some of their claims to expertise. Traditional disciplines such as English studies were entangled with history, religion, and films. This fusion replaced the modern single disciplines.

These changes in humanities had their effects on biblical studies. The discipline that had hitherto acted as an enclave free from outside influences was now faced with an invasion of critical theories and methods minted elsewhere. The two critical categories that made their entrance in biblical studies in the 1980s were literary or narrative criticism and social-science criticism. Both indirectly paved the way for postcolonial biblical criticism. The literature on these two forms of criticism is enormous (for an easy entry to the field, see works by Powell and Elliott[30]). Both forms were at that time hailed as necessary correctives to a field which was groaning under the tyranny and undisputed rule of the historical-critical method.

Literary criticism initiated the idea of viewing a text as a whole and coherent narrative rather than as an atomized and loosely related composition. It reintroduced the nineteenth-century notion popular among certain critics of treating the Bible as literature and subjected it to techniques often employed in literary criticism. Readers were encouraged to look for the plot and setting of the story, characterization, speech patterns, irony, symbolism, the implicit author and implicit readers in the text. Such a narrative pursuit replaced the earlier search for forms, sources, pericopes, author, original meaning, and the first intended readers, made fashionable by historical criticism. What the literary critics were telling their readers was to get immersed in the alluring designs of the narrative and not in the historical undertones evident in the text. This effectively presumed that texts were politically and historically innocent. This meant overlooking the context and especially the colonial context out of which these writings emerged.

The other critical category to emerge in the 1980s was social-scientific criticism. Its main task was to study the text in its relation to cultural and social contexts through the employment of models and theories supplied by social science. In their attempt to understand Near Eastern cultures, those who engaged in this enterprise were trying to speak for the Mediterranean culture through the materiality of its texts, customs, and communitarian behavior and render its mysteries simple for the West, especially the American audience. In doing so, these biblical scholars inadvertently reorientalized the Orient and regurgitated the old stereotypes.

A cursory glance at these writings will reveal two astonishing assumptions that the authors routinely make. The first is their confident generalization. The literature is peppered with statements such as that persons of Mediterranean origin are perfectly "free to lie to and deceive out-group members with impunity";[31] and in reference to in-group societies like those of the Middle East, "every group suspects that all other groups are plotting evil against it" and "village children are trained to spy out the secrets of other families while keeping secrets of their own families intact."[32]

Second, these writings are littered with exaggerated differences between the familiar America and the strange Middle East. "We" the Americans are progressive, rational, autonomous, tolerant, secular, peaceful, and upholders of family values, whereas "they" the Mediterranean societies are none of these things. This vision recreated for modern times an absolute demarcation between the two worlds envisaged by the earlier Orientalists, based on the assumption that the Mediterranean region and its cultures were static and its values absolutist. These writings, which purport to unveil the strange behavior of the Mediterranean people, go on to establish that what is aberrant from the American point of view is normal for a Middle Eastern person. To give an example, when discussing the resurrection appearances of Jesus, John Pilch observes that it would be "normal and common" for the Mediterranean culture to experience the phenomenon of resurrection through a state of altered consciousness. He then goes to claim that they "know how to enter and exit this dimension of human experience as easily as Westerners know how to drive a car, program VCRs and enjoy their CDs."[33] Mark how the contrast is made between the spiritually aware Mediterranean and the technologically savvy North Americans. This kind of attitude comes with being a politically strong culture which slots, referees, and makes assumptions about the "other." So, like the Orientalists of old, these biblical scholars are able to penetrate, grapple with, and give form and sense to the great Asiatic mystery. What social-scientific criticism did was to unwittingly replicate the rhetoric of Orientalism. I shall return to this in Chapter 4 with further illustrations.

To sum up this section: the absence of a colonial focus in literary criticism and overtly Oriental tendencies in social-science criticism provided the preparatory space for postcolonial biblical criticism to enter the field.

Another factor that led to the entry of postcolonial biblical criticism was the stagnation of Latin American liberation hermeneutics and its failure to take note of the postcolonial reality of multiculturalism. Postcolonialism shares some of the preoccupations of liberation hermeneutics such as addressing those victimized by economic exploitation. Liberation hermeneutics, however, locked itself into a narrow economic agenda, and, important though it was, overlooked the diverse religious and cultural traditions of the people. Its focus on analysis of the economic structure that underpinned society diverted its attention from the culture and institutions that buttressed that system. Its hermeneutical work, informed by a historical material reading of biblical texts emphasizing poverty and powerlessness, missed the discursive potential of texts which control power relations. Its embracement of a salvation-history model and the prophetic tradition were not always sympathetic to those who belonged to indigenous or pluralistic cultures. The employment of sacred history events such as the Exodus was harmful to the native people, just as it was to the biblical Canaanites. Liberation theologians were also wedded to the idea of a prophetic call for social justice. However laudable, the prophetic vision was partial and limited. The Hebrew Prophets had little time for ethnic, cultural, and religious diversity. They espoused the ideals of monoculturalism and a monotheistic god which were detrimental to plurality and diversity. In addition, liberation theologians were in thrall to both the authoritative and the liberative roles of the Bible, thus overlooking their unsavory aspects. While finding textual affirmation for fighting against economic oppression and exploitation, liberation hermeneutics tended to overlook the support, approval, and furtherance of empire and imperial values enshrined in several biblical narratives.

Finally, the changing face of the academy, especially regarding curriculum and constituency, played a critical role in ushering in postcolonial biblical criticism. The 1990s was the decade of identity studies. There was a proliferation of courses on African-American, Asian-American, and Hispanic-American studies. The impetus was provided by the presence of a large contingent of interpreters from Asia, Africa, and Latin America in the West, especially in North America, who were looking for an alternative reading practice to the dominant Western methods which did not address their newly found political freedom and cultural confidence.

Postcolonial Biblical Criticism and Its Concerns

The primary aim of postcolonial biblical criticism is to situate empire and imperial concerns at the center of the Bible and biblical studies. In doing so, it has added a number of new hermeneutical agendas to biblical studies.

First, it has brought to attention the importance of biblical empires – Assyrian, Egyptian, Persian, Greek, and Roman – central to many biblical books and providing the social, cultural, and political framework. The Reformation-driven Eurocentric attitude to the Bible hardly noticed or addressed the presence of empire and spent its energies on in-house ecclesiastical issues such as conflict over the synagogue participation of Jewish Christians, the Gentile converts and their reception into the Jewish-Christian world, or issues closer to the Protestant theology such as law and grace. While mainstream scholarship is restricted to theological, spiritual, and historical aspects of these narratives, postcolonial biblical criticism adds the often neglected dimension of empire and the politics of imperialism. In pursuit of this it interrogates the text in various ways, posing questions such as: how has the empire been depicted – as benevolent or evil? Does the text support the imperial intentions of the empire – does it perpetuate or contest them? Where do the loyalties of the author lie – with the imperial power or with those subjugated by it? How does the author represent the occupied – as victims or as grateful beneficiaries? Does the text provide space for their resistance?

Let me illustrate with two brief examples. When reading a text like the Book of Jonah, postcolonial biblical criticism would want to explore the presence of the Assyrian empire in the text rather than reading it as a typological literature foreshadowing the Jesus story. Similarly, it has been the practice among biblical scholars to place Matthew's Gospel as a document mainly focusing on disagreements with local Jewish groups or synagogues. What postcolonialism tries to do is to see Matthew not only as a theological or religious document but also as a document which emerged out of Roman imperial rule, and the troubling impact such imperial rule had on the text. To put it at its simplest, the aim of postcolonial biblical criticism is to set biblical texts within the fraught relationships of the imperial context and the narrative world of the biblical writers.

Second, postcolonial biblical criticism is vigilant about representation and asks how biblical interpreters in their exegetical works, philological studies, and commentaries on biblical books represent the empire. Do they reflect the imperial perspective of the Western powers or neo-colonial impulses, or do they try to unsettle colonial ambitions? How do they represent the land, and the people mentioned in the Bible whose land has been taken away from them? What kind of Oriental images appear in their work, and how does so-called liberal scholarship recycle the Oriental images of the "other" as "lazy" and "unreliable" in their writings, tacitly or overtly? I shall return to this again, with examples, in Chapters 4 and 5.

Third, postcolonial biblical criticism has embarked upon retrieval hermeneutics, and three tasks can be identified here. The first is to retrieve sidelined, silenced, written-out, and often maligned biblical figures and biblical incidents and restore their dignity and authenticity. One such maligned figure is Mary Magdalene. Utilizing the discarded Gospel of Mary, postcolonialism attempts to reconfigure the story of Mary Magdalene, showing how a once exemplary leader has been turned into a repentant sinner by later male ecclesiastical writers. The idea is not to make a heroine or an ideal figure out of Mary but to point out that there were figures like her, venerated and flawed, who were part of the continuum which made up the early Christian story.

The second task is to unearth the imaginative ways in which those once colonized had formulated their response to the empire and how they resisted some of the missionary hermeneutical impositions. It will also show how, in this process, they appropriated the Bible and its narrative power and demonstrated that the very Bible had counter-narratives opposing the teaching of the missionaries. Their story had been left to molder in the mission archives and was discarded by mainstream biblical scholarship as not worthy of enquiry because it lacked technical sophistication. These stories tell how the victims often situated themselves in the very narrative that was supposed to oppress them, and turned the tables in order to confront their oppressors and balance the unequal situation in which they were placed. Taking advantage of the biblical idea of salvation history, the victims of colonialism were able to justify both their resistance to colonial rule and their defense of their disparaged culture. Colonial hermeneutics is littered with many such examples: Sam Sharpe of Jamaica (1801–1831), the Baptist deacon, who drew inspiration from the Bible that human beings were equal, saw the Baptist missionaries as allies of the slaves in their rebellion against the slave owners; Hong Xiuquan (1814–1864), who announced himself as the younger brother of Jesus, and set out on a mission to purge the moral depravity of the foreign Munchu of the Quing dynasty and establish a Heavenly Kingdom of Peace based on biblical teachings; Olaudah Equiano (1745–1797), the freed slave, who worked tirelessly for emancipation before Wilberforce stole the limelight, and who among other biblical sources used Paul's letter to Philomen, the very text which served as the founding text for slavery, as a manual for freedom; William Apes (1798–1839), the native American who wrested away the biblical symbols and stories which were meant to subjugate his own people and used them as weapons of mass emancipation; Isaiah Shembe (1870–1935), the pioneer of the African independent churches, who found a textual ally in the Hebrew scriptures which validated some of the Bantu cultural practices disparaged by the missionaries; and Pandita

Ramabhai (1858–1922), a social reformer and activist, who spent her energies on producing a vernacular Bible in Marathi which was aimed at women and children and was easier to read than those produced by the British and Foreign Bible Society, which were littered with Sanskrit, Persian, and Arabic words. Not all resistance was based on and driven by Christian scriptures. Some new converts like K.M. Banerjea were able to relink with their own scriptural traditions which had been disparaged by the missionaries. This enabled them not only to draw attention to god's presence in their own religious traditions but also to claim, in certain cases, that the spiritual insights in their own scriptures were far more illuminating than those in the Bible. Banerjea's declaration that the Hindu Vedas contained superior notions of the sacrificial lamb is a notable case in point.

The selection of texts and interpretations by these men and women showed that they not only had mastered the text but also could invert it and use it devastatingly against their rulers. These resistant discourses were a timely reminder that the colonized were capable of recovering and restoring the "pure gospel" which had been distorted by the vested interests of Western denominationalism and cultural imperialism. While celebrating the hermeneutics of these lost voices, postcolonial biblical criticism is uneasy about the interpretations of the marginalized which glory in texts, biblical incidents, and figures to support and validate nationalistic, sectarian, and identitarian images.

The third retrieval task is to recover the hermeneutical works of the missionaries and European administrators who were part of the colonizing process but ambivalent about the purpose and the logic of the empire. They were conspicuously close to the empire and yet not so close as to share in its predatory success or to be blamed for its darker deeds. They showed another face of the empire, caring and humanitarian. These were the men and women who broke rank with their own compatriots and engaged in what I call dissident hermeneutics. They, too, employed the same Bible their fellow colonizers used to bolster the empire in order to unsettle and rattle its core ambitions. These include, among others, Bartolomé de las

Casas (1484–1566), the Spanish Dominican priest, a complicated figure who was horrified by the atrocities of his own people against the indigenous people, and who drew from the Bible a gentler and kinder form of evangelization; William Knibb (1803–1845), the Baptist missionary, popular among the slaves in Jamaica for his stance against his European plantation owners; John Colenso (1814–1883), the Society for the Propagation of the Gospel (SPG) missionary who supported the political cause of the Zulus and used insights from what was thought to be its contaminated culture to open up some of the Pauline mystery in the Epistle to the Romans; and James Long (1814–1887), an Anglican who worked for the Church Missionary Society in Bengal, India, who sided with the indigo workers and was imprisoned for translating a play, *Nil Darpan*, which highlighted the plight of the peasants, but more importantly went against the dominant complicated and abstract Pauline hermeneutics of work/grace, and introduced Indian popular literature as way of easy entrance into the biblical world. None of these was in favor of granting full independence. They all justified the empire as long as the Christian message was preached in a peaceful and tolerant way.

Fourth, postcolonialism has been able to intervene in the area of biblical translation and repair some of the cultural and theological damage done in that process. Biblical translatory activity gives contradictory signals. Positively, it has helped to revitalize a number of languages and finesse their grammar. Negatively, culturally insensitive theological injections carried out in the name of certain Christian theological values have neutralized some egalitarian values intrinsic to local cultures. An illustration of this is the missionary version of the Shona Bible, where the Supreme Being of the Shona people, who has no gender specificity, was transformed into a male god. Postcolonial translation also draws attention to the King James version which was used as the benchmark to set standards not only for vernacular versions but also for introducing notions such as the original and literal sense of texts, especially in oral cultures which brim with plural narratives and multiple meanings. It also tries to identify the native translators who are often forgotten but played a critical role along with missionaries in vernacular Bible production.

Finally, postcolonialism has been vigorous in addressing issues caused by the movement of people, such as diaspora, migrancy, multiculturalism, hybridity, and nationhood. These issues were the resultant effects of colonialism and postcolonialism. The presence of a sizable number of Asians and Latinos in the West and in particular in North America has given birth to what is now known as diasporic hermeneutics. Those who are engaged in such an enterprise are a mixture of second- or third-generation Asian- and Hispanic-Americans and newly arrived professional migrants located largely in Western academies. Diasporic hermeneutics incorporates a wide variety of ethnic experiences and records numerous views on the Bible. This varies from a wholesale adoption of biblical tenets to complicating and at times rejecting the Bible in favor of other life-enhancing sources from the wisdom traditions of Asia. Taking advantage of their hyphenated status, these interpreters have come up with refreshing readings of biblical characters buried deep in the narratives, such as the unnamed concubine in Judges 19 and Uriah the Hittite – both hailed in the USA as radical outsiders trying to figure an identity. In an often hostile context where diasporans are placed outside of and in opposition to the imagined wider white community, these hermeneutical efforts seek to make sense of their race, ethnicity, and sexuality.

To these one could add postcolonialism's scrutiny of the public nature of biblical studies through its professionalized and specialized guilds and bodies. How do these organizations structure themselves? Whose interests do they serve? What religious ideology do they reflect? What kinds of critical theories and reading practices get attention in these academic gatherings? Does the institutionalization of biblical studies make the discipline docile and conform to the status quo? Whose values do these bodies represent? In their annual meetings and gatherings, what sort of space is given to minority hermeneutics?

Concluding Remarks

The response of Western systematic theologians and biblical scholars to colonialism is pitiful. By and large, Western theologians reflect the liberal position that, in spite of the atrocities committed by the West, colonialism is still seen as offering a better, more compassionate, and more enlightened alternative to the degenerate state of the colonized. To put it bluntly, biblical scholars have yet to address the relation between European imperial impulses and the rise and collusion of their discipline in this expansion.

Postcolonial biblical criticism did not suddenly appear on the scene, but grew out of earlier interpretative strategies. It developed out of such reading approaches as "nationalistic," "liberationist," and "contextual," or was identified with specific geographical markers, Asian, African, and Latin American, or was linked with larger spatial categories such as "Third World" or "Two-Thirds World" or "Fourth World." Postcolonialism engages with the issues raised in these hermeneutics and extends the debate to include colonialism and the after-effects of colonialism on peoples and cultures. Its distinctiveness lies in challenging and rectifying the defamatory and lopsided colonial discourse which not only was interested in superintending other people's cultures, stories, and texts but also wanted to act as their trustees. It also serves as a watchdog against newer forms of cultural and economic imperialism.

At this point, clarification of some misconceptions about postcolonial biblical criticism is in order. First, contrary to popular perception, postcolonialism is not simply anti-Western or anti-missionary. In this chapter and elsewhere in my writings I have provided examples of exemplary missionaries and colonialists who not only broke ranks with their own compatriots and sided with the political causes of the "natives" but also offered liberative readings of the Bible which in most cases challenged the triumphalist missionary version. Postcolonialism is equally critical of both the triumphalist missionary's Eurocentrism and nationalist native revisionism, and is particularly severe on both for the way they have shaped and produced knowledge. Postcolonialism, however, is not in the business of inducing guilt feelings among the present generation of the West for the transgressions of their forebears, or interested in demanding apologies. Its chief concern is to rectify the defamatory representation of the "other" by the West and the unsavory aspects of the nationalist discourse, and more importantly, to use the phrase of *The Guardian* columnist Seamus Milne, to "act as an inoculation" against falling into imperialism again. Second, not all biblical hermeneutics emanating from Asia, Africa, Latin America, the Caribbean, and the Pacific – or the minority interpretation that claims to champion the victims – is postcolonial. Some of this type of work adopts and imitates the habits and outlook of the mainstream and has little interest in structural inequality or seeking reparations. Third, it is worth pointing out that although most of the biblical narratives come out of a colonial context, there is much material in the Bible which does not easily lend itself to postcolonial inquiry. Not all biblical accounts are preoccupied with political oppression, resistance, and protest. The focus of some biblical texts falls outside the concerns of postcolonialism. One such example is the sensuous love relationship of the unnamed lovers in the Song of Solomon; another would be the affirmation of the wonders of creation in the Book of Job.

The question I posed at the end of the last chapter – whether postcolonial criticism had changed anything – is equally valid for postcolonial biblical criticism. The answer is yes and no. The practice of referring to European or Western interpretation without cultural qualification, while routinely qualifying other regional interpretations as Asian, African, or Chinese, continues. There is still the unwarranted assumption that in order to qualify for inclusion, a minority, ethnic, or gender work must conform to the rules or criteria developed within the Western tradition. What is not considered as universal (read Western) is still denounced as anthropological, atavistic, and/or sociological. Indigenous resistance, critical independence, and imagination are treated as vernacular venting. The change of tone is notable. The earlier Western condescension which described African and Asian interpretations as "quaint," "exotic," "fantastic," and "bewitching" has, in these days of political correctness, given way to more measured descriptions such as autobiographical, sentimental, and journalistic. The earlier disdainful cultural condemnation has turned into a discursive critique. In other words, the control continues but is less strident.

There is also the continuing danger that the hermeneutical efforts of postcolonial biblical criticism replace one stereotype with another: the colonial god with a postcolonial god, evil imperialists with nice indigenes, native informer with diasporic intellectual. This last one is particularly relevant to those diasporans who engage in hermeneutical work in Western academies, who may unwittingly, to use an overworked phrase, reorientalize the Orient.

The enduring achievement of postcolonialism in biblical studies is that it has pushed the issues of colonialism, empire, and imperialism to the center of critical and intellectual debate. It has cautioned that interpreters who claim to be liberal and progressive and work under a veneer of objectivity and humanitarianism can err in unwittingly reinforcing dominant values and regurgitating Oriental images. Postcolonial criticism has succeeded in exposing the frequent assumption that biblical texts, biblical interpretation, and biblical interpreters are innocent. Biblical interpretation should be understood and studied as part of the cultural and political process. Postcolonial reading has made Western biblical interpretation more accountable and sensitive to the "other." It is also a reminder that there exist other worlds of thought apart from the forms of thought and representation fostered by mainstream biblical scholarship. Its impertinent inquiries into and exposure of Orientalist tendencies in some biblical scholarship may not have threatened the mainstream's hold, but at least it has made some of the dominant interpreters and their interpretations look awkward, arrogant, and insensitive.

Notes

1 David Daniell, *The Bible in English: Its History and Influence* (New Haven: Yale University Press, 2003), p. 417.

2 Din, a character in Tash Aw's novel *Map of the Invisible World* (London: Fourth Estate, 2009), p. 23.

3 Robert P. Carroll, "Cultural Encroachment and Biblical Translation: Observations on Elements of Violence, Race and Class in the Production of Bibles in Translation," *Semeia* 76 (1996), p. 41.

4 Christopher Columbus, *The Book of Prophecies Vol. III*, ed. Roberto Rusconi, trans. Blair Sullivan (Berkeley, CA: University of California Press, 1997), p. 75.

5 Columbus, *The Book of Prophecies Vol. III*, p. 73.

6 Columbus, *The Book of Prophecies Vol. III*, p. 69.

7 Richard Hakluyt, *Discourse of Western Planting*, eds David B. Quinn and Alison M. Quinn (London: Hakluyt Society, 1993), p. 8.

8 George Smith, *The Conversion of India: From Pantaenaus to the Present Time* A.D. *193–1893* (London: Murray, 1893), p. 3.

9 Smith, *The Conversion of India*, p. 6.

10 Keshub Chunder Sen, *Keshub Chunder Sen in England: Diaries, Sermons, Addresses and Epistles*, reprint 1980 (Calcutta: Writers Workshop, 1871), p. 85.

11 Sen, *Keshub Chunder Sen in England*, p. 182.

12 Sen, *Keshub Chunder Sen in England*, p. 85.

13 James Emerson Tennent, *Christianity in Ceylon: Introduction and Progress under the Portuguese, the Dutch, the British, and American Missions: With an Historical Sketch of the Brahmanical and Buddhist Superstitions* (London: Murray, 1850), pp. 270–271.

14 Tennent, *Christianity in Ceylon*, pp. 258–259.

15 Rammohun Roy, *The English Works of Raja Rammohun Roy*, ed. Jogendra Chunder Ghose (New Delhi: Cosmo, 1906), p. 146.

16 Klaus Koschorke, Frieder Ludwig, and Mariano Delgado, eds, *A History of Christianity in Asia, Africa, and Latin America 1450–1990: A Documentary Source Book* (Grand Rapids, MI: Eerdmans, 2007), pp. 15–16.

17 Henry A. Lapham, *The Bible as Missionary Handbook* (Cambridge: Heffer, 1925), p. 82.

18 Lapham, *The Bible*, p. 82.

19 Lapham, *The Bible*, p. 82.

20 Sen, *Keshub Chunder Sen in England*, p. 252.

21 Sen, *Keshub Chunder Sen in England*, p. 321.

22 Lapham, *The Bible*, pp. 85–86.

23 Halvor Moxnes, Ward Blanton, and James G Crossley, "Introduction," in *Jesus Beyond Nationalism: Constructing the Historical Jesus in a Period of Cultural Complexity* (London: Equinox, 2009), p. 2.

24 Spence R. Hardy, *The Sacred Books of the Buddhists Compared with History and Modern Science* (Colombo: Wesleyan Mission Press, 1863), p. 3.

25 Hardy, *The Sacred Books*, p. 3.

26 Hardy, *The Sacred Books*, p. 68.

27 Hardy, *The Sacred Books*, p. 146.

28 Rhys T.W. Davids, *Buddhism: Being a Sketch of the Life and Teachings of Gautama, the Buddha* (London: Society for Promoting Christian Knowledge, 1910), p. 87.

29 Rhys T.W. Davids, *Lectures on the Origin and Growth of Religion, as Illustrated by Some Points in the History of Indian Buddhism: The Hibbert Lectures 1881* (London: Williams and Norgate, 1891), p. 36.

30 Allan Mark Powell, *What is Narrative Criticism?* (Minneapolis: Fortress, 1990); John H. Elliott, *What is Social-Scientific Criticism?* (Minneapolis: Fortress, 1993).

31 Bruce J. Malina, *Windows on the World of Jesus: Time Travel to Ancient Judea* (Louisville, KY: Westminster/Knox, 1993), p. 15.

32 John J. Pilch, *The Cultural World of Jesus: Sunday by Sunday, Cycle A* (Collegeville, PA: Liturgical, 1995), p. 100.

33 John J. Pilch, *The Cultural World of Jesus: Sunday by Sunday, Cycle B* (Collegeville, PA: Liturgical, 1994), p. 72.

3

Postcolonial Biblical Studies in Action
Origins and Trajectories
Ralph Broadbent

> "When I use 'postcolonial,'" Humpty Dumpty said, in a rather scornful tone, "it means just what I choose it to mean – neither more nor less."
> "The question is," said Alice, "whether you can make words mean so many different things."
> "The question is," said Humpty Dumpty, "which is to be master – that's all."
> Through the Looking Glass (with apologies to Lewis Carroll)

The aim of this chapter is to provide a short overview of the origins and main themes of postcolonial biblical criticism. It is one of the most exciting methods of reading the Bible to have emerged in recent times. It provides challenge, insight, and a new way of thinking about the biblical texts and their exegesis which would have been unthinkable only a few years ago. Like its secular counterpart, it has served to enrage traditionalists and called into question established ways of doing business within the academy. As mentioned at the end of the previous chapter, how successful this has been is another matter.

Exploring Postcolonial Biblical Criticism: History, Method, Practice, First Edition.
R. S. Sugirtharajah.
© 2012 R. S. Sugirtharajah, with the exception of Chapter 3 © 2012 Blackwell Publishing Ltd.
Published 2012 by Blackwell Publishing Ltd.

So what exactly is postcolonial biblical criticism? The dilemma facing Lewis Carroll's fictional characters will have become clear from the earlier chapters of this volume. What exactly is meant by the term "postcolonial"? The multiple variations in "secular" discussions are equally well reflected within biblical postcolonial criticism. In some cases, postcolonial has come to mean little more than biblical exegesis vaguely originating in some sort of Third World context – the historical-critical method of criticism originating with a thin non-European veneer.[1] In other cases, postcolonial has become an excuse for biblical scholars to regurgitate scholarly summaries of the more abstruse aspects of postcolonial theory which make complex medieval theological questions, such as angels dancing on pinheads, seem models of clarity, sweetness, and light. Paul's remarks to the Corinthians concerning dark mirrors and seeing face to face can seem rather apposite.

It would, however, be unfortunate if these elements of dullness or obscurity served to hide the radical challenges presented by postcolonial biblical criticism. This chapter will try to present an overview of how postcolonial theory and biblical scholarship have interacted. An initial section will examine the early attempts to make use of the theory (in all its complexity). This will be followed by themed sections (e.g., postcolonialism and feminist exegesis) which will give an insight into the main themes which have emerged.

Origins

As might be expected, postcolonial biblical criticism has multiple origins and precursors. But in strict chronological terms, the first published systematic attempt to outline postcolonial biblical criticism as a possible programmatic way forward for biblical studies came from the pen of R.S. Sugirtharajah in a 1996 article in the *Asia Journal of Theology*.[2] Other important works were also appearing at this time which took imperialism and colonialism seriously: Philip Chia's postcolonial reading of the first chapter of Daniel, Keith Whitelam's *The Invention of Ancient Israel*, Michael Prior's *The Bible and Colonialism*, and Richard Horsley's collection of essays on *Paul and Empire*.[3] Interestingly, with the exception of the last, these initial offerings were from outside North America. We will return to these works below, along with a volume of the journal *Semeia* which also played an important catalytic role in the dissemination of postcolonial biblical criticism. However, as a starting point we will examine Sugirtharajah's article and use it as some sort of initial benchmark, looking at what was proposed and then, as the chapter develops, looking at how these initial early proposals were taken up, developed, changed, and challenged by the subsequent flood of material which was to follow over the next decade and a half.

If one had to answer the question of where and how postcolonial biblical studies originated, at least one answer would have to be the chance encounter between R.S. Sugirtharajah and Edward Said's *Orientalism* in a now long-defunct Birmingham bookshop called Hudson's. This encounter underpinned the initial article, "From Orientalist to Post-Colonial: Notes on Reading Practices."

The article highlighted three existing categories or styles of biblical interpretation, Orientalist, anglicist, nativist, and a possible way forward beyond their competing and limited claims – a postcolonial reading. The first reading category, "Orientalist," tried to show the "interconnection between Vedic texts and biblical narratives."[4] Just as the Orientalist tradition (identified by Said) had, during the imperial era, tried to recover India's ancient languages and traditions with a view to controlling and shaping these traditions and exercising power over them (and thus the natives), so one of the main aims of this mode of scriptural interpretation was to recover the learned Brahmanical tradition and show how these Indian scriptural traditions, bypassing the Hebrew scriptures, led directly to (New Testament) Christianity.

The second reading category, "anglicism," took a different approach. It imported into India "Western reading techniques in the form of historical criticism … and … biblical theology with its grand-themes [of] the Bible as a theologically unified whole … also … the view that narratives are objects with determinated meanings, and hence the commitment to discover *the* meaning of the text."[5] The outcome of this was that Indian religious texts were labeled as valueless, mere myths and fables (as per Macaulay's famous quote about a shelf of Western books being more valuable than all of India's writings). The fluid Indian storytelling tradition whereby new meanings come through retelling (and changing) stories is now replaced by so-called objectivity, and truth is no longer to be found in India and its traditions, but comes from elsewhere – that is, the Hebraic/Hellenistic tradition. As Sugirtharajah points out, this anglicist approach is still used, for example, in the Indian journal *Bible Bhashyam* which has enough Bultmann and Käsemann to keep the most traditional Westernized biblical critic happy.

The third reading category, "nativism," was the response to the first two approaches. Those who had had enough of high-flown, learned Sanskritic theories and equally dense Western academic theories turned to their own "performance traditions and [vernacular] textual tradition."[6] This could be seen as some sort of liberation approach, though not without shortcomings, as we will see later.

In response to these approaches, Sugirtharajah proposes a postcolonial approach. This new approach would challenge the "universalist, totalising forms of European interpretation." It would see that the modernist values of the other modes of interpretation "such as objectivity and neutrality are expressions of political, religious and scholarly power." These modernist values would be challenged with the "perception of truth as mapped, constructed and negotiated." The postcolonial approach would also highlight the stories and accounts of hidden or invisible groups, "women, minorities, the disadvantaged, and the displaced." Two other features of postcolonial reading are that "oppositional or protest voices in the texts" would be highlighted and that Christian sacred texts would be placed side by side with Hindu, Buddhist, and Confucian sacred texts.[7]

In this short article, there is what might be termed the Urmanifesto of postcolonial biblical interpretation. A series of challenges is thrown down to traditional Western exegesis: truth is not confined to the text and is not singular, but can take many forms;

non-Christian sacred texts are as important as Christian texts; the biblical text is not unique or the sole bearer of truth; the voices of the marginalized are to be heard and recovered. But within this, there is a critique not only of the Western, modernist, anglicist tradition, but also of the older Orientalist tradition and the more recent nativist tradition. All readings, both Eastern and Western, are open to critique. Just because something is "native" does not make it more true or authentic, just as what is Western and heavily footnoted is likewise not necessarily the bearer of truth. As we will see later, these themes were to be developed further and refined, but the crucial point is that Sugirtharajah had developed some sort of programmatic framework.

In the same year that Sugirtharajah's Ur-manifesto appeared, Keith Whitelam's book *The Invention of Ancient Israel* was published with the not uncontroversial subtitle, *The Silencing of Palestinian History*. It is noteworthy that this book is unmentioned in the various accounts of the development of postcolonial biblical scholarship. On the one hand, this may be just one of those historical accidents. On the other, it could be either that most scholars involved in postcolonial biblical studies have been NT specialists rather than Hebrew scripture scholars, or simply that the whole argument of the book was too hot to handle. Whatever the reason, Whitelam presents a long and detailed description of the ideological bias of much of what passes for OT scholarship. Importantly, from our perspective, the book makes detailed reference to the postcolonial work of Edward Said and also the work of the Indian-based Subaltern Studies Group.[8]

Whitelam outlines the three main models or schools of ancient Israelite history put forward by scholars to explain the arrival of the people of Israel in the promised land of Cannan: the Alt and Noth "peaceful" immigration/infiltration model; the Albright and Bright conquest/invasion model; and the Mendenhall and Gottwald model of some sort of internal, religious revolution or peasants' revolt driven by a materialist reading of history.[9] Whitelam's point is that these pictures of ancient Israel are not the result of the scholarly sifting of evidence, either archaeological or textual, but are all ideologically driven constructs. So, "ancient Israel was invented in terms of the European nation state."[10] Whitelam argues:

> The driving force of biblical studies has been the need to search for ancient Israel as the taproot of Western civilization, a need that has been reinforced by the demands of Christian theology in search of the roots of its own uniqueness in the society which produced the Hebrew Bible. This has been reinforced with the foundation of the modern state of Israel, giving rise to a search by Israeli scholarship for its own national identity deep in the past.[11]

This exposes,

> the power of the discourse of biblical studies which has projected an aura of objective scholarship when it is quite clear that subjective and unconscious elements have played a key role in constructions of the imagined past of ancient Israel.[12]

Thus,

> The mirage of the Davidic "empire," the retrojection of the modern state of Israel into the Iron Age, has completely distorted the representation of the history of the region.[13]

In all of this, Whitelam provides a carefully worked out example of Said's work on the ideology and power of European colonialism and its ability to shape history ideologically, as well as using the work of the Subaltern Studies Group ("history from below") in trying to recover submerged ancient Palestinian history. Whitelam's volume was to be followed a few years later by another important volume on the Hebrew scriptures, Kim's *Decolonizing Josiah*, which built on some of the insights Whitelam had provided, but used the Asian-American context as an interpretative tool and also unpacked, among other things, the craft of writing history from a postcolonial perspective.[14]

Like Whitelam's book, Michael Prior's 1997 work *The Bible and Colonialism* had an important subtitle, *A Moral Critique.*[15] Moore rightly notes that this is also a book that "has not received the attention it deserves within postcolonial biblical criticism."[16] While referring to Edward Said's work (though, interestingly, not to *Orientalism*), Prior's main concern was to uncover how the Hebrew scriptures, with some of the central themes such as "land," "Exodus," "conquest," and the destruction of Canaan and its peoples, allegedly by divine mandate, came to serve as a paradigm for current events in Israel/Palestine, and in earlier times for Christian missions in Latin America and South Africa.[17] Prior contrasts the effect these biblically inspired themes have had with basic secular human rights legislation and asks how it is possible that biblical critics have largely avoided critiquing both the biblical texts and their own lack of involvement in exposing injustice. For Prior, biblical scholars are not "justified in maintaining an academic detachment from significant engagement in real, contemporary issues."[18] A similar problem also arises with those liberation theologians who have in some ways uncritically adopted the Exodus paradigm as the basic foundation for their theologies. For Prior, there is no question that the Bible is an imperialist text. He notes:

> it is not without irony that the Bible, and its use as a legitimating document for the colonial ventures we have discussed, is applied against the interests of peoples for whom the biblical text had no corresponding authority. The very application by outsiders, Christian and Jewish, of the world view of the Bible to a people for whom it had no authoritative standing is a striking example of religious and political imperialism.[19]

But Prior is not simply critical of the Christian Bible:

> in the light of history one must question whether *the values of the Torah, the Koran and the Bible* can be relied upon to promote justice and peace, and underpin the imperatives of human rights.[20]

63

Here, Prior is unafraid to look at the complexities of the main religious texts implicated in the problems of the Middle East and question their usefulness, particularly alongside the strength and usefulness of secular human rights legislation.

The third early piece noted was an article, "On Naming the Subject: Postcolonial Reading of Daniel 1," which first appeared in the Hong Kong journal *Jian Dao*.[21] This article appeared at the time of and was influenced by the handover of Hong Kong from British imperial control to the neo-colonialism of Chinese rule on July 1, 1997. As Chia notes:

> This essay is dedicated, in memory of Hong Kong, named as a British Subject for more than a hundred years, and shall be renamed as a "special administration region" when it returns to China's sovereignty; and to those Chinese nationals who hold BNO passports, a subject with hybrid identity.[22]

Chia makes specific reference to two of Frantz Fanon's works, *The Wretched of the Earth* and *Black Skin, White Masks*. Using insights from Fanon, Chia argues that Daniel 1 has lessons for postcolonial Hong Kong as it becomes subject to neo-colonialism. The figure of Daniel allows resistance to the "dominating power of the colonizer."[23]

In his detailed exegesis of Daniel 1, Chia teases out the story of Daniel's resistance. The scene is set in the opening verses which allow the voices of the colonized to be heard and "the identity of the colonized as a superior subject" to become clear.[24] Nebuchadnezzar's strategy for colonization is revealed in this post-colonial reading. It is a project which begins by separating the elite from the people, a colonial strategy of divide and rule. This small elite will be required to learn the Chaldean language and be educated in Chaldean culture (just as the Indian elite were taught English during British rule in India and the Algerian elite were taught French during the period of Fanon's writing). The effect of this is to suppress, or at least label wholly inferior, native culture while at the same time reinforcing and labeling the imperial culture as superior. Furthermore, those thus educated are given or required to take Chaldean names; the colonizer gains the power of controlling meaning.[25] In turn this leads to hybrid identity for the colonized.

However, resistance is possible for the colonized. Daniel and his companions swap the rich food and wine provided by the king for plain vegetables and water. Their health and appearance become noticeably better than their Chaldean contemporaries.[26] This, in turn, leads to successful resistance because when Daniel and the others are questioned on all manner of things by the king, they are found to be wiser than the native Chaldeans.[27]

The fourth early text is Richard Horsley's edited collection *Paul and Empire*.[28] This collection is important because it marks the beginning of what has come to be known as "Empire studies." Instead of reading Christianity exclusively against Judaism, Christian history is now seen as something to be read over against Roman imperial history. We will return to this strand of postcolonial biblical studies in due course. For now, a quote from Horsley's opening will give a taste of what was being proposed:

> Christianity was a product of empire. In one of the great ironies of history, what became the established religion of empire started as an anti-imperial movement. Although some would still view Jesus as an innocuous religious teacher, it is becoming increasingly evident to many that he catalyzed a movement of the renewal of Israel – a movement over against Roman rule as well as the Jerusalem priestly aristocracy. While some still read Paul through the lens of Lutheran theology, it is becoming increasingly clear that, in anticipation of the termination of "this evil age" at the parousia of Christ, Paul was energetically establishing *ekklēsiai* among the nations that were alternatives to official "assemblies" of cities such as Thessalonica, Philippi, and Corinth. As expressed in the baptismal formula Paul quotes in Gal. 3:28, the principal social divisions of "this world … that is passing away" (1 Cor. 7:29, 31) were overcome in these communities of the nascent alternative society.[29]

What Horsley is proposing is that the early Pauline Christian communities were anti-imperial resistance groups of some kind. This line of thinking clearly builds on earlier work on the gospels by figures such as Crossan.

The final text I want to mention in this section on origins is the journal *Semeia* and the volume edited by Laura Donaldson, *Postcolonialism and Scriptural Reading*. This is often seen as an originating text for postcolonial biblical studies, and its printed date (1996) suggests this is the case. However, as was the nature of that particular journal series, chronologically it did not make its appearance until February 1998, rather later than some of the works already mentioned.[30] Whatever the chronology, however, the volume contained a diverse set of essays on the Bible and postcolonialism. Its editor (interestingly teaching English, women's studies, and American Indian/Native studies at the University of Iowa, rather than mainstream biblical studies) saw the essays as linked by a "critical focus on imperialism, neo-colonialism, and Eurocentrism" and, influenced by Said's *Orientalism*, investigating how these themes were "embodied in literary and theological forms."[31] Like Prior, she questioned the appropriateness of the Exodus tradition for liberation (perhaps not unexpectedly given her own Native American heritage and how the Exodus tradition had been used to justify the European colonization of North America),[32] noted the "myopia" of many ardent feminist scholars regarding colonialism,[33] and called for an investigation into the Great Commission (Matt. 28.19–20) and its link to imperial conquest.[34]

An essay in the journal by Jon Berquist served to show further the problematic nature of the biblical texts.[35] Berquist argued that in writing about the "Second Temple" period (the era of the rebuilding of the Jerusalem Temple after the exile) scholars have often assumed that even though Judah was controlled by the Persian empire, Judaism still had religious freedom. But if we take Said's insights seriously (particularly his *Culture and Imperialism*) it is unlikely that any such "religious" freedom existed. Everything, including religion, is ideological and controlled by the forces of empire. Thus, the first moves towards an authoritative OT canon in this period were imperial acts designed to give power to Cyrus and his imperial-colonizing project.[36] As Berquist puts it, "[c]anon is a function and expression of power, specifically imperial power."[37]

Elsewhere in his essay, Berquist argued that postcolonialism needed to "be informed by a careful class analysis if it [was] to succeed at its academic task of describing the effects of colonization or its ethical goal of decolonization in today's world."[38] The language used in this part of Berquist's essay has clear echoes of thinkers such as Gramsci and Althusser (e.g., "the social forces of production," the "ideological superstructure").[39] Berquist's essay concludes with a strong call for a complete re-evaluation of the scriptural canon, which is worth quoting at some length:

> to understand the canon as a postcolonial literature must first entail abandoning the absolutizing assertions about the developing canon. No longer can we assert that Judah's religious devotion was the ultimate force within society ... Likewise the fiction of a postexilic restoration must be rejected ... No one who went into exile "returned" although some of their children and grandchildren moved to Yehud as colonists. ... there was no master plan, only a colonizing impulse that took many of the same forms as Persian imperialism did in other neighboring areas.[40]

As can be seen, Berquist's essay continues and develops the postcolonial outlook with its questioning and exploration of canonical authority, the received historicity of the OT, the role of ideology, and the role of the biblical scholar.

One feminist scholar not guilty of Donaldson's charge of feminist "myopia" concerning colonialism is Musa Dube from Botswana. Her essay, "Reading for Decolonization," analyzes the story of the Samaritan woman in the Gospel of John. Referring to Said, Dube argued in this essay that the gospel describes the Samaritan woman as something empty, in need of colonization. These were the terms used in the high colonial period of European history to describe lands colonized by the imperial powers: the land was empty and the few natives that there were begged the imperial powers to help them. Of course, postcolonial criticism has shown this view of colonized nations to be an ideological construct to support imperial expansion. But there is an irony here. The "Johannine community embraces an ideology of expansion, despite the fact that they are themselves victims of imperial expansion and struggling for their liberation."[41] In other words, the Johannine community, despite being colonized by Rome, is happy to colonize the Samaritan community.

Dube further argues that this colonizing paradigm, embedded in the gospel text, would later come to provide scriptural authorization for "Christian disciples/readers/believers to travel, to enter, to educate, and to harvest other foreign lands for the Christian nations in a literary fashion that is openly modelled on imperialist values."[42] Dube backs up this assertion by an analysis of the story:

> the Samaritan woman is characterized as an ignorant native (v. 10) and in need of help (v. 10). She is constructed as morally/religiously lacking, that is, she had had five husbands, and the one she has is not her own (vv. 17–18), and she does not know what she worships (v. 22). On the contrary, Jesus, a superior traveller, is knowledgeable (vv. 10, 22); powerful (vv. 14, 25, 42); sees everything about her past (vv. 17–18, 29); knows and offers answers for her society (vv. 21–26); and teaches her and her people (vv. 21–23). The ignorance of the Samaritan woman is pathetic. ... Ignorance here is furthered by employing female gender.[43]

A final important point is made by Dube's essay. She notes that "the Johannine Jesus emerges fully clothed in the emperor's titles" as "Savior of the World."[44] The Johannine community has installed a new emperor to replace the one in Rome. This theme was to become a key part of postcolonial exegesis.

Other essays in the volume raised questions concerning the relationship between postcolonial exegesis and liberation theology. Hector Avalos makes the claim that postcolonial literature includes the works of liberation theologians such as Gutiérrez and Segundo and paraphrases of the psalms by Cardenal.[45] Kimberley Rae Connor sees the tradition of slave spirituals as falling in the postcolonial tradition. Slaves were written out of history, of little consequence.

So the spirituals provide "a difficult and highly complex means of working one's way back into history."[46] How do the colonized resist, or to put it in postcolonial phraseology, can the subaltern speak?

The final part of the volume contains responses to the essays. Of particular note is the response by Elsa Tamez. She notes that there is a difference between the colonialist reading of the biblical texts, which believe in objectivity and universality, and the popular readings of those discriminated against because of class, race, or gender. The latter readings not only challenge the colonial myth of objective readings, but "the very sacred texts in themselves even when they are read from an anti-colonial perspective":

> This is because the hermeneutical battle is framed in the dominant Western culture. The daily experiences, the perspectives from different worlds, and the multiple experiences of God have not found a place in the biblical readings nor in the biblical texts themselves. ... When the new theories of text reconstruction are applied, it is crucial to cross the boundaries of the canon, search for different texts, and write new gospels with inclusive categories.[47]

It may be that Tamez has here, at least in part, answered the question about the difference between liberation exegesis and postcolonial exegesis. The former is well aware of the difficulties with traditional exegesis and tries to remedy those defects while trying to rescue the biblical text. The latter realizes that exegesis is not the only problem. The real problem is that the biblical text itself is inadequate for the needs and experiences of many people and so may need to be put to one side while new texts and scriptures are written. This ambivalence about scripture, to save the text or not to save the text, will emerge as a key debate, at times explicit, at times implicit, within postcolonial biblical studies.

Building the Picture

After the initial period of postcolonial criticism outlined above, the discipline began to put down deeper roots. Sugirtharajah continued to produce a string of works, both edited volumes and books. Other voices also became prominent in the discipline, particularly Fernando Segovia. Other names include Steven Moore, Musa Dube, and Roland Boer. A series of volumes appeared, from 1998 onwards, under the series title *The Bible and Postcolonialism*, initially published by Sheffield Academic Press, with an editorial board gathered by Sugirtharajah of Fernando Segovia, Kwok Pui-lan, Sharon Ringe, Ralph Broadbent, and Marcella Althaus-Reid. It would be difficult to give even brief summaries of each of the volumes that appeared, so in this section we will examine some of the main themes which began to appear.

In 1998, Sugirtharajah published a volume entitled *Asian Biblical Hermeneutics and Postcolonialism: Contesting the Interpretations*. The chapters in this volume served to reinforce his earlier attempts to outline a "manifesto" for postcolonial biblical studies. Of particular note are the chapters on Indian readings of the Bible from the nineteenth-century colonial period and the Bible commentaries that were written a little later towards the end of the Victorian era. These illustrate aspects of the battle between native exegesis and missionary exegesis in the colonial era. Rammohun Roy argued that the missionaries' picture of god, Jesus, and the Bible was, in fact, marred by heathenism and unacceptable to Indians. He wrote:

> I am sorry to say ... the idea of a triune-God, a man-God, and also the idea of the appearance of God in the bodily shape of a dove, or that of the blood of God shed for the payment of debt, seem entirely Heathenism and absurd.[48]

As Sugirtharajah puts it, Rammohun Roy "was reminding the missionaries that the Jesus they projected was not an Englishman, and that the Christian message they promoted was by no means an English people's religion, because Jesus himself was an Asiatic and reflected the sentiments and ethos of Asians."[49]

In contrast to this, Sugirtharajah's exploration of the Indian Church Commentaries, heavyweight tomes similar to today's International Critical Commentaries, reveal the mainstream missionary position. Hinduism is seen as the demonized "other" of Christianity and is thus, by definition, an inferior faith. As Sugirtharajah remarks, "Christianity is presented as a historical, practical, and relevant religion, whereas the other faiths are projected as ritualistic, idolatrous, and superstitious."[50]

Using postcolonial language, Sugirtharajah summarizes the commentaries in this way:

> not surprisingly these commentaries persistently fall back on binary distinctions of Christians and heathens, believers and unbelievers, "us" and "them." The construction of the demonized "Other" serves to validate the superiority of the Christian faith. The unfamiliar sights and sounds associated with Hindu religious practices are perceived as antithetical to Christianity and are therefore presented as inferior to Christian religious practices. The effect of all this is to establish British dominance, and to provide the moral imperative for imperial intervention, subjugation, and the prolongation of the British presence in a heathen land.[51]

This all raises the question of resistance to Western imperializing Christianity and shows clearly that the natives could speak back.

The native speaking back and contesting imperial Christianity has been documented in other colonial contexts. In Zimbabwe, the Shona people were colonized through the colonization of their deity Mwari. Once this deity had been equated to the biblical god, the only real way to follow their own deity was to become Western and abandon their own Shona identity.[52] Yet this classic colonizing move was not always successful. In a study of Tamil translations of the Bible from the early nineteenth century, Israel has shown that Protestant Tamils were not simply at the mercy of the colonial missionaries and their translations, but "adopted and translated the Bible and its languages on their own terms."[53]

Now while resistance was sometimes possible, the power of colonial Bible translations should not be underestimated. These colonial translations served to reinforce colonial attitudes and self-confidence among the colonizers. As a result, Indian texts containing fables were seen as defiled and in need of cleansing. Native interpreters were deemed unreliable and the "colonizer has an inalienable right to explain and speak on behalf of the natives."[54] Thus, "colonial translations justified the colonizer's civilizing mission, and established the inherent superiority of the colonizer's culture."[55] Additionally, there were consequences for the Indian hermeneutical tradition. The Bible and its translation into native languages affected other religious traditions.[56] The process introduced the idea of "a fixed holy text which acted as an objective marker of a religious community." It forced Hindus to come up with their own fixed versions of texts such as the *Bhagavad Gita*, the *Vedas*, and the *Upanishads*. It also introduced (artificial) concerns for "accuracy, authenticity, and being true to original texts," whereas "Indians were more interested in the aesthetic flavor than literal accuracy." Retelling, modifying, and changing texts was the Indian norm.[57]

The idea of a fixed versus fluid tradition also had consequences for portrayals of Jesus. Sugirtharajah welcomes various recent portrayals of Jesus by scholars such as Vermes, Crossan, Borg, and Horsley which "have gone a long way to rectify the images of an abstract, ahistorical, and imperialistic Christ." But because Eurocentric scholarship has always looked to "Greece for its intellectual and philosophical roots" and Judaism for "its religious roots," these new portrayals have "effectively silenced and erased any possible influence of Eastern religious thought on the lifestyle and thinking of Jesus."[58]

Yet it would be equally possible to argue that the picture of Jesus as a wandering preacher fits the Buddhist tradition better than the Israelite prophetic tradition. Likewise, the Q source for the gospels could be some sort of adopted Buddhist text and the thought patterns of John's Gospel may be closer to Buddhism than Jewish or Hellenistic categories.[59] For Sugirtharajah, an awareness of this sort of interfaith cross-fertilization would serve to remind followers of all faith traditions that "no religion develops on its own, but grows in interaction with others, fashioning at least some of its own distinctiveness by new combinations of existing elements." This could also serve as a starting point for interfaith dialogue which could not only catalogue the similarities and differences between different faiths, but also "engage in an ideological and cultural critique of both Christian and other religious traditions and expose their virulent sides."[60] Again, we can see here that postcolonial biblical criticism ranges rather more widely than the narrow confines of the traditional historical-critical method.

This lack of attention by Western scholars to "Eastern" traditions and history is explored elsewhere in Sugirtharajah's work. He draws attention to the artificial structures of Church expansion in the Acts of the Apostles. The so-called "missionary journeys" of Paul in Acts are an invention of the imperial era. Both early Christian writers, such as Irenaeus and Jerome, and later writers such as Erasmus and Calvin failed to detect any missionary itinerary in Acts.[61] In fact, what "the author of Acts fails to record is that there was another history of the founding of the Church east of the Euphrates and throughout the Persian Empire, whose territorial control extended to the borders of India."[62] Further possible Eastern influences on the New Testament are also noted, for example, giving one's body to be burnt in 1 Cor.; the gospel source M may have originated in Edessa on the Silk Road; stories about Jesus's childhood might likewise have had Eastern influences.[63] Thus, a postcolonial reading "will celebrate the hybridized and eclectic nature of religious stories," "will refuse to be limited by religionist and preservationist imperatives," and will "ascribe fluidity to the texts."[64]

This fluidity of the text is a theme taken up by Musa Dube in an essay on John's Gospel which appeared in 1998. She picks up the need (in an African context) to uncover the colonizing readings of the biblical texts and instead to read them for what she terms "liberating independence." Thus the biblical text can be read for liberation. But she also notes the necessity of finding readings which "highlight the biblical texts and Jesus as undoubtedly important cultures, which are, nonetheless, not 'above all' but among the many important cultures of the world."[65]

While we are noting the foundational texts and ideas, attention should also be drawn to the work of Fernando Segovia. Based at Vanderbilt University in Nashville, Segovia has been a leading and pivotal figure in the development of postcolonial biblical criticism, particularly in the USA. In what has become something of a foundational text for the discipline, "Biblical Criticism and Postcolonial Studies: Toward a Postcolonial Optic," Segovia set out some of his ideas.[66]

Segovia notes that postcolonialism is a congenial discipline for him personally as he comes from the margins, resides in the center, and has devoted himself "to the struggle for liberation and decolonization."[67] He makes three important points. First, the ancient texts of Judaism and Christianity inevitably reflect their varied imperial contexts. The reality of these empires "is of such reach and power that it inevitably affects and colors, directly or indirectly, the entire artistic production of center and margins, of dominant and subaltern, including their respective literary productions."[68] Second, the last 500 years of Western empires needs to be taken into account: "the shadow of empire in the production of modern readings of the ancient texts should also be underlined."[69] Third, it is important to take into account modern historical trends – the postcolonial and the neo-colonial – which influence the construction of meaning and interpretation.[70] These nuanced thoughts made the important point that there are many varieties of imperialism and empires. Unfortunately, this variety has not always been noted by some subsequent writings which claim to be postcolonial but where postcolonial has been little more than a code word for some sort of continuing victimhood.

In a later essay, Segovia gave a critical overview of the various theoretical approaches to postcolonial studies. He noted the many and varied distinctions within the field and the difficulties of definition. He also noted the apparent omissions in the field. For example, British imperialism is usually the defining imperialism while the imperialisms of the ancient world, Latin America, the Soviet Union, and the USA are passed over. Segovia's own preference at this point would be to replace "postcolonial" with "imperial-colonial" which he believes would allow for a wider debate and also allow transcultural and transhistorical discussions.[71]

The picture continued to be built by two major volumes by Sugirtharajah published in 2001 and 2002: *The Bible and the Third*

World: Precolonial, Colonial and Postcolonial Encounters, and *Postcolonial Criticism and Biblical Interpretation.* Both volumes will repay careful study and are full of newly developed insights. Here we will pick out some of the main themes which moved the discipline forwards.

The first volume had as its overall purpose "to trace how the Christian Bible, the ur text of European culture ... has been transmitted, received, appropriated and even subverted by Third World people."[72] An important first chapter traces aspects of the transmission of the Bible, particularly in the East, in the precolonial period. Its title, "Before the Empire: the Bible as a Marginal and Minority Text," sets the tone. Sugirtharajah draws attention to the importance of the Nestorian Eastern Bible in Syriac, the Peshitta, which was different to the Western canon.[73] This Eastern canon was very definitely a minority text, even more so than the Bible in the West. For example, in India the Syriac Bible was largely incomprehensible to Indian Christians, and Christianity survived in India not because of the Bible, but because of the Liturgy of the Apostles Addai and Mari. This was much like medieval England where the scriptures were in Latin and there was little demand for an English translation. The point Sugirtharajah is arguing is that the idea of a "Bible-based spirituality is something recent and Protestant in its origin and orientation."[74]

Even when the Bible was translated in the East, there was no obsession with an exact translation. Nestorian Christians in China

> used the Christian text as a springboard rather than an immobilizing anchor. The documents demonstrate that translation was for them an independent transcreative act, an experience of freedom. Unlike the colonial preoccupation with exact philological equivalents, a way of assuming control, Nestorians were looking for parallel expressions in Chinese culture.[75]

The central chapters of the book explore in more detail the Bible and its interpretation in the colonial period, filling out the picture sketched in earlier works. The final chapters make two important claims, central to Sugirtharajah's work. Chapter 7 begins to explore in more detail the connection or overlap between liberation hermeneutics and postcolonial hermeneutics. On the former, Sugirtharajah is clear about its shortcomings:

> When it emerged, liberation theology gave the impression that it was going to be a great force in altering the way we do theology itself, and in ushering in an era of radical changes. Sadly these failed to materialize. In its interpretive proposals, liberation hermeneutics continued to be conservative. In its appropriation of the Bible, in its expositions, in its obsession with Christ-centred hermeneutics, it remained within conventional patterns. ... It did not engage in an overall reappraisal of, nor did it desire, a reconfiguration of the basic theological concepts ... Instead of being a new agent in the ongoing work of God, liberation hermeneutics has ended up reflecting upon the theme of biblical liberation rather than being a liberative hermeneutics.[76]

Sugirtharajah makes an important point here, particularly (though by no means exclusively) in relation to Latin American versions of liberation theology. It would have been good to see this critique unpacked further, possibly using the work on ideology developed within cultural studies. The works of Gramsci, Althusser, and Stuart Hall might have given a deeper understanding of the ideological forces at work in the "conservatism" of liberation theology, though without altering Sugirtharajah's conclusion in any significant way.

In his final chapter, Sugirtharajah makes clear what he thinks a postcolonial reading might involve. It means moving beyond the confines of biblical texts and Church documents.[77] Postcolonial biblical criticism would not necessarily abandon the Christian tradition, but it would not confine itself "to a particular religious source."[78] One might ask, at this point, if postcolonial *biblical* criticism is something of a misnomer. However, for Sugirtharajah:

> Postcolonial space refuses to press for a particular religious stance as final and ultimate. As a point of entry, individual interpreters may have their own theological, confessional and denominational stance,

but this in itself does not preclude them from inquiring into and entertaining a variety of religious truth-claims. It is the multi-disciplinary nature of the enterprise which gives postcolonialism its energy. It sees revelation as an ongoing process which embraces not only the Bible, tradition, and the Church but also other sacred texts and contemporary secular events.[79]

Sugirtharajah's second volume, *Postcolonial Criticism and Biblical Interpretation*, continues to fill out the picture. Again, it should be seen as a compulsory part of the postcolonial curriculum. Here, however, we will draw attention to certain aspects. Postcolonial criticism is specifically seen as challenging the status quo. It "instigates and creates possibilities, and provides a platform for the widest possible convergence of critical forces, of multi-ethnic, multi-religious, and multi-cultural voices, to assert their denied rights and rattle the centre."[80] Sugirtharajah is also more explicit about how biblical scholars might involve themselves in the wider postcolonial agenda. Subjects for careful consideration would include "race, nation, translation, mission, textuality, spirituality, representation" as well as "plurality, hybridity, and postnationalism" along with a rethinking of "slaves, sex-workers, the homosexual divide, [and] people of mixed race."[81] In doing this, postcolonial biblical criticism tries to go "beyond the Christendom model, and seek[s] to place biblical scholarship in a non-missionary and less apologetical context."[82] But, as in his earlier volume, Sugirtharajah sees that postcolonialism demonstrates "that the Bible itself is part of the conundrum rather than a panacea for all the ills of the postmodern/postcolonial world ... [it is] an unsafe and a problematic text."[83]

The volume ends with a final plea for the relativity of scriptural texts:

> Scriptures are only pointers and not an end in themselves. Texts, dogmas, and creeds are not the only access to reality. I end with a quotation from a text which advocates both embracement and eventual abandonment, attachment and detachment from text. It comes from an ancient Indian text, *The Upanishads*. It contains this apparently sacrilegious thought: "Read, study and ceaselessly ponder the

> Scriptures; but once the light has shined within you, throw them away as you discard a brand which you have used to light your fire" (*Amritanada Upanishad* 1).[84]

This issue of the place of scriptures is, to use the current colloquialism, "the elephant in the room" (that which everyone is aware of but no one talks about). It applies to all textually based religious traditions, whatever ancient century provides their origin. Fundamentalists of all traditions shout loudly for a return to the true ancient text, but the circle cannot be squared and postcolonialism recognizes the difficulty and suggests a way forward. In the context of the Bible, the next section of this chapter gives a brief overview of one attempt to square the circle.

Postcolonialism and the Modern Empire: Or, American Biblical Studies Meets "The West Wing"

It is no coincidence that what has become known as the "empire studies" segment of postcolonial biblical studies emerged in very much the same period as the liberal (and sadly fictional) American president Josiah Bartlett and his staff of Leo, Toby, CJ, Josh, Sam, and Donna in the television series "The West Wing." In the same way that these fictional characters strove to rescue the American political system from right-wing lunacy, so the scholars involved in "empire studies" strove to rescue Jesus, Paul, and the biblical texts from right-wing fundamentalists.

A leading exponent of this type of postcolonial criticism has been the already mentioned Richard Horsley. His work emerged independently of postcolonial studies, perhaps being better described as a First World type of liberation theology in its early stages. But over time, this has become conflated with postcolonial biblical studies as the two strands have interacted and affected one another. Horsley's many works can be straightforwardly summarized: "Jesus ... led a prophetic movement to renew Israel among Galilean and other villages, revitalizing the traditional Mosaic covenantal principles of communal mutuality and justice, in resistance to oppressive Roman imperial rule."[85] Elsewhere Horsley argues that Mark's Gospel narrative is similar to the history from below produced by the Indian Subaltern Studies Group:

> Mark sharply opposes both alien imperial rule and its collaborators among the local "colonial" aristocracy. ... Mark exhorts an indigenous people's movement of resistance to the imperial order to embody an alternative social order ... In contrast with Luke-Acts ... Mark calls hearers/readers in the movement back to the villages of Galilee (presumably to continue the project inaugurated in Jesus' ministry; 14.23; 16.7). Jesus and his movement take an active and uncompromising stance against the temple-state in Jerusalem.[86]

Quoting Edward Said on the subject of the power to either allow or block narratives from emerging, Horsley argues that established Christianity coopted Mark's (radical) Gospel and that Western biblical studies have prevented the true submerged story of Christianity's radical beginnings from re-emerging.[87]

Horsley further argues that Paul is also part of this anti-imperial resistance movement. "Read from a postcolonial perspective ... Paul appears to resemble more recent anti-colonial leaders or postcolonial intellectuals in important respects."[88] Paul's "adamant uncompromising opposition to the Roman imperial order and his formation of communities as a kind of international anti-imperial alternate society, may be causes for reflection in the current postcolonial context."[89]

Within this strand of postcolonialism, similar views are put forward by Warren Carter whose work has concentrated on Matthew's Gospel. In his original large work, *Matthew and the Margins*, he describes the gospel as "a counternarrative."[90] For Carter, the "Gospel's audience resists the values, commitments, and agendas of the Roman empire."[91] In fact, it "constructs an alternative world. It resists imperial claims. It refuses to recognize that the world has to be ordered on those lines. It offers an alternative understanding of the world and human existence centered on God manifested in Jesus. It creates an alternative community and shapes anti-imperial praxis."[92] Writing a few years later (2007), Carter still takes the same view of Matthew, but his thought has developed and he is more aware of the limitations within Matthew. In ascribing "all authority" to Jesus (28.18) Carter notes that "the Gospel mirrors and replaces one system of absolute authority with another."[93] Thus Matthew is now a complex and contested text. On the one hand, the "exposure of Roman injustice and of the devastating impact of its reign is laudable." On the other hand, "the Gospel's imitation of imperial practices and mindset is not."[94] Likewise, Carter is aware of the limited nature of the gospel's exclusive claims and sees the need to look for god working in all peoples and in non-biblical texts, and to move beyond the language of "the empire/reign/kingdom of God."[95]

There are, of course, problems raised by this "empire studies" aspect of postcolonial biblical studies. First, much of it originated in the USA during a period of Republican political hegemony which raises the question of how much of it is wishful thinking. Some scholars have argued that, for example, Mark's Gospel is not a counter-imperial text at all.[96] Sugirtharajah has warned of the danger of being lulled "into believing that the Bible was a counter-imperial document."[97] Roland Boer makes a similar point, but goes on to raise a further question:

> The increasingly voluminous literature on "empire" and the New Testament has been trying to argue that Paul and indeed the whole New Testament offers resistance to the Roman Empire. Apart from my misgivings at such an effort to detoxify and rescue the text once more (a deeply confessional effort), it does not measure up.[98]

Boer is raising the important point of whether or not we should even try to rescue the biblical text when it is, as Sugirtharajah put it, a document which has been "used to sanction war, colonialism, annihilation of cultures, annexation of lands, racism, and imperial intentions."[99] Another difficulty with rescuing the text is that it may reinscribe authority to one single text and exclude (Carter's caveat above notwithstanding) non-biblical scriptures and writings.

It would, I think, be possible to argue that because of the particular circumstances of the USA and the role the biblical texts play in public life, the "empire studies" variation of postcolonialism with its emphasis on the biblical text was a necessary move in North America. Its aim was to provide a counterweight to the right-wing fundamentalist view of America as a "chosen nation under God" for the moral rearmament of the world. It might also be the case, however, that such studies have temporarily unbalanced the radical nature of the postcolonial project (however defined) and moved it back into the narrower confines of a single tradition. However, despite this, progress continued to be made and the next section will look at some examples of this.

The Postcolonial Commentary on the New Testament Writings

In 2007, under the editorship of Segovia and Sugirtharajah, *A Postcolonial Commentary on the New Testament Writings* was published. A few references have already been made to this work above, but in this section I want to give some examples of the exegesis it contains in order to provide some sort of feel for the breadth of concerns that postcolonialism covers. Virtually every page of this one-volume commentary will repay careful study and reflection.

Liew's commentary on Mark, for example, offers a very different take on the gospel than that of Horsley above. Liew's commentary builds on an earlier essay on Mark in which he had argued that "Mark has indeed internalized the imperialist ideology of his colonizers."[100] Liew goes on to note that "by defeating power with more power, Mark is, in the final analysis, no different from the 'might-is-right' ideology that has led to colonialism, imperialism and various forms of suffering and oppression. Mark's Jesus may have replaced the 'wicked' Jewish-Roman power, but the tyrannical, exclusionary and coercive politics goes on."[101]

Another difficulty Liew identifies in his commentary is that human beings (like the passive natives of colonial times) are objects that are acted upon rather than subjects who act. The only true actors are God and Satan and, as Satan's hold on the world is so strong, God has decided that only direct, violent intervention through the parousia will solve the problem: "This intervention will bring salvation to some and destruction to others; either way, human beings remain objects instead of subjects of agency."[102] Additionally, Liew sees Mark's Gospel as irredeemably patriarchal. Women will only ever be subjects in the domestic sphere and "will always be subjected to the men and the needs of the family."[103] The outcome of all this is that Liew feels he "must appraise the actions and attitudes that Mark endorses and excludes rather than assuming them to be timeless truths."[104] In other words, the gospel text is no longer authoritative.

Perhaps, unsurprisingly, the picture of the imperial Christ in the gospels also causes some difficulty for the commentators on the epistles. The authors of the commentary on Colossians write from the context of the Philippines. There the letter has been used to control indigenous traditions:

> the author asserts the supremacy and absolutism of Christ over all other religious and political claimants (1.13–20; 2.8–3.4). These texts have been a powerful tool in the history of the colonial missionary enterprise, a weapon used to reject indigenous rituals, practices and beliefs of colonized and converted peoples. Still today, these texts are used in the Philippines by pastors attempting to curtail the persistence of traditional, indigenous rituals, especially in rural settings. In particular, these texts have targeted earth-based spiritualities of the indigenous peoples and have annihilated their religious functionaries.[105]

This is the classic "anglicist" position of destroying native culture. But it is also a reminder that such things are not confined to a long-lost "colonial" past but are still very much present.

Other NT texts are found to be more congenial to the interpreter. Sharon Ringe writes on the letter of James, a favorite of liberation theologians. Western commentators have long domesticated the discussions about the rich and poor in this epistle, usually through talking of "spiritual" riches and poverty rather than the hard realities of the latter. For Ringe, James is a "postcolonial voice" calling "for a response to the imperial reality" which is concrete rather than some sort of "inner or spiritualized religion." This response is still required today and is based on "the author's affirmation of the inherently destabilizing values of the gospel – parity, community and integrity or coherence of life – that tenaciously resist imperial challenges, whether from Rome or a later day."[106]

There are many other insights in this volume, but I want to end this section by drawing attention to Jennifer Bird's commentary on Ephesians. Among the points she makes is the observation that in "the process of the exaltation of Christ, Jesus loses that which made him human, and his followers are simply trading in one ruler for another."[107] However, the practical effect of this is that as Christians have "their true citizenship in a heavenly empire, their dealings on earth matter very little, and thus submission to the ruler of this world's empire, for the sake of peace or the avoidance of persecution, is quite reasonable."[108] It is one of Bird's final comments that is, perhaps, the most devastating in a postcolonial context. For the Ephesians, "in order for their counter-empire to make any sense, the earthly empire must be maintained."[109] While she does not pursue this further, the simple sentence raises the question of how Christianity might survive without imperial language within its doctrinal formulations. It also raises the intriguing question of what shape Christianity might take in North America when (as is probably the case) American neo-colonialism comes to an end.

Postcolonialism and Feminism

It is always difficult for any scholar to define the exact relationship between two such amorphous terms as postcolonialism and feminism. Kwok Pui-lan makes a good attempt in an essay first published in 2005, "Making the Connections: Postcolonial Studies and Feminist Biblical Interpretation." She sees these two disciplines as creating "a space" so that women in "colonial and semicolonial situations can be remembered in order to enliven our historical and moral imagination."[110] To traditional, male-dominated, historical-critical scholarship the idea of "moral imagination" may seem improper, but Whitelam's argument should be remembered here: that ancient Israel has, within traditional scholarship, been both "subjective" and "imagined" and little more than "midrashic historiography."[111] Likewise, the free-flowing patristic traditions of biblical interpretation also remind the reader that strict historical-critical interpretation is a rather recent invention.

Kwok goes on to note that within postcolonial criticism, male critics in particular have paid scant attention to gender issues.[112] She argues that certain themes are central to postcolonial feminist scholarship, whatever methodological tools are adopted. First of all, these scholars "want to investigate how the symbolization of women and the deployment of gender in the text relate to class interests, modes of production, concentration of state power, and colonial domination."[113] Second, Kwok argues that special attention should be paid to biblical women in the "contact zone" in biblical stories. She defines a contact zone as "the space of colonial encounters where people of different geographical and historical backgrounds are brought into contact with each other, usually shaped by inequality and conflictual relations. One such figure is the prostitute Rahab."[114] Third, postcolonial feminist critics are suspicious of "metropolitan interpretations."[115] Also, these metropolitan scholars have often "failed to question the ideology of mission in the text and continue to assume that biblical traditions are universally valid for all cultures."[116]

A fourth point Kwok makes is that postcolonial feminist critics will emphasize "the roles and contributions of ordinary readers," thus enlarging "the interpretive community" and bringing to the fore the suppressed knowledges that are often dismissed by "academic elites."[117] Linked to this is Kwok's final point. She calls to mind what the biblical scholar Mary Ann Tolbert has called "the politics and poetics of location." Kwok interprets this as "the complexity of one's social background, such as gender, race, and sexual orientation, as well as one's national and institutional context and economic and educational status, which determine who speaks and who is likely to listen."[118] The themes outlined by Kwok appear in many other postcolonial feminist readings. For example, Laura Donaldson's "The Sign of Orpah" specifically mentions the "contact zone."[119]

Another approach adopted by postcolonial feminist scholars is to take particular scriptural passages which involve women and to exegete them using not only a hermeneutic of suspicion (well known in feminist criticism) but also tools and themes provided by postcolonial criticism. As already mentioned above, Jennifer Bird's commentary on Ephesians displays an acute awareness of imperial ideology. Her reading strategy has four specific aspects to which she wants to direct suspicion: "(1) resonances with the methods of imperial propaganda, (2) imagery that counters, yet reinscribes, an imperial order, (3) constructions of gender roles that perpetuate the subordination of women to men, which is one of many particular manifestations of imperial order and (4) potential glimmers of hope for a liberationist subversion of the author's own construction."[120] When she reads Ephesians with those concerns, Christianity becomes a tool for social conformity and inequality.

In a similar way, Dora Mbuwayesango discusses the role of women, both Canaanite and Israelite, in the book of Deuteronomy. She notes in her subtitle that this is potentially at the "intersection of sexism and imperialism."[121] The deuteronomic law codes "normalize males as property owners. Women in general and female sexuality in particular are assumed to be and treated as properties of men."[122] Now, this is pretty well indisputable, but so what? Deuteronomy is clearly a sexist, imperializing, colonizing text. But what is the next step, in terms of either moving beyond the text or ensuring the equality of women? This we are not told.

One possible answer to this dilemma comes from an essay by Karen King, "Canonization and Marginalization: Mary of Magdala."[123] Writing in a feminist context, King argues that to do justice to the importance of Mary Magdala, it will be necessary to problematize the biblical canon "as a starting point for both historical reconstruction and theological reflection." That is to say that the process of canonization was part of a move towards "orthodoxy" which was designed to exclude women from leadership and condemn as "heretical" anyone who took women's leadership seriously.[124] Here again, we can see the whole problem of biblical authority raised.

Postcolonial Biblical Criticism: Some Critical Voices

The postcolonial approach does, of course, bring its own dangers and is open to critique. From those still pursuing the traditional approach to biblical studies it is, as has been pointed out elsewhere, something too hot to handle, as it challenges many "orthodox" positions in both the academy and the ecclesiastical world.[125] There is also the danger of theoretical obsession. As Sugirtharajah pointed out in his introduction to *The Postcolonial Biblical Reader*, if the volume was to succeed as a reader, it would

> not be in championing or contradicting the theory [postcolonialism], but in fostering whatever response is possible in the field of political action. Ultimately, as the late Edward Said made abundantly clear in his writings, political responsibility must take priority over theoretical engagement.[126]

Other scholars have drawn attention to the lack of a Marxist perspective within postcolonial biblical studies (though the work of the Subaltern Studies Group in India has been influenced by Marxist theory). Among scholars making this point are Roland Boer,[127] David Jobling,[128] and Gerald West.[129] All of these scholars worry that postcolonialism has become too bland or theoretically concerned to be truly oppositional. A good parallel can be seen in cultural studies. In its original form, cultural studies made use of Marxist insights to critique the writing of (for example) history and to uncover ideological biases within the standard accounts. However, as cultural studies became more mainstream, so its cutting or critical edge became rather blunted. The same danger is there for postcolonial biblical studies.

By way of a brief conclusion to this chapter, it seems clear that postcolonial biblical studies has produced some remarkable insights into the biblical text and the shortcomings of the practice of both academic and popular exegesis. Certainly still largely unfulfilled is the engagement with non-biblical traditions and texts, whether religious or secular. What this means for the future of biblical studies is a question still to be answered. As we have examined various aspects of postcolonial biblical studies, there has been a tension between keeping and reinterpreting the text and the other option of abandoning the text (or at least putting it alongside other ancient traditions). Postcolonialism also presents wider challenges to so-called "doctrinal orthodoxy" for all religious traditions. It may be simply too hot to handle for too many people.

Notes

1 See for example the Indian biblical journal *Bible Bashyam*.
2 R.S. Sugirtharajah, "From Orientalist to Post-Colonial: Notes on Reading Practices," *Asia Journal of Theology* 10, 1 (April 1996), 20–27.
3 Philip Chia, "On Naming the Subject: Postcolonial Reading of Daniel 1," in *The Postcolonial Biblical Reader*, ed. R.S. Sugirtharajah (Oxford: Blackwell, 2006), pp. 171–185; Keith W. Whitelam, *The Invention of Ancient Israel: The Silencing of Palestinian History* (London: Routledge, 1996); Michael Prior, *The Bible and Colonialism: A Moral Critique* (Sheffield: Sheffield Academic, 1997); Richard A. Horsley, *Paul and Empire: Religion and Power in Roman Imperial Society* (Harrisburg, PA: Trinity, 1997).
4 Sugirtharajah, "From Orientalist to Post-Colonial," p. 21.
5 Sugirtharajah, "From Orientalist to Post-Colonial," p. 22.
6 Sugirtharajah, "From Orientalist to Post-Colonial," pp. 22–23.
7 Sugirtharajah, "From Orientalist to Post-Colonial," pp. 24–25.
8 Whitelam, *Ancient Israel*, p. 7 and passim.

9   Whitelam, *Ancient Israel*, pp. 71ff.

10 Whitelam, *Ancient Israel*, p. 70.

11 Whitelam, *Ancient Israel*, p. 119.

12 Whitelam, *Ancient Israel*, p. 120.

13 Whitelam, *Ancient Israel*, p. 231.

14 See Uriah Y. Kim, *Decolonizing Josiah: Toward a Postcolonial Reading of the Deuteronomistic History* (Sheffield: Sheffield Phoenix, 2005), and on history especially Chapter 3.

15 Prior, *The Bible and Colonialism*.

16 Stephen D. Moore, *Empire and Apocalypse: Postcolonialism and the New Testament* (Sheffield: Sheffield Phoenix, 2006), p. 16.

17 Prior is, of course, well aware of the different critical views of these themes and narratives – their chronological lateness and lack of historicity – but his point is that the narratives taken at face value and read uncritically have served to sanction genocide and apartheid in various contexts.

18 Prior, *The Bible and Colonialism*, pp. 295–296.

19 Prior, *The Bible and Colonialism*, p. 290.

20 Prior, *The Bible and Colonialism*, p. 40.

21 Chia, "On Naming the Subject."

22 Chia, "On Naming the Subject," p. 182 n1. British National (Overseas) (BNO) passports were issued to those in Hong Kong who wanted a British passport. These documents, however, gave the holder no right to settle in the United Kingdom.

23 Chia, "On Naming the Subject," p. 173.

24 Chia, "On Naming the Subject," p. 174.

25 Chia, "On Naming the Subject," pp. 175–176.

26 Chia, "On Naming the Subject," pp. 178ff.

27 Chia, "On Naming the Subject," pp. 180ff.

28 Horsley, *Paul and Empire*.

29 Horsley, *Paul and Empire*, p. 1.

30 I am gently taking issue with the idea that the *Semeia* volume marked the beginning of postcolonialism and biblical studies. Certainly it drew the attention of American scholarship to this school of biblical criticism, but its origins are not North American.

31 Laura E. Donaldson, "Postcolonialism and Biblical Reading: An Introduction," *Semeia* 75 (1996), 1.

32 Donaldson, "Postcolonialism," p. 11.

33 Donaldson, "Postcolonialism," p. 10.

34 Donaldson, "Postcolonialism," p. 6. This is in some ways similar to Prior's position on the land/conquest traditions in the Hebrew scriptures.

35 Jon L. Berquist, "Postcolonialism and Imperial Motives for Canonization," *Semeia* 75 (1996), 15–35.

36 Berquist, "Postcolonialism," p. 22. It might be possible to argue here that some sort of hybridity might be going on which would serve to resist the imperial project, albeit in a small way (see Chia above), but that is not the point Berquist is trying to make.

37 Berquist, "Postcolonialism," p. 28.

38 Berquist, "Postcolonialism," p. 30.

39 Berquist, "Postcolonialism," p. 31.

40 Berquist, "Postcolonialism," p. 32.

41 Musa W. Dube, "Reading for Decolonization (John 4: 1–42)," *Semeia* 75 (1996), 47.

42 Dube, "Reading for Decolonization," p. 49.

43 Dube, "Reading for Decolonization," p. 51.

44 Dube, "Reading for Decolonization," p. 49.

45 Hector Avalos, "*The Gospel of Lucas Gavilán* as Postcolonial Biblical Exegesis," *Semeia* 75 (1996), 88.

46 Kimberly Rae Connor, "'Everybody Talking About Heaven Ain't Going There': The Biblical Call for Justice and the Postcolonial Response of the Spirituals," *Semeia* 75 (1996), 109.

47 Elsa Tamez, "The Hermeneutical Leap of Today," *Semeia* 75 (1996), 204–205.

48 R.S. Sugirtharajah, *Asian Biblical Hermeneutics and Postcolonialism: Contesting the Interpretations* (Maryknoll, NY: Orbis, 1998), pp. 46–47.

49 Sugirtharajah, *Asian Biblical Hermeneutics*, p. 48.

50 Sugirtharajah, *Asian Biblical Hermeneutics*, p. 63.

51 Sugirtharajah, *Asian Biblical Hermeneutics*, p. 61.

52 Dora R. Mbuwayesango, "How Local Divine Powers Were Suppressed: A Case of Mwari of the Shona," in *The Postcolonial Biblical Reader*, p. 266.

53 Hephzibah Israel, "Cutchery Tamil versus Pure Tamil: Contesting Language Use in the Translated Bible in the Early-Nineteenth-Century Protestant Tamil Community," in *The Postcolonial Biblical Reader*, p. 282.

54 Sugirtharajah, *Asian Biblical Hermeneutics*, pp. 87–88.

55 Sugirtharajah, *Asian Biblical Hermeneutics*, p. 88.

56 Cf. with Prior's point, above, about scriptures which have no authority for a people nonetheless being used to determine their life and culture.

57 Sugirtharajah, *Asian Biblical Hermeneutics*, pp. 90–91.

58 Sugirtharajah, *Asian Biblical Hermeneutics*, p. 113.

59 Sugirtharajah, *Asian Biblical Hermeneutics*, pp. 115–116.

60 Sugirtharajah, *Asian Biblical Hermeneutics*, p. 117.

61 R.S. Sugirtharajah, "A Postcolonial Exploration of Collusion and Construction in Biblical Interpretation," in *The Postcolonial Bible*, ed. R.S. Sugirtharajah (Sheffield: Sheffield Academic, 1998), pp. 101–102.

62 Sugirtharajah, "A Postcolonial Exploration," p. 104.

63 Sugirtharajah, "A Postcolonial Exploration," pp. 107–111.

64 Sugirtharajah, "A Postcolonial Exploration," p. 111.

65 Musa W. Dube, "Savior of the World but Not of This World: A Post-Colonial Reading of Spatial Construction in John," in *The Postcolonial Bible*, p. 133.

66 Fernando F. Segovia, "Biblical Criticism and Postcolonial Studies: Toward a Postcolonial Optic," in *The Postcolonial Bible*, pp. 49–65.

67 Segovia, "Biblical Criticism," p. 54.

68 Segovia, "Biblical Criticism," p. 57.

69 Segovia, "Biblical Criticism," p. 60.

70 Segovia, "Biblical Criticism," p. 61.

71 Fernando F. Segovia, "Mapping the Postcolonial Optic in Biblical Criticism: Meaning and Scope," in *Postcolonial Biblical Criticism: Interdisciplinary Intersections*, eds Stephen D. Moore and Fernando F. Segovia (London: Clark, 2005), pp. 23–78.

72 Sugirtharajah, *The Bible and the Third World: Precolonial, Colonial and Postcolonial Encounters* (Cambridge: Cambridge University Press, 2001), p. 1.

73 Sugirtharajah, *The Bible and the Third World*, p. 15.

74 Sugirtharajah, *The Bible and the Third World*, pp. 21–22.

75 Sugirtharajah, *The Bible and the Third World*, p. 29.

76 Sugirtharajah, *The Bible and the Third World*, pp. 242–243.

77 Sugirtharajah, *The Bible and the Third World*, p. 261.

78 Sugirtharajah, *The Bible and the Third World*, p. 262.

79 Sugirtharajah, *The Bible and the Third World*, p. 262.

80 R.S. Sugirtharajah, *Postcolonial Criticism and Biblical Interpretation* (Oxford: Oxford University Press, 2002), p. 13.

81 Sugirtharajah, *Postcolonial Criticism*, p. 25.

82 Sugirtharajah, *Postcolonial Criticism*, p. 71.

83 Sugirtharajah, *Postcolonial Criticism*, p. 100.

84 Sugirtharajah, *Postcolonial Criticism*, p. 207.

85 Richard A. Horsley, "Renewal Movements and Resistance to Empire in Ancient Judea," in *The Postcolonial Biblical Reader*, p. 76.

86 Horsley, "Renewal Movements," p. 157.

87 Horsley, "Renewal Movements," p. 161.

88 Horsley, "Renewal Movements," p. 163.

89 Horsley, "Renewal Movements," p. 170.

90 Warren Carter, *Matthew and the Margins: A Sociopolitical and Religious Reading* (Maryknoll, NY: Orbis, 2000), p. xvii.

91 Carter, *Matthew and the Margins*, p. 2.

92 Carter, *Matthew and the Margins*, p. 43.

93 Warren Carter, "The Gospel of Matthew," in *A Postcolonial Commentary on the New Testament Writings*, eds Fernando F. Segovia and R.S. Sugirtharajah (London: Clark, 2007), p. 97.

94 Carter, "The Gospel of Matthew," p. 100.

95 Carter, "The Gospel of Matthew," p. 102.

96 Werner H. Kelber, "Roman Imperialism and Christian Scribality," in *The Postcolonial Biblical Reader*, pp. 98–99; Stephen D. Moore, "Mark and Empire: 'Zealot' and 'Postcolonial' Readings," in *The Postcolonial Biblical Reader*, p. 199.

97 Sugirtharajah, *The Postcolonial Biblical Reader*, p. 133.

98 Roland Boer, "Resistance versus Accommodation: What To Do with Romans 13," in *Postcolonial Interventions: Essays in Honor of R.S. Sugirtharajah*, ed. Tat-siong Benny Liew (Sheffield: Sheffield Phoenix, 2009), p. 119.

99 Sugirtharajah, *The Postcolonial Biblical Reader*, p. 133.

100 Tat-siong Benny Liew, "Tyranny, Boundary, and Might: Colonial Mimicry in Mark's Gospel," in *The Postcolonial Biblical Reader*, p. 209.

101 Liew, "Tyranny," p. 215; Tat-siong Benny Liew, "The Gospel of Mark," in *A Postcolonial Commentary*, p. 117.

102 Liew, "The Gospel of Mark," p. 123.

103 Liew, "The Gospel of Mark," p. 128.

104 Liew, "The Gospel of Mark," p. 131.

105 Gordon Zerbe and Muriel Orevillo-Montenegro, "The Letter to the Colossians," in *A Postcolonial Commentary*, p. 295.

106 Sharon H. Ringe, "The Letter of James," in *A Postcolonial Commentary*, p. 378.

107 Jennifer G. Bird, "The Letter to the Ephesians," in *A Postcolonial Commentary*, p. 266.

108 Bird, "The Letter to the Ephesians," p. 267.

109 Bird, "The Letter to the Ephesians," p. 278.

110 Kwok Pui-lan, "Making the Connections: Postcolonial Studies and Feminist Biblical Interpretation," in *The Postcolonial Biblical Reader*, p. 45.

111 Whitelam, *Ancient Israel*, pp. 120, 224.

112 Kwok, "Making the Connections," p. 47.

113 Kwok, "Making the Connections," p. 48.

114 Kwok, "Making the Connections," p. 49. For an example of postcolonial feminist criticism on Rhab see Musa W. Dube, "Rahab Says Hello to Judith: A Decolonizing Feminist Reading," in *The Postcolonial Biblical Reader*, pp. 142–158.

115 Kwok, "Making the Connections," p. 49.

116 Kwok, "Making the Connections," p. 49.

117 Kwok, "Making the Connections," pp. 49–50.

118 Kwok, "Making the Connections," p. 50.

119 Laura E. Donaldson, "The Sign of Orpah: Reading Ruth through Native Eyes," in *The Postcolonial Biblical Reader*, p. 160.

120 Bird, "The Letter to the Ephesians," p. 265.

121 Dora Rudo Mbuwayesango, "Canaanite Women and Israelite Women in Deuteronomy: The Intersection of Sexism and Imperialism," in *Postcolonial Interventions*, pp. 45–57.

122 Mbuwayesango, "Canaanite Women," p. 56.

123 Karen L. King, "Canonization and Marginalization: Mary of Magdala," in *The Postcolonial Biblical Reader*, pp. 284–290.

124 King, "Canonization," pp. 288–289.

125 I have made various suggestions about this elsewhere. See Ralph Broadbent, "Writing a Bestseller in Biblical Studies or All Washed Up on Dover Beach? *Voices from the Margin* and the Future of (British) Biblical Studies," in *Still at the Margins: Biblical Scholarship Fifteen Years After* Voices from the Margin, ed. R.S. Sugirtharajah (London: Clark, 2008), pp. 139–150; and "One Step Beyond or One Step Too Far? Towards a Postcolonial Future for European Biblical and Theological Scholarship," in *Postcolonial Interventions*, pp. 296–309.

126 Sugirtharajah, *The Postcolonial Biblical Reader*, p. 2.

127 Roland Boer, "Marx, Postcolonialism, and the Bible," in *Postcolonial Biblical Criticism*, pp. 166–183; "Remembering Babylon: Postcolonialism and Australian Biblical Studies," in *The Postcolonial Bible*, pp. 24–48.

128 David Jobling, "'Very Limited Ideological Options': Marxism and Biblical Studies in Postcolonial Scenes," in *Postcolonial Biblical Criticism*, pp. 184–201.

129 Gerald O. West, "What Difference Does Postcolonial Biblical Criticism Make? Reflections from a (South) African Perspective," in *Postcolonial Interventions*, pp. 256–273.

4

Enduring Orientalism
Biblical Studies and the Repackaging of Colonial Practice

I am an Oriental writing back at the Orientalists, who for so long have thrived upon our silence.[1]

The East is ours, we are its heirs, and claim by right our share in its inheritance.[2]

One important aspect of colonial discourse analysis is the idea of Orientalism. The book that acted as a catalyst and became the founding text was Edward Said's *Orientalism*. In Said's words, "Orientalism is a generic term that I have been employing to describe the Western approach to the Orient; Orientalism is the discipline by which the Orient was (and is) approached systematically as a topic of learning, discovery and practice."[3] Basically, Orientalism is about how Europe invented the idea of the Orient and how this idea was used as a weapon to control and subjugate the "other." It is a suspect type of thinking.

Exploring Postcolonial Biblical Criticism: History, Method, Practice, First Edition.
R. S. Sugirtharajah.
© 2012 R. S. Sugirtharajah, with the exception of Chapter 3 © 2012 Blackwell Publishing Ltd.
Published 2012 by Blackwell Publishing Ltd.

East–West Relations: Earlier Attempts

Orientalism is a textual construct of the Orient and is a potent discursive instrument. Traces of Orientalism can be gleaned from a loosely knit group of Western writings which consist of factual reports (official minutes, travel narratives), imaginative literature (colonial novels), religious tracts (sacred texts, rituals), historical documents, and anthropological findings. As Said has outlined, Orientalism signals a number of things. For our purpose, it can be narrowed down to the following. First, it is a "corporate institution for dealing with the Orient – dealing with it by making statements about it, authorizing views of it, describing it, settling it, ruling over it: in short, Orientalism as a Western style for dominating, restructuring, and having authority over the Orient."[4] Second, Orientalism is about power relations: "Orientalism is more particularly valuable as a sign of European-Atlantic power over the Orient than it is a veridic discourse about the Orient."[5] In this power relationship, the "West is the actor, the Orient a passive reactor. The West is the spectator, the judge and the jury, of every facet of Oriental behaviour."[6] Third, Orientalism is about "distillation of essential ideas about the Orient – its sensuality, its tendency to despotism, its aberrant mentality, its habits of inaccuracy, its backwardness – into a separate and an unchallenged coherence."[7] Fourth, Orientalism is about representation:

> How does one *represent* other cultures? What is *another* culture? Is the notion of a distinct culture (or race, or religion, or civilization) a useful one, or does it always get involved either in self-congratulation (when one discusses one's own) or hostility and aggression (when one discusses the "other")? ... How do ideas acquire authority, "normality," and even the status of "natural" truth?[8]

Although such a discourse gives the impression that these representations are interested in the Orient, the motive apparently is to establish control over the "other." Said's book questioned not only "the possibility of nonpolitical scholarship but also the advisability of too close a relationship between the scholar and the state."[9] Even the handful of Oriental scholars who showed a deep affinity with and love for the cultures and peoples of the Orient could not entirely get rid of their Eurocentrism and have involuntarily contributed to the ascendancy of the West. Orientalism is about the uneven and often unfair and manipulative contact between the East and the West. The Western representation of the "other," with all its good intentions, has not only damaged literature about the Orient but also, at times, colluded with the dominant power.

Although Said's book was seen as pioneering the discourse, there had been other attempts by both Western and Eastern scholars who studied European images of non-European peoples. Said did not initiate the study of the troubled relationship between the West and the East. Cultural, intellectual, and mercantile exchanges between the East and the West had been scrutinized before. There were other thinkers and writers both in the East and in the West who had studied the uneasy association between the Occident and the Orient. There were Arabist and Islamic scholars such as Abdul Latif al-Tibawi, the Palestinian historian and educationist;[10] Syed Hussein Alatas, the Malaysian sociologist;[11] Anouar Abdel-Malek, the Egyptian philosopher;[12] Hitchem Djait, the Tunisian historian; Indian writers such as K.M. Panikkar[13] and K. Ananda Coomaraswamy;[14] and East Asian thinkers like Tenshin Okakura, who highlighted the unfair, distorted, and highly opinionated rendering of the Orient by the Occident.[15] Among Western scholars who drew attention to the lop-sided account of East–West relations were Marshal G. Hodgson, the American historian of Islamic civilization, and Bryan S. Turner, the sociologist.

Said's book not only sharpened and expanded these earlier contributions, but also added a few new critical dimensions. In his own words, it "married the two things" that he was "most interested in: literature and culture, on the one hand, and studies and analysis of power, on the other hand."[16] A great enhancement was to add to studies of the reports of colonial administrators, anthropologists, geographers, and travelers one more category – literary fiction, thereby exposing colonial assumptions and empire values entrenched in the Western literary canon. He exposed how some of these great Western literary works accommodated colonial endeavors and practices. For instance, he demonstrated how Jane Austen's *Mansfield Park* was untroubled by slavery or exploitation in the sugar plantations, and how Kipling's Kim colluded with the interests of the British empire by being a loyal servant. The tainted nature of such novels, in Said's view, did not warrant dismissal of these authors or substitution of their work with an Eastern canon, but they did require a decolonizing critique. His preferred solution was to engage these novels in contrapuntal reading, a discursive strategy which aims to juxtapose the writings of the mainstream and the subaltern and to "connect them all together – to understand wholes rather than bits of wholes."[17] Besides examining literary texts, Said's book addressed systematically the complex and contentious problem of knowledge and power. His work combined the various interpretative realms of historical, cultural, literary, and humanistic scholarship, and also political concerns through his analysis of how power and hegemony play a vital role in knowledge creation and production. In other respects also, Said differed from earlier exponents. While most of their work was confined to a single discipline, Said's approach was ecumenical. He shepherded together an assortment of disciplines, concepts, and even resistance movements. In his work he brought together fields such as Islamic studies, Indic studies, and philology; critical concepts such as Romanticism and Enlightenment, humanism and liberation; and politically effective oppositional and resistance movements. He merged these incongruent elements into an effective but at the same time a contentious discourse which he called Orientalism. Whereas the previous attempts were carried on within the confines of single disciplines, Said's work cut across several scholarly fields and looked for connections across disciplines. He wanted to paint a larger picture rather than confine himself to narrower specialisms which tended to shut out other fields such as art, politics, and history.

Said's work was distinguished from the earlier writings on the Orient by the considerable impact it made outside the academy. He offered his findings to a wider audience, rather than restricting them to the safe confines of the academic cloisters. *Orientalism*, while espousing truth, freedom, agitation, and resistance as worthy and legitimate causes for academic writing, simultaneously exposed the limitations and the fatal flaws in what was claimed as serious scholarship. More to the point, it made it unequivocally clear that the virtues of Western scholarship – neutrality and objectivity – are in fact hostile and harmful to the people of the "Orient." Said expected scholarship to be not only erudite but also ethical and committed to serving the dominated rather than the dominant.

The other distinguishing mark of Said's book was that it had a personal and autobiographical tone to it. It came out of his experience of living as an Arab Palestinian in the West, especially in America which was, in his words, "disheartening." It also drew on his experience of growing up as an Oriental child in two British colonies – Palestine and Egypt. *Orientalism* has a revealing subsection called "The personal dimension" where he recalls the historical circumstances which necessitated the writing of the book: troubled East–West relations, the regurgitating of stereotypical images of the Orient in the electronic and print media as exotic and menacing, and the invisibility and total absence of a Palestinian voice in the dominant discourse. Unlike the earlier writers on Orientalism, as Said remarked, he was "able to put to use my humanistic and political concerns for the analysis and description of a worldly matter, the rise, development, and consolidation of Orientalism."[18] The book, scholarly though it is, was also a personal testament and a witness to being an Oriental in the West. He was, as he acknowledged, a "personal beneficiary" of Western education and grateful for the critical tools he acquired through it, but "in none of that, however, have I ever lost hold of the cultural reality of, the personal involvement in having been constituted as an 'Oriental.' "[19] Conspicuously, the book was both an assessment and a self-appraisal.

98

Biblical Studies as an Oriental Project

Biblical studies has been struggling with the question of its own identity, and with which academic discipline it should align itself. Given the way that mainstream biblical studies habitually reinforces the inherent prejudices of Orientalism in its work, I think its rightful place is in Oriental studies, and it should be seen as an essential component of and heir to Oriental scholarship. Orientalism is not to be seen exclusively in terms of East–West cultural enterprise; rather, as Edward Said has pointed out, it includes "such disparate realms" as the study of "the biblical texts and the biblical lands."[20] In its method and scope biblical studies resembles Oriental studies and has a number of affinities with it. While Orientalists study the entire Asian terrain, biblical scholars focus on the Near East. Like the Orientalists, biblical scholars collect, catalogue, edit, and translate ancient manuscripts. For the former the texts are Sanskrit, Arabic, Persian, and Chinese, and for the latter they are Hebrew, Greek, Aramaic, and Sumerian. Both communities of scholars do a detailed and patient philological study of their texts. Both have accumulated textual treasures and artefacts belonging to Asian, Arabian, and African communities and transported them to the capitals of European cities. Both Orientalists and biblical scholars excavate and study ancient sites, cultures, religions, and rituals of bygone eras. Both devote their attention to the past and hardly pay any attention to the needs and questions of the contemporary world. For both, the main readership and market are not the indigenous populations but North Americans, Europeans, and Israelis. Like the Oriental discourse, biblical Orientalism has constituted itself as an object which has to be studied and structured and has distanced itself from the concerns of the region. Biblical Orientalism has paid little attention to what the indigenous people in the Mediterranean thought about its knowledge production.

Other disciplines in humanities such as history, English literature, and anthropology have all moved on from their long history of colluding with colonialism and of opposing the marks of Orientalist scholarship within their field. By contrast, biblical studies has remained totally distant from and unaffected by the Oriental aspects of its enterprise.

There are a number of reasons for this indifference and reluctance to be self-critical. First, biblical studies flourishes when empires flourish. Biblical studies is thriving in America at a time when America is projecting herself as the new imperium. This new national self-importance, coupled with the belief that the Americans are the new chosen race, blinds its scholars to the presence of imperial impulses enshrined in the biblical texts. This was the case at the height of British imperialism when there were hardly any biblical interpreters who raised their voices against the British imperial adventure. Even those who expressed dissent, like Bishop Colenso, did not contest the concept of colonialism as such, which they all thought was good for the natives. Their disagreement was with the atrocities and cruelties committed by the imperial forces. While the British were a dominant force in the world, a generation of biblical scholars like Westcott and Lightfoot were engaged in the task of how to convert India. In the 1960s when the massive decolonizing process was going on in Africa and an influx of immigrants was arriving in the UK, Nineham was trying to demythologize the Gospel of Mark for English audiences, a demythologizing process with which the Germans were already familiar. Simillarly, Stephen Neil's *The Interpretation of the New Testament, 1861–1961*, which has a classic status, hardly mentions colonialism – the background against which most Victorian biblical scholarship was undertaken. Current American biblical scholarship, in Hector Avalos's view, is in the business of protecting its profession by keeping "alive a text that is repeatedly used as an authority for violence, racism, sexism and the like." To this list of atrocities encouraged by biblical texts, one could add colonialism as well. In such a mood of self-preservation, one can hardly expect any severe ideological scrutiny of the text. Instead of helping the world to view the ancient texts with detachment, these scholars indulge in what Avalos calls "bibliolatry."[21]

The second reason for the shyness on the part of mainstream biblical scholars to offer a critique of Orientalism is their failure to use theories originating from outside biblical studies to investigate biblical texts. Critical theories do not usher in the kingdom, but they intervene and ask awkward questions and unsettle the status quo. They introduce into the agenda a giddy challenging mixture of politics and ideology – an agenda hitherto controlled by traditionalists who assumed they were above bias and vested interests. Even those involved in the study of biblical empires hardly engage with colonial discourse analysis. Illustrative of this is the recent issue of *Journal for the Study of the New Testament* on the Imperial Cult and the New Testament. Except for a single reference to Homi Bhabha, none of the essayists engage with the conceptual or theoretical clarifications provided by Said, Spivak, African anti-colonial writers and activists such as Fanon, and Indian subaltern studies, in order to face up to empire anew and confront its threats, dangers, and predatory capabilities. Far worse is the essayists' refusal to draw out contemporary implications when modern empires like the US model themselves on images of the earlier Roman empire. David Horrell's introduction to the volume assures his readers with these soothing words: "Any who suspect, therefore, that the current interest in the New Testament and Empire is a fad, driven more by contemporary political interests than historical substance, should find those suspicions thoroughly laid to rest."[22] Empire, imperialism, identity, and displacement are crucial questions of our time, and critical theory helps to answer them. If theory is used at all, it is employed by those who are engaged in minority hermeneutics – feminists, Asian-Americans, African-Americans, and Hispanic-Americans – who utilize theories vigorously to expose the patriarchal and racial nature of both the text and the interpreters.

The third reason for the reluctance to scrutinize Oriental tendencies in biblical scholarship is the unshakeable belief among scholars that their scholarship is unsullied and unswayed by ideological or religious bias. The tool these scholars employ – historical criticism – effectively shuts them out from the concerns of the contemporary world in order to focus on their study of ancient texts. In their philological work, these scholars are so concerned with the original meaning and the reception history of the Hebrew, Greek,

Aramaic, and Sumerian terms that they fail to detect the ambiguous political and propagandist content of the biblical lexicon. Under the pretense of technical competency, they fail to raise doubts about the imperialism embedded in biblical words and phrases. Biblical scholarship is in essence an ideological project, with its own political biases. On surveying the way that a professional guild such as the Society of Biblical Literature, its forums and its journal, work in America, Avalos's conclusion is that a disproportionate interest is shown in ancient cities, pottery, and inscriptions rather than in the masses and the problems they face such as health care. Most biblical scholarship is driven by a religious agenda which is conservative.

Finally, biblical scholarship, which is inclined to be politically conservative, became more so during the Cold War era and in the aftermath of the 1967 War between Israel and the adjacent Arab countries. Crossley has shown that strong support for Israel by the USA, UK, and European countries is reflected implicitly in biblical interpretation and Jesus scholarship.[23] It is not the political allegiances of these interpreters but their pre-understandings and the models they work with that concern us. What is said of the old Orientalists could well be said of biblical scholars. They are "technocratic deconstructionist[s], discourse analysts, new historicist[s]" and they "retreat into a nostalgic celebration of some past state of glory."[24] The reactionary nature of biblical scholarship reminds one of Said's estimation of Dr Casaubon in George Eliot's *Middlemarch*, "sterile, ineffectual, and hopelessly irrelevant to life."[25]

Current Biblical Scholarship and Recycling of Orientalist Practices

The Oriental project is very much alive in biblical studies today, and there a number of orientalizing tendencies are evident. Biblical scholars are no exception when it comes to fixing, codifying, and structuring the Orient. A proneness to Orientalism is particularly evident in the work of biblical scholars who employ social-scientific methods. Since the literature in this field is so vast, I will focus on

John Pilch's *Cultural World of Jesus* and Bruce Malina's *Windows on the World of Jesus*. The reason for choosing these two volumes is that both are aimed at a mass market readership. Pilch's three-volume reflections on the gospels are assigned for each Sunday in the Roman Catholic lectionary. Malina provides interesting scenarios of various kinds of cultural behavior, attitudes, and life views of the Middle East as contrasted with those that prevail in America. He then goes on to relate these life situations to a related passage in the New Testament. The publication of these volumes is also politically significant. They came out soon after the first Iraq War when there was so much negative portrayal of Iraqi people and the Middle East in the media and in the public discourse. These volumes, instead of repairing the defamatory portrayals of the Middle East and in the process educating congregations, refurbish the clichés of prejudice, giving them a respectable academic form. The works of Pilch and Malina require a much closer and longer scrutiny. My engagement with them is restricted to the specific needs of this chapter. As readers will notice, I also bring in examples from the writings of other biblical scholars to demonstrate the prevalence of Orientalism in biblical scholarship.

One of the standard Orientalist traits is labeling the "other." Biblical scholars come up with an array of labels to identify the geography of the biblical lands. The area is variously described as "Israel," "Land of Israel," "Judah," "Holy Land," "Palestine," "Syro-Palestine," "Mediterranean," "the Levant," "World of Jesus," "Cultural World of Jesus." To an outsider these descriptions may look like innocuous, interchangeable, and non-aligned neutral terms. But basically they are ideologically charged rhetoric and markers of Eurocentric and Christian-centric conceptualizations of that part of the world. For instance, in an essay on the "Geography of the Holy Land," Phythian-Adams confirms that "it is only by Jews and Christians that it has been remembered as the 'Land of Israel.'" [26] Denis Baly's calling Palestine the "country of the Bible"[27] is another indication of how theological presuppositions play a key role in defining a region. Terms like "Middle East" and "Ancient Near East" inadvertently rule out the significant presence of African nations and silence the voices of the African people mentioned in the Bible. Naming is not an innocent activity or an honest desire to describe reality. It is the way of intruders – claiming, particularizing, dividing, and taking possession of the land for themselves. It is a form of control and domination and of managing the "other."

Closely linked to the above is the conception of the "other" as blank, abandoned, and empty and thus ready for development, expansion, and exploitation. The way biblical scholarship has treated Palestine is a notable case in point. There are a number of Orientalist characteristics at work. First, scholars declare that as a land it belonged to no one, so everyone has a claim to it. W.J. Phythian-Adams, in an article written in a one-volume commentary, vividly paints a picture of Palestine, its different regions, its mountains and rivers, its climatic conditions, and the numerous racial groups who have inhabited the region, but he still pronounces that "for centuries" the region was a "No Man's Land or Any Man's Land."[28] The inference is clear: the land is there for anyone to occupy.

Second, interpreters depict inhabitants as a loosely knit group of vulnerable people who, from time to time, "succumbed to a stronger power."[29] The implication is that the indigenes are weak and vulnerable and are in need of a stronger power. Third, scholars introduce a Christian monotheistic god as the one who can provide such leadership. To do this, they expose the local polytheistic gods as ineffectual and the natural religion which sustains such ideas as useless. They portray these gods as "always calm and never a disturber of the established order,"[30] and that allegiance to such gods results in "weakness, trouble and defeat for the worshippers."[31] Natural religion produces, according to W.E. Wright, "passionate man" and "silent man." Such a benign and soft state of affairs prompts the classical Oriental prescription: that land, its people, and its resources belong to those who are best able to develop and provide strong theological and political management. Such superior guidance was seen as supplied by Israel and the West, the former providing religious rejuvenation and the latter technology and modernity. To this passive, accommodative, and sleepy environment, Israel was seen as offering a superior and energetic monotheistic idea of god who, Wright reckoned, was "an utterly different God from the gods of all natural, cultural and philosophical religion."[32] Such a god was known not through "numinous awareness of nature" but "based on historical event."[33] This monotheistic ideal, according to Wright, was not something that gradually evolved out of primitive and polytheistic phases but something which was present and preserved in every significant point in the life of Israel. The indigenous gods who were perceived as lackadaisical were replaced by a sexless, dynamic being, who was "engaged in the active direction of history."[34] Heralding this "Divine Lord," the prophets "created an extraordinary atmosphere of social and political reform entirely unknown in polytheistic circles."[35] Unlike the polytheistic gods, whose main task was to maintain the status quo, the god of Israel was projected as "authoritative and decisive."[36] In place of gods whose values were seen in terms of rhythm, balance of nature, and integration, Israel was seen as introducing to the region a divine being who was imposing authority rather than coexisting with the local deities.

While Israel supplies a strong religious tone, the West is seen as providing modernity in the form of various Western industrial inventions to the region. George Adam Smith, the Scottish biblical scholar, proudly recounts how a "few hundred thousands of colonialists and warriors, though the sword was not out of their hand, organized the land into a feudal kingdom as fully assigned, cultivated, and administered as any part of the contemporary France or England."[37] Under this European care there were agricultural settlements, cultivation of wine and the silk worm, and various capitalistic enterprises, but the "most important material innovation from the West," according to Smith, was "the railway,"[38] the line completed between Jaffa and Jerusalem, which would be of "immanent strategic value."[39] Western intervention has made this province of Asia, as Smith put it, "a bit of the West."[40] Palestine became the perfect canvas for the fulfillment and true realization of Israel's religious ideals and the West's modern inventions. Thus Palestine had no inherent significance of its own but provided an empty space for the display of the monotheistic god and for the West to demonstrate its industrial achievements.

Orientalism's conventional habit of caricaturing and ideologically silencing the "other" continues to appear. One habit is to perpetuate the Orientalist conception of the "other" as lazy, passive, fatalistic and incapable of taking any initiative on their own. To give one example, the Acts of the Apostles records an incident (Acts 16:13–40) where Paul and Silas are put in prison at the instigation of the owners of a slave girl who has a spirit of divination. While in prison, Paul and Silas are praying and singing when there is a sudden earthquake which makes the foundations of the prison shake. As a result the doors are opened and the chains of the prisoners loosened. To the surprise of the jailor, no prisoner escapes. Commenting on this incident, E.M. Blaiklock, using the words of William Ramsay, comes up with an answer which is an example of "pure" Orientalism. The reason that the prisoners not did not try to escape was because the "excitable Oriental people" lacked "the northern self-centred tenacity of purpose and presence of mind."[41] The implication is that the Orientals are mercurial, emotional, impetuous, and not capable of taking the initiative.

Biblical scholars continue to reiterate the classical Orientalist message. One standard Orientalist perception is the idea of a static Orient. The Orient is something which "remained fixed in time and place for the West."[42] In an introduction which appears in all three volumes, Pilch informs his readers that the Mediterranean people "share many cultural elements unchanged over several millennia."[43] There are many examples in these volumes which reinforce the unchanging nature of Middle Eastern culture. One such example is the use of cooking utensils. While Americans use a gas or electric stove, modern Middle Eastern people use a clay oven which has been the case since ancient times. When a missionary discussing the Parable of the Two Sons (Matt. 21.28–31) with a group of modern-day Middle Easterners, asked which of the two was the better son, the vast majority of them choose the son who said yes to the father and did not go to work. Pilch's unsubstantiated explanation recycles the fixed and static nature of Oriental thinking. The fact that the son did not go to work was, in Pilch's view, beside the point. For these people, the son's reply was honorable and respectful because in the Middle East "it was *always* honor"[44] which took precedence over other values. When looking at any contemporary Mediterranean city, it is customary for scholars to perceive it as something that has remained untouched by any changes. For instance, one of the captions for a photograph in Dorothee Soelle and Luise Schottroff's *Jesus of Nazareth* has these words: "The life of children in rural Egypt today is still very like that of children in the time of Jesus."[45] Even feminists who are alleged to be progressive participate in reorientalizing the Orient in such direct and naïve ways.

Essentializing is another favored technique of Orientalism. It is a methodology which reduces cultures to certain essentials. It was a hermeneutical tactic employed by the colonial and imperial powers to typecast and degrade the "other." Scholars who employ social-science and anthropological methods routinely essentialize Mediterranean culture. They reduce complex cultural features to a set of core values such as honor and shame, or patron and client, and portray them as common throughout the Mediterranean world irrespective of the fact that the region is composed of different cultures and countries. People are labeled as belonging to defined and neat cultural categories. Reducing Mediterranean culture to a series of core values impoverishes its vitality and its ability to change and transform. Another mark of essentializing is to represent human frailties and flaws as natural and normal human behavior. Pilch informs his readers, without any proof, that in Mediterranean culture "secrecy, lying, and deception are key strategies."[46] He claims that children are expected to find things out by wandering into other people's homes, and at the same time are warned by their parents not to divulge family secrets to others.[47] Basically for Pilch, people of the Middle East "delight in deception and lying."[48] He goes even further in claiming that " adultery is a strategy by which one male shames the another male."[49]

Essentialism thrives on gender stereotyping. Women in the ancient Mediterranean world were considered to be "lascivious, and untrustworthy," so much so that the husband never knew for sure whether a child was actually his.[50] When the Samaritan woman broke the rules and discussed publicly "masculine" politico-religious topics like the Messiah and the Temple, John's Jesus, in Plich's view, steers her back to "feminine" topics. Pilch hails this as a "revolution."[51] Women in the Middle East were seen as needing protection because they were "oversexed" and as requiring constant vigilance by a key male member of her family – by a father over his daughter (Sir. 42.9–10), a brother over his sister (2 Sam. 13.7–39), a husband over his wife (Sir. 26.1–9), and a son over his mother.[52]

In the Orientalist mode of operation there is simultaneous acknowledgment and disparagement. Even virtues which have a positive value are described as being inexplicably linked to some sinister motive. When talking about fasting, Pilch says that for the people of the Mediterranean, a fast is a public event aimed at getting attention and impressing the onlookers with the fasters' asceticism. This self-humiliating act is a way of begging for assistance, whereas in America people cry for help out of their humiliating experience of loss of employment, dispossession of home, and loss of medical care.

The other mark of Orientalism is the contrastive way of thinking which places so much emphasis on the characteristics which differentiate the East and the West. Said has drawn attention to the fact that such dichotomizing tendencies create and help to define both the East and the West. The way it works is to polarize the differences so that the Orient becomes more Oriental and the West more Western. In the biblical social-science literature, America is portrayed as modern, progressive, and active, whereas the Mediterranean culture is depicted as traditional, static, and passive. Such a classification itself becomes a tool by which Mediterranean culture is deprived of any inner dynamic and capacity for change and development. The inferior values of the Orient are pitted against the superior values of the West. Americans are "scientifically sophisticated," whereas the Mediterraneans rely on "amulets, formulas or other symbols to ward off" spirits.[53] Pilch writes: "In the ancient and contemporary Mediterranean world, people believe in a huge, diverse and a very real spirit world ... It is difficult for modern, scientifically minded Western believers to appreciate the conviction by our ancestors in the faith that these spirits were very powerful for good and ill."[54] Healing in the Mediterranean world is done by touch of hands and feelings, whereas in America it is about "microscopes, 'cat scanners,' and an impressive array of modern drugs."[55] Middle Easterners are noisy, loud, and spontaneous.[56] Americans are prompt and punctual at dinner parties because they have clocks and calendars. "Mediterranean Judeans" are sluggish because they measure time by the location of the sun, moon phases, and cock crowing.[57] So the West is portrayed as rational, disciplined, democratic, and enlightened, whereas the Orient is impulsive, unruly, despotic, and benighted.

When it comes to discussing biblical concepts like faith, love, witness, and peace, there is a tendency to exaggerate and overplay the differences. Faith for Americans is seen as having a strong intellectual feel to it and is based on rational thinking rather than a matter for heart and will, whereas in the Middle East, faith is about group loyalty and solidarity. The example Pilch cites is the case of the beloved disciple who, in spite of troubling evidence such as an empty tomb, no corpse, and abandoned wrappings, believed in the resurrection because he was "loyal no matter what."[58] Similarly, love for Middle Eastern people is about attachment and bonding rather than showing affection, as most Americans do. Public prayer in Palestine was to move god to act, because the Mediterranean people did not have control over their lives and needed god's intervention. In contrast, Americans are masters of their own destiny and hence their prayers are "composed with greater concern to impress or edify human listeners."[59] The notion of witness in the Middle East is not about factual veracity or eyewitness testimony which Americans relish, but is about "what one feels, imagines, presumes, or desires, especially if it will help a friend in need."[60] Peace is understood not as in the American sense of "silence, stillness and everything is in its orderly place" but as expressed through a delightful array of acts such as children yelling and adults shouting or quarrelling. Moreover, peace is maintained through family rivalry and intrigue. The example that Pilch provides to support his claim is that of Rachel advising her son Jacob to dupe his father in order to gain the inheritance.[61]

This caricature of Orientalism is matched by a hyped-up opinion about the West, especially about America. It is a form of Occidentalism which derives from a position and an authority which speak in terms of simple contrasts. Pilch tells his readers that Americans believe in the "equality of all persons," whereas such a notion is alien to the Middle East. Americans are the "most individualistic people who ever lived on the planet" and have "a personal social security number and many other distinctive and singular identities." This is in contrast to the Mediterranean people "who have no sense of their individuality" and depend on others to "help them know who they are."[62] Americans of humble origins can rise to a greater position than came with their birth, whereas such a notion is unthinkable in the Mediterranean culture which is tied to an honor-based system where one is required to maintain and preserve the system. Getting ahead in life in the Mediterranean culture is perceived as divisive to a communal way of living.[63] In dealing with conflictual situations, Americans depend on tact, diplomacy, and dialogue, whereas Middle Easterners rely on confrontation and insult.[64]

One of the oldest tricks of Orientalism is simultaneously to isolate and incorporate the "other." Natives who constantly challenge the system are segregated as misfits and turned into the image of the colonizer. The Orientalist tactic is to identify as enlightened natives those local persons who question and rebel against indigenous cultural rules and customs and who speak the language of the rulers. This is what happens in the construal of Jesus, both in the Jesus Seminar and in social-scientific approaches.[65] Jesus is portrayed as one who is secure in his culture yet critical of it. Repeatedly he is seen as a person who, to use Malina's phrase, sought to "re-arrange Mediterranean values."[66] Those who employ social-scientific methods provide plenty of examples of such reorderings by Jesus. One example was unsettling the patron–client system and the brokerage that went with it. Jesus did so by constantly being on the move, by healing people, and more importantly by refusing to settle down in Nazareth and become a patron and enjoy the privileges that came with it. The reason his family rejected him, according to Crossan, was that he was repudiating a system which was believed in by a vast majority of the people. Similarly, Jesus redefined honor culture. In a society where almsgiving, prayer, and fasting were seen as seeking attention and thereby winning honor from the onlookers, Jesus encouraged his disciples "to do the same good deeds in secret."[67] On a number of occasions, Jesus is depicted as inverting the cultural values of the time. When Martha, true to the role assigned by her culture, was engaged in "doing" domestic tasks, she was directed to imitate Mary's example of "being" which was exemplified in Mary's spontaneous response to Jesus. Instructions get reversed when Jesus tells his male disciples that "being" attached to him is not enough and that they should be seen as "doing" the commandments.[68] Jesus was presented as differing over the popular beliefs of his own people. While the Mediterranean people were seen as obsessed with the present, which is reflected in the saying of the Lord's Prayer, "Give us today our bread," Matthew's Jesus was able to "force his present-oriented people to think of at least a slightly remote, if not yet very far off, future."[69] Jesus's advice and behavior, in Pilch's view, make his "teaching a counter-structural rather than counter-cultural."[70] What emerges is a picture of a Jesus who is isolated from his Middle Eastern culture and made almost an American. Pilch reconfigures him as an American mentor. Just like a mentor who helps people to achieve excellence and success, Jesus is seen as a "faction founder" who builds a group of followers or disciples around him.[71]

These writings also exhibit the Orientalist trait of appropriating values and characteristics from the "other" that are missing in America, but have the potential to make American life even better. The books of both Pilch and Malina are littered with examples from Middle Eastern life which are missing in American life. A notable absentee is the medical care prevalent among Mediterranean communities, which poses a "stirring challenge" to the privatized and expensive health care that Americans are used to. Another aspect which has nearly disappeared from American life is mystery and wonder. Excessive rationalization in American thought patterns has robbed Americans of the beauty of the liturgy and the likely experiential impact of the sacrament. Mediterranean parables (Luke 16.1–13), too, carry a warning for Americans who are raised on capitalistic ideals: money isn't everything! Zacchaeus is projected as an exemplar for millions of Americans who have low self-esteem. Pilch also wonders whether missing values, such as showing hospitality to strangers, should not be imported into contemporary American life.

Pilch informs his readers that the cultures of the Mediterranean and America are dissimilar. Their problems are different and the solutions the Mediterranean cultures offer may not work for Americans. But he keeps drawing lessons for America and shows the desire to appropriate the simpler Oriental life patterns into his vision of America. In this desire to recreate missing nobler values, Pilch finds a perfect complement for an idealized picture of America in the imperfect copies of the "other." Such an idealization of the "other," and the freedom to borrow in order to supplement the missing ideals and quality of life, come with the privilege of being a strong culture.

To bring this section to a close: biblical scholars such as Pilch and Malina, who employ social-scientific biblical criticism, have reignited the idea of the Orient which has been either lying dormant in other disciplines or regarded as a degenerate affair best forgotten. The work of these biblical scholars retains old ideas with a few added politically incorrect riders. What emerges is a Mediterranean world wrapped in tradition, cruelty, and despotism. They describe the Orient in modern Occidental terms and lift it out of its obscurity through the clarity of modern social science. The end result is a fair amount of abridgment, misrepresentation, reduction, and overstatement. Their caricatures and embellishments are reminiscent of colonial travel writings. The Orient reflected here is a hermeneutical foil to emphasize the classical standards of American behavior, values, and civility: individualism, honesty, hard work, and punctuality. What these scholars have done is to indulge in the standard

Orientalist practice of reshaping the Orient from one thing into something else. It is done not only for the sake of the American constituency these scholars represent, but, as was often claimed by the old Orientalists, for the sake of the Oriental. The impetus for the process of manufacturing the Orient is linked to and supplied by the prevailing cultural and political norms of the West. Their work draws heavily for its authority from contemporary social-science models and theories which lend status but make the "other" look vulnerable.

While criticizing the traditional historical-critical method for not addressing cultural and anthropological issues, social-science criticism ends up forging stereotypes for Americans and non-Americans which mutually confirm an idealized portrayal of North America and a degraded picture of the Middle East. Unfortunately, these scholars replicate the worn-out images and conventional hallmarks of Orientalism which were not only ethnocentric but also patronizing and condescending.

These popular volumes of Pilch and Malina give the impression that every male Mediterranean person wakes up in the morning and thinks about how he is going to preserve his honor by committing adultery with female members "embedded in him," namely wife and unmarried daughters. Or about what deeds he should avoid which will bring shame to him or to his in-group; or how he is to maintain the client–patron relationship which does not disturb social cohesion. This is like expecting Americans to get up daily and think about the civil rights and liberties enshrined in their constitution, or about how they are going to fulfill the American dream, or what sort of dividends they are going to get from their investments. People go about their lives, and they do not consciously and constantly think about core cultural values or scriptural prescriptions.

Everything that is said about the Middle Eastern people in the volumes of Pilch and Malina – about how they lie and deceive, about their confrontational and vengeful nature, their group mentality, and the licentiousness of their women, about how their witnesses mislead, and how their prestige depends on dominating others – can be equally true of Americans. These characteristics are consistently seen as customary, typical, and to be expected from Middle Eastern people. Such portrayals not only homogenize the people as if every individual is the same, but also lead to racial stereotyping. Like all human beings, Americans are duplicitous, argumentative, and rancorous; their women can be immoral; and they have a strong racial identity. Even those who have a casual interest in politics will find it hard to sustain the claim that the US administration relies on negotiation and diplomacy while Mediterraneans resort to confrontation. The recent American involvements in international affairs make such claims difficult to uphold.

Malina's astonishing claim that when dealing with present anomalies Americans look to the future whereas Mediterraneans delve into their past history, appeal to the word of god in scripture, and invoke the ancestors, is simply exaggeration. When faced with a crisis, American presidents have sought scriptural validation and consolation for war, such as George Bush over Iraq. American politicians often recall the founding fathers, Jefferson and Lincoln, for inspiration, and the American military regularly explore past historical events like Pearl Harbor to stir them into action. Malina and Pilch routinely claim that their exegetical practice is culturally sensitive, but their volumes are full of culturally and politically tactless assertions. Pilch makes a curious statement that Americans would be "stunned at the normal palace politics that made Solomon king."[72] Americans, too, have their political shenanigans; they have only to remind themselves of Watergate and the political intrigues that ensued. What we see is that the cultures of the Mediterranean world are viewed from a white North American perspective which becomes the new benchmark for all human civilization. The aim seems to be to demonstrate and highlight the difference between cultures rather than to arrive at an understanding of how similar human beings are in an increasingly complicated world.

The work of social-scientific biblical scholars has all the hallmarks of American Orientalism. According to Malini Johar Schueller, American Orientalism is a "contemporary projection of a proto-imperial narrative for the nation based on versions of the dichotomies of US American righteousness, morality, energy, and vibrancy versus Oriental corruption, deviance, lassitude, and passivity, dichotomies which helped mystify internal racial schisms."[73] American Orientalism is not a mere imitation of the British variety but an indigenous discourse gaining its momentum from theories of Western civilization, America's socio-political status, and the idea of the USA as the new empire. Biblical scholars like Pilch and Malina, while claiming that they are trying to reshape the Orient in order to understand it, end up replicating the American vision of the "other."

Orientals and Their Orientalizing Praxis

Orientalism is not something which is confined exclusively to the Western mode of thinking. Its marks are found even in the discourse of some Asian scholars. This happens in two ways. One is the unthinking repetition of some Western perceptions of the East. Asian interpreters have routinely parroted a reduced and impoverished Orientalist characterization of the East as spiritual and mystical, lacking a historical sense, valuing the oral over the written. The Asian mind is seen as good at synthesizing rather than showing critical awareness. A classic case is the way some Indian Christians have interpreted St John's Gospel, recycling precisely the categories devised by Orientalists. Surveying the Indian interpretation of St John's Gospel, M.R. Spindler concludes that Indian readings emphasize "the mystical aspect of the Fourth Gospel, either in some continuity with the advaitic tradition, or in the line of the Bhakti tradition of Hinduism."[74] While India has produced various religions and philosophies, it is also a place of deep-seated religious skepticism and rationalism and has produced agonistic and atheistic literature. Amartya Sen has recently demonstrated this against the commonly held prejudice that rationality, reasoning, science, tolerance, liberty, and justice are exclusively Western. These are found in the Eastern traditions as well as in the West.[75]

115

The other example of Orientals making use of Orientalism is the adoption of Oriental discourse and redirecting it to the very people who helped to construct it. The European discoveries of ancient civilizations and manuscripts aroused national consciousness and prompted some nationalists to make exaggerated claims about their cultures and traditions, and then to use them as potent weapons of resistance, ironically against the very people who had uncovered them. This redirection is done with a triple purpose of rectifying the Western defamation of their culture, reconfiguring their identity which was sullied by Western negative portrayals, and exposing the double standards of the West. I shall return to this in Chapter 5 where I shall provide examples of how some Asians used Orientalism as a convenient strategy to intimidate, shame, and humiliate the West for its failure to practice what it preached, and also as a serviceable tool to redefine Asian identity.

Conclusions, Critical Reflections

The origins and rise of Orientalism are linked to old European colonial practices. What Orientalism does is to imprison people within predetermined cultural ghettos. Its rebirth and flourishing in North America might be connected to the emergence of the USA as a neo-colonial power. In attempting to document the "other," America came to document itself.

Behind the Orientalist manipulation of the "other" lies what Anouar Abdel-Malek calls the hegemonism of possessing minorities.[76] It is the privilege of the West not only to supervise the non-Western world but also to possess it. Orientalism is a measure of assessing the "other." Its utility lies in structuring knowledge and information. It is a stable and enduring testimony to the superiority of Western civilization, and a perpetual justification for the West's control of the non-West. Orientalist thinking remains intact and manifests itself in a subtle, serene, and sophisticated manner.

Orientalism is not always about misconception and manipulation of the East by the West. There is another aspect of Orientalism which has been positive and which serves as a reminder that the story of Orientalism is not always about maneuvering and misrepresentation. In the field of Indic, Arabic, Persian, and Chinese studies, the contributions of European scholars were enormous. There were the Europeans who painstakingly unearthed ancient textual treasures, mastered various vernaculars and regulated their grammars, examined religious practices, and were genuinely fascinated with the cultures of the people whom they ruled. Unfortunately, they were the exception and they remained only a small minority. This knowledge production was not exclusively an European effort. In most cases it was a joint attempt in which countless nameless indigenes participated. For a collaborative effort between the Europeans and the Indians see Trautmann;[77] for the role played by local Christians in Bible translation see Strandenaes;[78] and for the role of Indians in the vernacular productions of the Bible see Hooper.[79]

The problem is not with these Orientalists and their exemplary achievements, but with what was made of their work and to what purpose it was turned. In some cases their scholarship was turned into a system of generalizations which reinforced racial, ideological, and imperialist stereotypes. As Said observed: "As a system of thought about the Orient, it always rose from the specifically human detail to the general transhuman one; an observation about a tenth-century Arab poet multiplied itself into a policy towards (about) the Oriental mentality in Egypt, Iraq, or Arabia. Similarly, a verse from the Koran would be considered the best evidence of an ineradicable Muslim sensuality."[80] Put at its simplest, "one voice becomes the whole story."[81] Orientalism's failure is the failure to identify with human experience. In an attempt to clarify his often misunderstood position, Said wrote that nowhere did he argue that Orientalism was "evil, or sloppy, or uniformly the same in the work of each and every Orientalist."[82] What he fiercely resisted was when the good work of Oriental scholars was pressed into the service of imperialism. His quarrel with Orientalism was when it was reshaped into "a particular system of ideas"[83] and "structure of attitudes," and when Orientalists complied with the "imperial power."[84]

The task is to arrive at an East–West discourse which is free from an inherited colonial legacy. These inherited representations are so persistent and detrimental and they are continually being reinvented. What is evidently clear is that the answer to Orientalism is not a reverse gaze upon the Occident. In the concluding section of his book, Said made his view abundantly clear:

> Above all, I hope to have shown my reader that the answer to Orientalism is not Occidentalism. No former "Oriental" will be comforted by the thought that having been an Oriental himself, he is likely – too likely – to study new "Orientals" or "Occidentals" – of his own making. If the knowledge of Orientalism has any meaning, it is in being a reminder of the seductive degradation of knowledge, any knowledge, anywhere, at any time. Now perhaps more than before.[85]

What Said advocated was to "study other cultures and peoples from a liberation, or a nonrepressive and nonmanipulative perspective."[86] It is vital that we arrive at a less discriminatory view of other people and their cultures. One way to do this is to be constantly vigilant and acutely conscious of what we think and write.

Notes

1   Edward W. Said, *Power, Politics, and Culture: Interviews with Edward Said*, ed. with introduction by Gauri Viswanathan (New York: Pantheon, 2001), p. 38.
2   Max F. Müller, *Chips from a German Workshop*, vol. IV (London: Longmans, Green, 1875), p. 342.
3   Edward W. Said, *Orientalism* (London: Penguin, 1978), p. 73.
4   Said, *Orientalism*, p. 3.
5   Said, *Orientalism*, p. 6.
6   Said, *Orientalism*, p. 109.
7   Said, *Orientalism*, p. 205.
8   Said, *Orientalism*, p. 325–326.
9   Said, *Orientalism*, p. 326.

10 A.L. Tibawi, *English Speaking Orientalists: A Critique of Their Approach to Islam and Arab Nationalism* (London: Luzac, 1964).

11 Syed Hussein Alatas, *The Myth of the Lazy Native: A Study of the Image of the Malays, Filipinos and Javanese from the 16th to the 20th Century* (London: Cass, 1977).

12 Anouar Abdel-Malek, "Orientalism in Crisis," *Diogenes* 44 (Winter 1963).

13 K.M. Panikkar, *Asian and Western Dominance: A Survey of the Vasco Da Gama Epoch of Asian History 1498–1945* (London: Allen and Unwin, 1959).

14 Ananda K. Coomaraswamy, *The Dance of Shiva: Fourteen Indian Essays* (New Delhi: Munshiram Manoharlal, 1970).

15 Tenshin Okakura, *The Awakening of Japan* (London: Murray, 1905).

16 Edward W. Said, "Orientalism and After," in *A Critical Sense: Interviews with Intellectuals*, ed. Peter Osborne (London: Routledge, 1996), p. 67.

17 Said, *Power, Politics, and Culture*, p. 261.

18 Said, *Orientalism*, p. 27.

19 Said, *Orientalism*, p. 26.

20 Said, *Orientalism*, p. 4.

21 Hector Avalos, *The End of Biblical Studies* (Amherst, MA: Prometheus, 2007), p. 321.

22 David G. Horrell, "Introduction," *Journal of Study of the New Testament* 27, 3 (2005), 254.

23 James G. Crossley, *Jesus in an Age of Terror: Scholarly Projects for a New American Century* (London: Equinox, 2008); "Jesus and the Jew since 1967," in *Jesus Beyond Nationalism: Constructing the Historical Jesus in a Period of Cultural Complexity*, eds W. Blanton, James G. Crossley, and Halvor Moxnes (London: Equinox, 2009), pp. 119–317.

24 Edward W. Said, *Humanism and Democratic Criticism* (New York: Columbia University Press, 2004), p. 70.

25 Said, *Humanism*, p. 57.

26 W.J. Phythian-Adams, "The Geography of the Holy Land," in *A New Commentary on the Holy Scripture Including the Apocrypha*, eds Charles Gore, Henry Leighton Goude, and Alfred Guillaume (London: SPCK, 1928), p. 635.

27 Denis Baly, *The Geography of the Bible: A Study in Historical Geography* (London: Lutterworth, 1957), p. 5.

28 Phythian-Adams, "The Geography of the Holy Land," p. 635.

29 Phythian-Adams, "The Geography of the Holy Land," p. 646.

30 G. Ernest Wright, *The Old Testament against Its Environment* (London: SCM, 1950), p. 44.

31 Wright, *The Old Testament*, p. 43.

32 G. Ernest Wright, "The Old Testament: A Bulwark of the Church Against Paganism," *Occasional Bulletin from the Missionary Research Library* 14, 4 (1963), 5.

33 Wright, *The Old Testament*, p. 22.

34 Wright, "The Old Testament," pp. 5–6.

35 Wright, *The Old Testament*, p. 46.

36 Wright, *The Old Testament*, p. 23.

37 George Adam Smith, *The Historical Geography of the Holy Land Especially in Relation to the History of Israel and of the Early Church* (London: Hodder and Stoughton, 1909), p. 17.

38 Smith, *The Historical Geography*, p. 20.

39 Smith, *The Historical Geography*, p. 21.

40 Smith, *The Historical Geography*, p. 17.

41 E.M. Blaiklock, *The Acts of the Apostles: An Historical Commentary* (London: Tyndale, 1959), p. 127.

42 Said, *Orientalism*, p. 108.

43 John J. Pilch, *The Cultural World of Jesus: Sunday by Sunday, Cycle A* (Collegeville, PA: Liturgical, 1995), p. xii.

44 Pilch, *Cycle A*, p. 142.

45 Dorothee Soelle and Luise Schottroff, *Jesus of Nazareth* (London: SPCK, 2002), p. 52.

46 Pilch, *Cycle A*, p. 83; see also John J. Pilch, *The Cultural World of Jesus: Sunday by Sunday, Cycle C* (Collegeville, PA: Liturgical, 1997), p. 91.

47 Pilch, *Cycle A*, p. 59.

48 Pilch, *Cycle C*, p. 6.

49 John J. Pilch, *The Cultural World of Jesus: Sunday by Sunday, Cycle B* (Collegeville, PA: Liturgical, 1994), p. 146.

50 Pilch, *Cycle B*, p. 14.

51 Pilch, *Cycle A*, p. 56.

52 Pilch, *Cycle C*, p. 61; see also p. 46.

53 Pilch, *Cycle C*, p. 49.

54 Pilch, *Cycle C*, p. 90.

55 Pilch, *Cycle B*, p. 103.

56 Pilch, *Cycle C*, p. 125.

57 Bruce J. Malina, *Windows on the World of Jesus: Time Travel to Ancient Judea* (Louisville, KY: Westminster/Knox, 1993), p. 158.

58 Pilch, *Cycle B*, p. 68.

59 Pilch, *Cycle A*, p. 86.

60 Pilch, *Cycle A*, pp. 22–23.

61 Pilch, *Cycle C*, p. 125.

62 Pilch, *Cycle A*, p. 127.

63 Pilch, *Cycle B*, p. 121.

64 Pilch, *Cycle B*, p. 132.

65 The Jesus Seminar is a group of biblical scholars who study the traditions about the historical Jesus in the early Christian writings.

66 Malina, *Windows on the World*, p. 78.

67 Pilch, *Cycle A*, p. 101.

68 Pilch, *Cycle B*, pp. 83–84.

69 Pilch, *Cycle A*, p. 3.

70 Pilch, *Cycle A*, p. 101.

71 Pilch, *Cycle C*, p. 145.

72 Pilch, *Cycle C*, p. 125.

73 Johar Malini Schueller, *U.S. Orientalisms* (Ann Arbor, MI: University of Michigan Press, 1997), p. ix.

74 H.R. Spindler, "Indian Studies of the Gospel of John: Puzzling Contextualization," *Exchange* 27, 1 (1980), 45.

75 Amartya Sen, *The Argumentative Indian: Writings on Indian History, Culture and Identity* (London: Allen Lane, 2005).

76 Anouar Abdel-Malek, "Orientalism in Crisis," *Diogenes* 44 (Winter 1963), p. 108.

77 Thomas R. Trautmann, ed., *The Madras School of Orientalism: Producing Knowledge in Colonial South India* (New Delhi: Oxford University Press, 2009).

78 Thor Strandenaes, "Anonymous Bible Translators: Native Literati and the Translation of the Bible into Chinese 1807–1907," in *Sowing the Word: The Cultural Impact of the British and Foreign Bible Society 1804–2004*, eds Stephen Batalden, Kathleen Cann, and John Dean (Sheffield: Sheffield Phoenix, 2004), pp. 121–148.

79 J.S.M. Hooper, *The Bible in India with a Chapter on Ceylon* (London: Oxford University Press, 1938).

80 Said, *Orientalism*, p. 96.

81 Said, *Orientalism*, p. 243.
82 Edward W. Said, *Orientalism* (London: Penguin Books, 2003), p. 342.
83 Said, *Orientalism*, p. 325.
84 Said, *Orientalism*, p. 342.
85 Said, *Orientalism*, p. 328.
86 Said, *Orientalism*, p. 24.

5

Postcolonial Moments
Decentering of the Bible and Christianity

Their books are also different from our own.[1]

We have to change our country by changing its representation.[2]

Postcolonialism is not a reference to a time that marked the formal
ending of empire. Rather, it refers to reactive measures undertaken
by people both during and after colonialism. It is a discourse that
engages simultaneously with and against colonialism. These rare
moments serve as a combative encounter with the empire.
Postcolonial moments are occasions when *a priori* claims for the
purity and wholesomeness of Christianity and the intellectual pre-
eminence of Europe are momentarily rattled. These awkward occasions are when Christianity's central position is replaced with
multiple centers. These are revelatory moments when the myth of
universality and the unique message of the Bible come under challenge. These are revelatory moments when religions are judged not
by the standard set by the Christian Bible, but in their own right as

Exploring Postcolonial Biblical Criticism: History, Method, Practice, First Edition.
R. S. Sugirtharajah.
© 2012 R. S. Sugirtharajah, with the exception of Chapter 3 © 2012 Blackwell Publishing Ltd.
Published 2012 by Blackwell Publishing Ltd.

transforming and evolving entities. These are the uneasy instances when there is a refusal to accept the binary notion of margin/center and of subordination and unequal comparison.

There were at least two such postcolonial moments during the height of colonialism which have a deep significance for the Christian Bible and Christianity. One was the publication of *The Sacred Books of the East* in 1879, and the other was the Parliament of Religions held in Chicago in 1893.

Living with Many Texts

The Sacred Books of the East was a monumental project undertaken by Max Müller, the German indologist who settled and pursued an academic career at Oxford. It was a 50-volume project (the last volume being the index) which spanned more than three decades (1879–1910). *The Sacred Books of the East* was a shining example of the kinder face of Orientalism. European Orientalists, with the help of local pundits, were responsible for unearthing some of the richest textual treasures of the East. Such an enlightened enterprise was undertaken by only a small minority of European scholars who showed a genuine interest in Eastern grammar, poetry, and numismatics. This discovery of ancient civilizations and textual records awoke national consciousness and pride among many Asians.

The books were the edited English translations of Buddhist sutras, Hindu shastras and law manuals, Zoroastrian scripture, and Chinese texts. Although the name of Müller endures as the editor of these volumes, it was Sir William Markby, a judge of the Calcutta High Court, who was responsible for expanding Müller's original idea. Markby extended the data on six Eastern religions and included Indian law books. These translations had an enormous utility value for both the British and the Indians. The books provided a fair knowledge of the people whom the British governed, and at the same time Indians themselves came to know not only about the richness of their religious tradition but also about the laws governing their own property and inheritance. It is, however, common among those involved in translation studies to acknowledge that translation is not merely rendering texts and that they are ideologically tainted products. This was true of *The Sacred Books of the East*. The Enlightenment and Protestant values set the tone for these translatory efforts. Except for two scholars from the East – Kashinath Trimbak Telang, an Indian judge who rendered the Sanskrit *Bhagavad Gita* into English, and the Japanese Junjiro Takakusu, a professor at Tokyo University who translated a Mahayana text – the translators were either English or Germans. Müller, James Legge, T.W. Rhys Davis, and Hermann Oldenberg were involved with six volumes each, and E.W. West and Julius Eggerling came next with five each. Just as the King James version was the product of a company of translators, *The Sacred Books of the East* was also the venture of a group of learned men.

Mysteriously, Christian testaments and scriptures which originated in West Asia were left out. Müller came up with an intriguing answer: "All religions are Oriental, and with the exception of the Christian, their sacred books are written in Oriental languages."[3] In a private letter, Müller added another reason: the Christian Bible was canonical, whereas the other texts were not. The latter half of the nineteenth century was a great period of translations. *The Sacred Books of the East* appeared at a time of Victorian fascination with the texts of ancient peoples connected with the biblical story and history. There were two significant publications, in this regard, at that time. One was the 12-volume *Records of the Past: Being English Translations of Assyrian and Egyptian Monuments* published under the editorship of Samuel Birch,[4] and the other was *Oriental Records: Monumental Confirmatory of the Old Testament Scriptures* by William Harris Rule.[5] The aim of these publications was to support and strengthen the case of the biblical narratives. Birch, in his preface to *Records of the Past*, wrote: "The value of these translations, to those interested in Biblical history and archaeology, cannot be estimated too highly by all who have turned their attention to the language, literature, and history of the nations of the East contemporaneous with the Hebrews, and conterminous to the land of Palestine."[6] Until then the Europeans, or the Northern nations as Max Müller put it, depended on Assyrian, Sumerian, and Egyptian sources for clarifying biblical material, but now "a new stream" was being introduced – "the stream of Oriental thought." This new Oriental stream, Müller points out in his opening address to the International Congress of Orientalists, would intimate that "there are other worlds besides our own, that there are other religions, other mythologies, other laws, and that the history of philosophy from Thales to Hegel is not the whole history of human thought."[7] These books, he goes on to say, have "supplied us with parallels, and with all that is implied in parallels, viz, the possibility of comparing, measuring, and understanding."[8]

The publication of these volumes challenged some of the cherished claims of biblical faith. The comparative study of these texts revealed that there were noticeable affinities between Christianity and these Eastern religions. First, the principal religious texts of the world demonstrated that there was a thirst for the supernatural in these natural religions. Second, the moral precepts which were the hallmarks of the revealed religions, such as Judaism and Christianity, had parallels or similarities in these Eastern texts. Müller showed that the two most important moral codes found in the Hebrew and Christian scriptures, namely the Ten Commandments and "love thy neighbor as thyself," have been known to every human being without the benefit of any special revelation. They occur "some times in almost the same words, in the Sacred Books of other religions."[9] Similarly, the highest truth of Christianity – love thine enemy – a central teaching of the biblical religion, was quite widespread among the Eastern religions. It has its counterparts couched in varying metaphors in the discourses of Lao Tzu, Confucius, and the Buddha. Müller acknowledged that among these various versions, the Hindu version was more poignant and modern than the one found in the New Testament: "Bar thy door not to the stranger, be he friend or be he foe. For the tree will shade the woodman, while his axe does lay it low."[10] As Müller explained, the Indian poets suggested that our love for our enemies should be like the perfume that the sandalwood tree sheds on the very axe that fells it. Müller ruled out any possibility of these religions borrowing such ideas

126

from the Hebrew or Christian scriptures because they were in cir-
culation even before the biblical religion came into existence.

Third, the notion of religion as a practical affair – living a godly
life after a new birth – was not confined to Christianity:

> And even this belief in a new birth is by no means an exclusively
> Christian idea. Nicodemus might ask, how can a man be born again?
> The old Brahmans, however, knew perfectly well the meaning of that
> second birth. They call themselves *Dvi-ga*, that is Twice-born, because
> their religion had led them to discover their divine birthright, long
> before we were taught to call ourselves children of God.[11]

Finally, the comparative study showed how all sacred texts, including the Christian Bible, have, theologically and spiritually, both
savory and unsavory aspects. As Müller put it in his Preface to *The
Sacred Books of the East*:

> There is much, no doubt, in their sacred books which we should toler-
> ate no longer, though we must not forget that there are portions in
> our own sacred books, too, which many of us would wish to be
> absent, which from the earliest ages of Christianity, have been regret-
> ted by theologians of undoubted piety, and which often prove a
> stumbling block to those who have been won over by our missionar-
> ies to the simple faith of Christ.[12]

The important lessons of such a juxtaposition of texts are: (a) that
"there is a common fund of truth in all religions,"[13] and (b) that "the
truths on which all religions agree" far exceed "those on which they
differ."[14]

Müller was not as open, liberal, and understanding as popular
perception portrays him. All these books were accommodated to fit
in with a European editorial mindset which privileged biblical faith.
His interest in these books of the East was mainly historical in the
sense that he was keen to demonstrate that these religions passed
through a stage which biblical religions had left behind long ago.
Said's estimation of Oriental scholars befits Müller: "the Orientalist
sees himself as accomplishing the union of Orient and Occident, but

mainly by reasserting the technological, political, and cultural supremacy of the West."[15] After spending so much energy and enthusiasm on studying the texts of the Eastern religions, he finally ends by privileging Christianity: "For with all that I have said in order to show that other religions also contain all that is necessary for salvation, it would be simply dishonest on my part were I to hide my conviction that the religion taught by Christ, and free as yet from all ecclesiastical fences and intrenchments, is the best, the purest, the truest religion the world has ever seen."[16]

Müller's comparative method would today come under heavy bombardment. Marks of Orientalism are clearly written all over his study of the parallel accounts of various religions. These religions of the East were subordinated to a textualist, essentialist, idealist, universalist, and salvationist vision as imagined by Orientalists. Despite Müller's attempt to compress these values to a manageable Oriental project, what the publication of these volumes did was to challenge, by the very existence of these texts, the then prevailing, ruling idea that the Christian Bible contained sufficient truth for all humankind. The significant implication was that the publication of these volumes loosened the biblical framework which acted as the benchmark for evaluating human affairs. The reference point was no longer Christian or Jewish texts but Vedic Hinduism, Buddhism, Zoroastrianism, Confucianism, and the text of Manu. This became manifestly clear at the Parliament of Religions held at Chicago in 1893.

The Parliament, Public Space, and People's Power

The Parliament of Religions brought together representative adherents of the religions represented in *The Sacred Books of the East*. The Parliament's usefulness, its impact, and its weaknesses have been dealt with competently elsewhere and there is no need to rehearse them here. For our purposes, the Parliament was significant for four reasons.

First, the speeches of the Eastern delegates exposed the incompatibility between biblical teaching and Christian life and practice. Their speeches featured instances of the wide gap that exists between biblical teaching and its application in daily life. These delegates highlighted the high-handed, bigoted, and racist attitudes of some of the missionaries and the behavior of the powerful nations of Christendom. The Japanese layman, Kinza Rigue M. Hirai, whose speech John Barrows the organizer of the Parliament wanted to suppress, listed the atrocities done to the Japanese by Western nations. His catalogue included western vessels smuggling seal fishery into Japanese seas; legal cases unfavorably decided by international authorities against Japan; and racism meted out to Japanese in San Francisco: "If such be the Christian ethics," Hirai told the assembly, "well, we are perfectly satisfied to be heathens."[17] He told the assembly that what mattered to the Japanese was not whether they were called Buddhists, or Shintoists, or Confucianists, but the constant application of the truth taught and its practice in private and international affairs: "Whether Christ saves us or drives us into hell, or whether Gautama Buddha was a real person or there was never such a man, is not a matter of consideration to us; but the constancy of doctrine and conduct is the point on which we put the greatest importance."[18] Similarly, Swami Vivekananda from India, who made a great impact on the Parliament, exploited the failure of missionaries to conform to the teaching of the Bible. He referred to the Bengal famine and the behavior of the missionaries during the time of starvation. While millions were starving, the Swami said, missionaries were busy building churches. The victims "asked for bread" and you "gave them stones."[19]

Second, the Parliament offered a public space for the followers of *The Sacred Books of the East* to scrutinize the Bible openly. The Bible had been through a thorough examination by rationalists and those who applied modern criticism, but that had been done by Christian scholars themselves. The difference this time was that the Bible was inspected by those who were outside its tradition. These were the very people whose own sacred books such as the *Bhagavad Gita*, the *Dhammapada*, and the *Analects* were constantly subjected to severe inspection by those outside the tradition. Now, these Eastern delegates took it upon themselves to make their own readings of the very book which was so often used against them. Hirai was able to take passages from the Sermon on the Mount and recontextualize them in order to mock the moral lapses of Western Christians:

> I read in the Bible, "whoever shall smite on thy right cheek, turn to him the other also," but I cannot discover there any passage which says: "whoever shall demand justice of thee smite his right cheek, and when he turns smite the other also." Again, I read in the Bible: "If any man will sue thee at the law and take away thy coat, let him have thy cloak also," but I cannot discover there any passage which says: "if thou shalt sue any man at law, and take away his coat, let him give thee his cloak also."[20]

While delegates like Hirai were exposing the questionable morality of Western Christians, Anagarika Dharmapala from Ceylon took advantage of the comparative study of religions undertaken by Oriental scholars of the time in order to expose the theological claims of Christians. He provided the assembly with parallels between the life of Buddha and the life of Jesus and the close resemblances in their messages, thus challenging claims to uniqueness in Jesus's teaching.

Third, the Parliament provided an opportunity for the delegates from the East to assert the virtues of Eastern faiths. It offered a public space to bring to a larger audience the universal virtues of Eastern faiths. Until that time, it was missionaries and Orientalist scholars who had the resources and power which made them the spokespeople for these faiths in the West. As Mozoomdar, an Indian delegate, put it, "we have not the resources of money to get men to listen to our message ... and the message that we could not propagate you have taken into your hands to propagate."[21] For the Eastern delegates, Asian religiosity, spirituality, piety, and tolerance were the compelling weapons against Western rationality, materialism, and intolerance. Vivekananda, Mozoomdar, Dharmapala, and Japanese delegates like Soyen were not only eulogizing the spirituality and tolerant nature of Asian faiths but also offering them as a potent antidote to the West's preoccupation with wealth and rationality. These representatives were not rejecting the Western achievements in science and technology. Theirs was not a one-sided attack on the West, with fulsome praise for the East. They were equally appreciative and critical of both the East and the West. Mozoomdar wanted the Parliament to "combine to support each other's strengths and supply each other's deficiencies. And that blessed synthesis of human nature shall be established which all prophets have foretold, and all the devout souls have sighed for."[22] He was proposing a strategic hybridization in which the East and the West borrowed equally from each other. The Asiatic ideals were projected and reconfigured as universal in scope, but this universal potency and range were contingent upon selectively drawing from both West and East. The synthetic religion that the delegates offered acted as a check upon the global advancement of Christianity. There was a strong belief among the Eastern delegates that the time of the East had come. The words of Vivekananda confirm this: "The star arose in the East; it travelled steadily towards the West, sometimes dimmed and sometimes effulgent, till it made a circuit of the world, now it is again rising on the very horizon of the East ... a thousand fold more effulgent than it was before."[23] Such an idea, in Mozoomdar's view, was not the dream of fanatics but had the support of biblical prophecy. Mozoomdar in his speech quoted the prophetic words of Ezekiel, "Behold, the glory of the Lord cometh from the way of the East."[24]

Fourth, the Parliament provided a forum for putting forward the case for independence for the Eastern nations that were under colonial rule. It offered an opportunity for the delegates who were under foreign rule to expose the exploitative nature of colonialism, to draw attention to political inequalities imposed on weaker nations, to seek for international justice, and to claim independence for Asian countries. B.B. Nagarkar, an Indian belonging to the Hindu reform group called the Brahmo Samaj, spoke to the assembly about the "heavy and crushing price" Indians were paying under British rule. Indians not only lost their liberty but were also deprived of some of their "noblest pieces of ancient art and antiquity which have been brought over to England for the purpose of adornment of, and exhibition in, English museums and art galleries." Nagarkar conceded that this loss of wealth and liberty had been compensated for by bestowing upon Indians "the inestimable boon of knowledge and enlightenment." He went on to say that "knowledge is a power" and warned that "it is with this power we shall measure the motives of the English rule. The time will come, as it must come, when if our English rulers should happen to rule India in a selfish, unjust and partial manner, with this same weapon of knowledge we shall compel them to withhold their power over us."[25]

A delegate who spoke more forcibly about the unfairness of the colonial West was Kinza Rigue Hirai. He highlighted the injustices of the treaties, especially that of 1858, imposed by America and other Western powers when diplomacy was "a quite new experience" for the Japanese.[26] Such unfair treaties resulted not only in putting the Japanese in a very disadvantageous position but also in depriving them of their rights.

These Eastern delegates skillfully invoked the freedom the Americans had gained from the British and said they believed that America would understand their plight. For Hirai, "the circumstances which made the American people declare independence" were "in some sense comparable to the present state"[27] of his country. Just as Americans wanted justice from their mother country, the Japanese, too, were asking for justice from these foreign powers. Hirai's plea must have made an emotional impact on the Americans when he said that he could not restrain his "thrilling emotion and sympathetic tears" whenever he read the Declaration of Independence.[28] What he and some of the Eastern delegates wanted for themselves was the same dignity of freedom that America enjoyed, and they hoped that the Americans were well placed to sympathize with their predicament and aspiration. Nagarkar ended his speech by asking the Americans, who lived in a free country, to give advice, extend cooperation, and bestow their blessings on "Young India" as she tried to realize her "social, political and religious aspirations."[29] This call for independence was remarkable because this was long before Gandhi started the freedom struggle. These delegates were soliciting the help of America, a freed country, to show by example that America was still the America of freedom and hope.

The publication of *The Sacred Books of the East* and the Parliament of Religions made several things clear. First, the great human qualities – love, charity, equality, fraternity, holiness, purity, justice – were not, contrary to what missionaries claimed, exclusive to Christianity. These qualities were to be found in the Eastern religions and these religions had produced men and women who had exhibited these characteristics. Second, there was a strong appetite among people who were under foreign occupation to rule themselves rather than be ruled by others. Linked to this was the staunch desire among the representatives of the Eastern religions to represent themselves in a public forum rather than to be represented by European Orientalists and Western missionaries. Third, the Parliament helped to vitalize and modernize movements in Asia and paved the way for the rise of religious nationalism in India, Sri Lanka, and Japan. Finally, these two events – the Chicago Parliament and the publication of the Eastern religious texts – are a reminder that, in scope, spirit, and complexity, postcolonialism is not restricted by time and period.

Colonial Struggles: Old and New

Anti-colonial struggles went on even at the height of European colonialism. The current postcolonialism is a continuation of that resistant streak, but differs from it in a number of ways. There were three types of resistance during colonialism: political, cultural, and moral. There were frequent political uprisings, rebellions, and mutinies in India, the best known and most extensive being the 1857 revolt. The 1857 uprising had a number of local manifestations beside the major one in the Indo-Gangetic plain. It was fueled by factors such as the offense caused to the religious beliefs of the people and the reduction of the ruling elite's power and wealth. It was not a popular uprising, with people leading the revolt and wanting to establish a democratic form of government. The 1857 revolt was hardly a fight for democratic rights. Rather, it was about restoring power to local chieftains who had lost it through the land-grabbing intervention of the East India Company. The rebels requested a monarch, the Mughal emperor Bahadur Shah Zafar II, the representative of an earlier conquering power, to lead them against the British. The idea of independence did not exist at that time and it emerged only in the early years of the twentieth century. It was only later that anti-colonialism developed into a political force, turned its attention to gaining independence from colonial rule, and went on to create new nation-states. Gandhi himself was an empire loyalist until 1918.

Current postcolonialism has a different challenge. The task today is not territorial emancipation but freedom from the control of the market, especially from Western-inspired corporate expansion as the norm for all. The new global order is not about controlling territories but about the market acting as a mediating agency and imposing its values such as profit for a few at the cost of the welfare of the people. As the former British prime minister Tony Blair put it in one of his foreign policy speeches: "it is about a battle of values and progress; and therefore it is one we must win." Phrased bluntly, it is about controlling ideas and values.

The anti-colonial struggle during the colonial period was undertaken within the context of the unequal positions that prevailed between the colonizer and the colonized. The ammunition for such a resistance was then supplied specifically by the Orientalists – as we have seen, a group of European scholars who retrieved manuscripts which were obscure and brought to public knowledge the long cultural history of the East (Chapter 4). The early protesters were guided by the vigilantly prepared roles assigned by some influential Orientalists to the East and the West. For instance, the nationalists made great purchase out of the binary thinking advocated by these Orientalists: Asia was spiritual and instinctive, whereas Europe was scientific and rational. The West dominates and controls nature, whereas India lives close to nature. One of those nationalists who made great use of this contrastive construc-

tion was Keshub Chunder Sen (1838–1884). He, in one of his Calcutta
Town Hall lectures, said:

> Europe, study botany like a scholar; we prefer to live as devotees in
> the garden of Eden. Europe, rise on the wings of science and study
> the stars in the firmament above; we shall indulge in the highest
> contemplation in the heavens above.[30]

By employing the very cultural discursive strategies of the
Orientalists which showed India in a positive light, the nationalists
were able to unsettle the colonial hold on its own terms. They made
profitable use of the images of the Orient supplied and controlled
by the Master in order to attack the Master himself. The current
postcolonial struggle, though it subscribes to the ruling modes
of thought, is not entirely subservient to them. Postcolonialism
speaks from the privileged position of the "other." Today's
postcolonialism is about questioning the anthropological insights,
scientific theories, theological presuppositions, racial stereotypes,
and linguistic maneuverings which legitimized and were central
to colonialism and now legitimize neo-colonialism. It is about unsettling these cultural ideas and causing their dislocation. The current
postcolonial resistance does not essentialize the tradition but draws
critically on both cosmopolitan and indigenous thought patterns. It
looks for hermeneutical possibilities and energies that emerge from
knowledge and practices accumulated during the long colonial
experience.

The solution to colonial rule that the early agitators came up with
was accommodation and reconciliation. Some of the Indian nationalists who were critical of British rule and its racial policies settled
for a harmonious life with the British because of the benefits British
rule bestowed on India. Raja Rammohun Roy (1772–1823) and
Keshub Chunder Sen were examples of such an attitude. Both were
critical of the British occupation of India and very much aware of
the evils of political subjugation, but both were moved and enthused
by its advantages. They conceded the greatness of the British
achievement in India and at the same time were proud of India's

own spiritual and cultural heritage. They advocated and hoped for a mutual dependence which would benefit both the ruler and the ruled. Their aim was reciprocal structural adjustments between the ruler and the ruled which would benefit both, rather than the overthrow of the British leading to full independence. Sen wrote:

> Thus shall we rectify each other's errors and supplement mutual deficiencies. Europe will correct and purify Eastern communion with the hard logic of science, and remove all the superstitious and idolatrous rites and all the mystical delusions which have encrusted around it in the course of ages. While on the other hand, we shall take the dry facts of Western science, fill them with the flesh and blood of Eastern sentiment, and spiritualize and vivify them with a living faith.[31]

This mutual amalgamation of each other's science and spirituality, in Sen's view, had an eschatological purpose: "When all nations and countries will thus eat and absorb each other's goodness and purity, then shall the inward kingdom of heaven be realized on earth, which ancient prophets sang and predicted."[32]

Rammohun Roy, a liberal, supported national aspirations elsewhere. He was supposed to have told Victor Jacquemont that "conquest is rarely evil when the conquering people are more civilized than the conquered." Roy, who was so concerned about political freedom for other nations, and greeted the progress of South America's struggle against the Spanish empire with great enthusiasm, was less condemnatory of British imperialism. He did not believe that India was fit or ready for such a free existence. He, like other nationalists at the time, was prompted by practical considerations. Roy wrote: "we frequently offer up our humble thanks to God, for the blessings of British rule in India and sincerely pray, that it may continue in its beneficent operation for centuries to come."[33] Roy wanted the link between Britain and India to be put on a strong and "a solid and permanent footing" provided that India were to be "governed in a liberal manner, by means of Parliamentary superintendence."[34] Both Roy and Sen were loyal and grateful recipients of all that British colonialism could offer to awaken India from her moral slumber and they had no qualms in acknowledging it publicly.

Sen's anti-colonial resistance took the form of endlessly reminding the British of their moral responsibility. The fact that Sen viewed the presence of the British as by divine providence did not prevent him from criticizing the racism and brutality that accompanied British rule. For Sen, the British had lost their moral authority because they paid only lip service to the teachings of Jesus. Sen's contention was that the bad behavior of a number of British Christians in India was the cause of the failure of Christianity to "produce any wholesome moral influence" on India.[35] He urged the British to use their power sensibly as a "means of raising and purifying not only a few individuals but a whole nation."[36] In a lecture Sen gave in Edinburgh in 1870, he harangued his audience: "will you go there [i.e., India] only to make money, and then come home; and will you not feel a moral interest in that country, in the welfare of its people?"[37]

Sen's attack on the insensitive behavior of the British does not make him an anti-imperial hero. His role during the Indian uprising of 1857 is unclear. According to his biographer, Sen spent the critical years 1856–8 studying philosophy under a Mr Jones, professor of philosophy. He and Western educated Indians at that time hardly entertained the notion of a free and independent India. At the most, what Sen expected was that India "under the direction and guidance of England, will be enabled to occupy a high position in the scale of nations."[38]

There was a hesitation on the part of the nationalists about antagonizing the rulers or seeking their expulsion. Both Roy and Sen rejected the idea of one group of people ruling over another, but they did not have any qualms about endorsing British colonialism. Colonialism was seen as an inevitable and, more importantly, as a necessary intervention to revitalize India. Their resistance agenda was to promote the needs of both parties, and they advocated a wholehearted cooperation based on the premise that the weak needed the strong for their survival. In this earlier form of resistance, the aim was to create a harmonious existence between the colonized and the colonizer.

The aim of this anti-colonial struggle during colonialism was to temper the territorial occupation with a moral governance, aided by the monumental role played by missionaries in fashioning this moral vision. Sen was tireless in reminding his audience that it was not Queen Victoria or Lord Lytton or Sir Frederick Haines who "secured attachment and allegiance of India"; rather, it was "through spiritual influence and moral suasion" that "India's hearts have been touched, conquered, and subjugated by a superior power. That power – need I tell you – is Christ? It is the Christ who rules British India and not the British government."[39] For Sen, like the Romantics, the quintessence of Christianity lies in its moral renewal presented by Christ. However, the Christ who was the source of this moral revival was not the all-conquering European Christ, but the Christ reimagined by Roy and Sen. For Roy, this Christ was a moral teacher, and for Sen it was the Christ who wore a saffron robe. The early nationalists like Roy and Sen were adopting the British tabloid method of naming and shaming. They were exposing the moral failures of the British in their day-to-day dealings with the Indians. They were appealing to the conscience and the good nature of the British character to rectify their moral lapses. They were invoking the moral conscience of the British to change their way of life without disturbing the existing power structure.

Current postcolonialism does not appeal to the moral virtues of the West and is wary of using such a tactic. The West's track record of dealing with countries over the last 200 years has shown that it has lost its moral fibre. Arbitrary military interventions, double standards in international politics, betrayals of promises (the Kurds), manufactured calamities like famines in Africa, the high-handed manner in which Western countries violate international rules, the redefinition of democracy to suit Western interests, have all made moral and ethical principles the last thing one can expect from the West. Postcolonialism does not appeal to the so-called superior moral principles of the West but uses values such as justice, equality, tolerance, and reason as a means to assert the right

138

of all people to enjoy the same freedom and have access to the same resources.

Postcolonial moments are those occasions when the colonized realize both the potential and the limitations of colonialism. While anti-colonial struggles of the past were not entirely sure about the removal of the occupying power, the postcolonial project today is about eradicating the deep assumption that the West knows best. It is one of those rare occasions when the subjugated people display their resentment towards their rulers, although their protest has only a limited ambition and purchase. In the past, it might not have unsettled the system but it caused consternation and eventually led to the dislocation of the empire. Today it provides a powerful critique.

Orientalism in the final analysis was not always as destructive as it was generally understood to have been. As a system, it has, to use Gauri Viswanathan's words, a "boomerang effect." It furnishes the Orientals with "a critical repertoire that ultimately is used, ironically to contest Orientalism's power and reach."[40] The redeployment of Oriental images by Rammohun Roy, Keshub Chunder Sen, Swami Vivekananda, and Kinza Rigue Hirai did exactly this.

Notes

1 Jorge Luis Borges, *Fictions* (London: Penguin, 1998), p. 18.
2 A character in Miguel Syjuco, *Ilustrado* (New York: Farrar, Straus and Giroux, 2010), p. 207.
3 Max F. Müller, *Chips from a German Workshop*, vol. IV (London: Longmans, Green, 1875), p. 344.
4 S. Birch, ed., *Records of the Past: Being English Translations of the Assyrian and Egyptian Monuments*, vol. 1 (London: Bagster, 1873).
5 William Harris Rule, *Oriental Records: Monumental Confirmatory of The Old Testament Scriptures* (London: Bagster, 1877).
6 *Records of the Past*, p. i.
7 Müller, *Chips*, p. 343.
8 Müller, *Chips*, p. 343.

9 Max F. Müller, *Physical Religion: The Gifford Lectures Delivered Before the University of Glasgow 1890* (London: Longmans, Green, 1891), p. 342.

10 Müller, *Physical Religion*, p. 362.

11 Max F. Müller, "The Parliament of Religions: Chicago 1893," in *Collected Works of the Right Hon. F. Max Müller XVIII, II, Essays on the Science of Religion* (London: Longmans, Green, 1901), p. 341.

12 Max F. Müller, "Preface to *The Sacred Books of the East*," in *The Sacred Books of the East Translated by Various Oriental Scholars*, ed. Max F. Müller (Oxford: Clarendon, 1879), pp. xxxvii–xxxviii.

13 Müller, *Physical Religion*, p. 346.

14 Müller, *Chips*, p. 345.

15 Edward W. Said, *Orientalism* (London: Penguin, 1978), p. 246.

16 Müller, *Physical Religion*, pp. 363–364.

17 Kinza Rigue M. Hirai, "The Real Position of Japan toward Christianity," in *The World's Parliament of Religions: An Illustrated and Popular History of the World's First Parliament of Religions Held in Chicago in Connection with The Columbian Exposition of 1893*, vol. I, ed. John Henry Barrows (Chicago: Parliament, 1893), p. 449.

18 Hirai, "The Real Position," p. 449.

19 Swami Vivekananda, "Hinduism," in *The World's Parliament of Religions*, vol. I, p. 129.

20 Hirai, "The Real Position," p. 448.

21 Protop Chunder Mozoomdar, "The Brahmo-Somaj," in *The World's Parliament of Religions*, vol. I, p. 351.

22 Protop Chunder Mozoomdar, "The World's Religious Debt to Asia," in *The World's Parliament of Religions*, vol. II, p. 1092.

23 Vivekananda, "Hinduism," p. 978.

24 Mozoomdar, "The World's Religious Debt to Asia," p. 1092.

25 B.B. Nagarkar, "The Work of Social Reform in India," in *The World's Parliament of Religions*, vol. I, p. 770.

26 Hirai, "The Real Position," p. 445.

27 Hirai, "The Real Position," p. 450.

28 Hirai, "The Real Position," p. 450.

29 Nagarkar, "The Work of Social Reform in India," p. 779.

30 Keshub Chunder Sen, *Keshub Chunder Sen's Lectures in India* (London: Cassell, 1904), p. 115.

31 Sen, *Keshub Chunder Sen's Lectures* (1904), p. 115.

32 Keshub Chunder Sen, *Keshub Chunder Sen's Lectures in India* (London: Cassell, 1901), p. 487.

33 Rammohun Roy, *The English Works of Raja Rammohun Roy*, ed. Jogendra Chunder Ghose (New Delhi: Cosmo, 1906), p. 198.

34 Roy, *The English Works*, p. 316.

35 Sen, *Keshub Chunder Sen's Lectures* (1901), p. 31.

36 Keshub Chunder Sen, *Keshub Chunder Sen in England: Diaries, Sermons, Addresses and Epistles*, reprint 1980 (Calcutta: Writers Workshop, 1871), p. 326.

37 Sen, *Keshub Chunder Sen in England*, pp. 384–385.

38 Sen, *Keshub Chunder Sen in England*, p. 464.

39 Sen, *Keshub Chunder Sen's Lectures* (1901), p. 361.

40 Gauri Viswanathan, "Introduction," in *Power, Politics, and Culture: Interviews with Edward Said*, ed. Gauri Viswanathan (New York: Pantheon, 2001), p. xv.

6

The Empire Exegetes Back
Postcolonial Reading Practices

The office of the interpreter is not to add another.[1]

Who knows how the word may be twisted, knotted and turned?[2]

Different reading practices open up different ways of looking at texts. This chapter provides three examples of what happens to biblical texts when they are subjected to postcolonial scrutiny. The first example uses Edward Said's contrapuntal reading method to look at the birth narratives of two religious founders – Siddhartha, the Buddha, and Jesus, the Christ. It shows how these birth stories which came out of different cultural, religious, and political contexts, and were constructed to meet different hermeneutical needs, can mutually enhance and critique and gain from each other without losing their individuality and vitality. The second example has benefited from what Edward Said called the late style, a concept he was trying to develop towards the end of his life. The late style is about how artists and writers change their minds and ideas over the years.

Exploring Postcolonial Biblical Criticism: History, Method, Practice, First Edition.
R. S. Sugirtharajah.
© 2012 R. S. Sugirtharajah, with the exception of Chapter 3 © 2012 Blackwell Publishing Ltd.
Published 2012 by Blackwell Publishing Ltd.

For instance, a radical artist might end up as a conformist or vice versa. I look at the writings of Paul and John using this concept as a way of explaining the contradictory resolution found in their last writings. One, an agitator in his early life, tries to bring harmony and serenity as he faces his end, and the other, initially a compromiser, ends up confronting the powers that be. The third example employs the rhetoric of representation to look at the Parable of the Rich Man and Lazarus and investigates how the rich and the poor are portrayed both in the text and in subsequent interpretations. What follows gives some flavor of how postcolonial biblical criticism operates.

Masters and Their Miraculous Births

The earlier comparative approach to the study of religions was aggressive, judgmental, and condescending. The observation of Ernest Wright neatly sums up this position: "The study of comparative religion can do nothing more than point out the distinctiveness, and perhaps the superiority, of the Biblical God."[3] It worked on the dominant Christian model and pointed out a plethora of deficiencies in other religious traditions: lack of a monotheistic ideal, of a personal savior, and of historically verifiable redemptive acts. These omissions provided a substantial contrast for establishing Christian superiority, and for scoring significantly against other religions.

A different approach is to be seen in contrapuntal reading, in which all texts are constantly impelled by a desire for connection and conversation. The aim is to produce not a harmonious reading but a reading which contains complexities and irresolvable differences. Contrapuntal reading is an activity which leads to a larger world of texts and enables an interpreter to see connections. It unveils what might have been buried or underdeveloped or obscured in a single text. As an example of contrapuntal reading, I would like to look at the birth stories of the Buddha and Jesus. These have both considerable common features and considerable differences.

To begin with, in neither story is the father the begetter, and in both the mother is a vehicle for a higher purpose. Both Buddhist and Christian accounts agree that Suddhodana, in the case of Siddhartha, and Joseph, in the case of Jesus, were not the biological fathers. Both narratives are silent about how the two mothers – Maya and Mary – became pregnant. The conversation between Mary and the angel Gabriel was not about how Mary conceived but a statement of assurance and trust. In the case of Maya, the mother of Siddhartha, it was she who told her husband on the day of her conception that she wished to "spend the night away" from him (*Mahavastu* ii.5).[4] In both cases, the annunciation takes the form of a dream. In the Buddhist version, before she conceived, Maya the mother of the future Buddha "saw in her sleep a white lord of an elephant entering her body, yet she felt thereby no pain" (*Buddhacarita* 1.4).[5] One striking difference between the Buddhist and the Christian versions is that in the Buddhist account it was the Buddha who chose his father, and in the Christian version it was the work of the Holy Spirit.

Both the Buddhist and Christian versions include an annunciation scene. In the Christian account the angel Gabriel announces the birth to Mary, and the message is mainly about preserving the house of David and perpetuating his dynasty (Luke 1.26–38). However, in the Buddhist story, when Maya thought that she was expecting a universal king, she was corrected by the devas – the celestial beings – who told her that her child would be called the "Exalted One" and that he would become the Buddha and not a universal king: "You bear one who is an elephant among men, the best of treasurers, the destroyer of the force and violence of intoxication, the dispeller of dark and murky folly, the storehouse of good qualities, the possessor of boundless wealth, a royal seer whose chariot wheel knows no obstacle, whose radiance is boundless" (*Mahavastu* 2.14). His assigned role was not to rule, but to remove ignorance and the causes for suffering.

Maya and Mary each conceived during the course of a vision. While Buddhist narratives insist on the painless nature of the child's growth in the womb and birth, the Christian text is silent. The

144

assumption is there was nothing unusual in the birth. When the Boddhisatva entered Maya's womb, she was comfortable in her movements. At the time of delivery, there was none of the usual screaming of the mother, tears, sweat, blood, pollution, and uncleanness normally associated with giving birth. The mothers were free of pain and their wombs remained unscathed and at ease. *Mahavastu* gives the reason for this pain-free birth: "Tahagatas are born with a body that is made of mind, and thus the mother's body is not rent nor does any pain ensue" (2.20). The gospels do not describe how Mary gave birth and there were no details of the actual delivery. Buddhist texts provide interesting information as to how it all happened. The birth took place in Lumbini Park. Maya's delivery was not like that of other women giving birth in a lying or sitting position. She delivered the Buddha standing. Feeling that the time had come she stretched out her hand to support herself by the branch of a tree. Standing thus, she gave painless birth to a child. The child came out from her side. The *Mahavastu* provides an explanation for such a birth: "For the Supreme of Men are born from their mother's right side; it is here that the all the valiant men abide when in their mother's womb" (2.20). Asavaghosa, believed to be the writer of a second-century account of the Buddha's life, elaborated on this unusual delivery by comparing the Buddha's birth to the great sages of the Vedic period, thus placing him in the line of great sages: "As with the birth of Aurva from the thigh, of Prthu from the hand, of Mandhatr, the peer of Indra, from the head, of Kaksivast from the armpit, such was his birth" (*Buddhacarita* 1.10).

There is an age difference between the two women. Mary was considerably younger than Maya according to a non-canonical text, which says she was "sixteen when these mysteries happened" (Proto-Gospel of James 12.3). Maya was 35 when she gave birth to the Buddha. Mary was the first and the only mother of the Messiah. There was no Jewish history of mothers giving birth to Messiahs. Maya, by contrast, was not the first mother of the Buddha. There were several mothers who had given birth to Buddhas. There was no suggestion that Maya was a virgin at that time. Interestingly, it was Jerome in CE 393 in his writing against Jovinianus who popularized the idea in the West that "the Buddha the founder of their religion, had his birth through the side of a *virgin*."[6]

The doctrine of the virgin birth is not mentioned in the earliest written New Testament writings such as Paul's Epistles. There is no reference in Mark, believed to be the first written gospel. There are variations within the Christian accounts of the birth of Christ. The narratives of virginal conception in Matthew and Luke differ. The Matthew version has dreams of Joseph, the visit of the Magi, and the massacre of the innocents, and has Joseph and Mary going to Nazareth only after returning from Egypt. His account centers around and is dictated by a prophecy of the Hebrew scriptures with forced interpretations: "Behold, a virgin shall conceive." When Matthew used the passage from the prophecy of Isaiah, he was quoting it from the Septuagint version, the Greek translation of the Hebrew scripture, which has *parthenos*, meaning virgin. Those who are familiar with the translation of the biblical text will know that the original Hebrew text does not have the specific term for virgin *bethulah*, but only *almah*, a young woman.

Luke places the birth of Jesus at the end of the rule of Herod. Luke has nothing to say about Herod, the magi, or bloodshed massacre of the babies. Contrary to Matthew, Luke paints a peaceful and homely scene. Luke's narrative is woven around the traditional events that were expected to happen to a Jewish boy. At the end of the eighth day he was circumcised (2.21). At the proper time (33 days: Lev. 12.4) the mother was purified and the son redeemed. At the age of 12 he becomes a bar mitzvah, demonstrating his knowledge before the rabbis and assuming a significant position of leadership (2.41–52).

Both the infants – the Buddha and Jesus – had visitations from wise men. The *Lalitavistara* mentions five foreign wise men paying homage to the Buddha. The Christian version, which some scholars believe was based on the Buddhist one, has some magi or magicians or Chaldean astrologers visiting the newborn Jesus. A Turkish text has it that the gifts these three kings offered, gold, frankincense, and myrrh, were three jewels of Buddhism – Buddha, Dharma, and Sangha.[7] Both these little boys were blessed and venerated by devout men: Asita the hermit ascetic in the case of the Buddha, and Simeon and the prophetess Anna in the case of Jesus (Luke 2:25–34).

The earliest Buddhist records are also silent about a virgin birth. The oldest documents such as *Mahjjhima-nikayas* and *Digha Nikya* do not mention it. The earliest text in which the idea of the virgin birth can be traced is the *Mahavastu* (the *Sublime Story*) – a collection of history and legends related to the Buddha. It does not have a single author and was compiled over a period ranging from the second century BCE to the third or fourth century CE.[8] Whereas there is written literature about Jesus between 30 and 100 years after his death and resurrection, there is no story of the founder of Buddhism that was written within the century or so after his death. Buddha's biography evolved slowly over the centuries.

It is the non-canonical writings that make the claim about and emphasize the virginity of Mary. One such is the Proto-Gospel of James, a second-century document which was supposed to have been written by James. In this, when Joseph found out that Mary was pregnant, he is worried and asks her, "You who have been cared for by God. why did you do this?" A distraught Mary answers: "I am pure and have not had sex with any man" (13.2–3). The same gospel even has salacious details about the virginal status of Mary. A skeptical Salome (who she was is not revealed) declares: "As the Lord my God lives, if I do not insert my finger and examine her condition, I will not believe that the virgin has given birth." After the inspection, a contrite Salome cries out: "Woe to me for my sin and faithlessness. For I have put the living God to the test, and see, my hand is burning, falling away from me" (19.3–20.1). Just like the women who attested to the risen Christ, here two women, in keeping with the Jewish expectation that two women were required as witnesses, attest to the virginity of Jesus's mother. Buddhist mythologizers even went further and declared that the Buddha's mother had "no thought of men connected with the senses" and that she suppressed her passion even for King Suddhodana. At her conception, she spent the night away from her husband. The baby entered her womb in the "form of a white elephant" and sat there in a posture of meditation. The Buddha's mother died seven nights after giving birth, because it was not fitting that she who bears the peerless one should afterwards indulge in love (*Mahavastu* 2.8).

The Christian accounts of the virgin birth do not make any reference to the pre-existence of Christ. There are, however, tales about the Buddha before he was in his mother's womb. These tales are magical and look absurd to those raised on rationalistic thinking. These pre-existence fables make the claim that the Buddha did not begin his journey as Siddhartha, but had embarked on his spiritual adventure long before his actual birth.

The myth makers of religions try to give their religious founders an aristocratic lineage. The Buddha must be born of a royal or priestly class, whichever was predominant at the time. He was born to Maya, the queen of King Suddhodana of the Sakya clan. Unlike the Buddha, Jesus did not come from the upper class, but the gospels try to make him part of the Davidic dynasty. Only the Proto-Gospel of James describes Mary as a daughter of a wealthy Jew, Joachim, and his wife Anna.

Birth stories of religious founders tend to revolve around either a matter-of-fact depiction or an overblown account. The birth narratives of the Buddha and Jesus fall into the second category. Records of the birth of these two masters are not bias free. The gospels, which were regarded as reliable historical sources for the biographical details of Jesus, were written from the different theological persuasions of the evangelists. There were disputes about the selection and interpretation of facts related to the life and work of Jesus. In the case of Buddhism, there are no documents comparable to the gospels, though the biographies of the Buddha which later emerged produced their own share of controversy and theological disputes.

The doubts about the virgin birth are not a recent phenomenon largely fueled by the Enlightenment. The skepticism was there even during the early days of Christianity. As the Gospel of Philip puts it: "Some say that Mary was impregnated by the Holy Spirit. They err. They do not know what they say. When did a woman become pregnant by a woman?" (v. 17). The other point is that no sacred text is entirely original or totally distinctive. Texts grow out of borrowing, or at times are influenced by the already prevailing oral traditions, texts, ideas, and concepts, and then transmute them through creative inventiveness and application.

The tendency among certain biblical scholars is to limit truth to history. The consequence of this is to accord a historical status to the gospel narratives. Biblical scholars treat the gospels as a privileged vehicle for transmitting and recognizing truth. Truth is revealed not only through texts and historical accounts but also through myths and metaphors. The Buddhist birth stories indicate that truth for a Buddhist can also be conveyed through fables, folklore, and imaginative constructions.

Contrapuntal reading means texts gaining from one another and at the same time not losing their vitality. Juxtaposed texts profit by opening themselves to new dimensions which are not present in their textual traditions. The juxtaposition of the birth stories forces Buddhists and Christians to rethink some of the cherished ideas and practices surrounding the infancy stages of their religious founders. One of the images the Spanish used in the colonies was the image of the infant Jesus. This harmless and helpless baby in the lap of his mother needs protection and those who protect him, especially the institutionalized Church and the empire, become his "guardians" and "Lords." Such a child Christ, according to Saul Trinidad, played a pivotal role in the "expansionist and military theocracy"[9] of Spain in the Americas. This child Christ adopted by his guardians does not speak against the powerful and is shorn of his liberative role. He is depicted in art as having a perpetual smile. The image of god as a vulnerable and pathetic child is a convenient way of distracting attention from the type of god who, as powerful despot and destroyer of indigenous culture, accompanied the colonialists. The infant Jesus is a suitable image because it has nothing to say about whether countries have a right to invade other people's territories or about how one treats the vulnerable. In the Buddhist tradition, the formative period of the Buddha's childhood has hardly any hermeneutical purchase. It was the grown-up teacher, and not the uninformed Siddhartha, that the Buddhists were concerned about.

Siddhartha's non-uniqueness as *the* Buddha (because there was a series of Buddhas in the Buddhist tradition) is a challenge to the often rigid and unrepeatable Christian claim made for the Jesus event. Siddhartha as the Buddha is a supreme model, a non-specific figure who exemplifies the truth of the previous Buddhas. There is no uniqueness attached to Buddhas. One of the alleged sayings of Siddhartha found in the *Lankavatra Sutra*, a Mahayana text, goes like this: "Between myself and (all the other) Buddhas, in this respect, there is no distinction whatsoever" (61.8).[10] There is a similar verse in *Milindapahana*, a text which is part of the Pali canon, which reiterates the same point: "There is no distinction between the Buddhas in physical beauty, moral habit, concentration, wisdom, freedom, cognition and insight of freedom ... in a word in all dhammas of Buddhas, for all Buddhas are exactly the same as regard the Buddha-dhammas."[11] This does not mean that all Buddhas are the same. As Richard S. Cohen has observed, "although all buddhas are equal in their wisdom, they differ through their compassionate deeds."[12] The difference between them is their compassionate action.

The historical dimension of Siddhartha's life is certainly vital to his role as religious leader and founder, but his contribution has to be seen in the much wider context of the compassionate activities of the earlier Buddhas. Siddhartha's non-uniqueness as the Buddha is central to his status as the founder: "One must acknowledge that Shakyamuni's [i.e., Siddhartha's] function as founder has not given him a singular status for Buddhists, who ironically use his teachings as a means for seeking, worshipping, emulating, and encountering *other* buddhas."[13] In contrast, Jesus's status is dependent not only on the historical events surrounding his life and death but also on the claim that he is the only son of god and a unique incarnation. The virgin birth, along with the miraculous activities of Jesus, his atoning work, his bodily resurrection, and his expected return, are a cornerstone of faith among Christians.

Christians see incarnation as a unique event. The miracle of incarnation is not possible without the miraculous conception of Christ in the womb of a virgin. This is seen as a once and for all event, and it assumes that revelation is something that happened only in the past. The Buddhist story assumes that revelation is an ongoing phenomenon. The historical Siddhartha is one among an infinite series of Buddhas who appear throughout history so that the Dharma can be constantly preached and rediscovered. Siddhartha was the seventh in the line of such dharmic incarnations. The Buddha will be followed by Maitreya, now a Bodhisattva in heaven.

The Buddhist story plays down the nationalistic aspect of religious figures. Buddha's saviorhood was expressly divorced from any one nation's triumphal longings and was unwaveringly focused on teaching people how to attain *nirvana*. The concept of Christ arose within the monotheistic Judaic culture, fulfilling the nation's longing for a liberating king. The idea of Bodhisattva emerged in ancient India which was full of gods and goddesses.

There is no devotion and theology about Maya comparable to Marian devotion. Mary has been coopted into various liberative causes, foreshadowing the trials and struggles of women of all time. More importantly, the devotees of Mary see her as a female counterpart of Jesus: "If Jesus was poor and suffered, so too was Mary. If Jesus healed, so did Mary If Jesus was the Lord, then Mary must have been a lady of sorts. If Jesus is King, so Mary is Queen."[14] The absence of a similar Maya veneration among the Buddhists could be attributed to two factors. First, she died soon, seven days after giving birth to Siddhartha. Such an end was in keeping with previous mothers of the Buddhas who passed away on the seventh day after giving birth. She is viewed largely as a receiver and a respondent rather than an as instrument for change. Second, Maya was not the only begetter of the Buddhas; there were six before her who had the privilege of bringing the Buddhas into the world. In spite of these reservations, Buddhists could learn from Christians and offer a deserved place to Maya and to other mothers of the Buddhas rather than simply seeing them as begetters of the Buddha.

These stories reinforce the notion that women's bodies are not their own. Their bodies are there to perform a higher, noble, and useful role on behalf of humankind. The bodies belong to all except to the women themselves. Such an idea plays into the hands of those who are obsessed with the idea of woman as ideal mother whose sole point in life is to carry out valuable duties for humanity.

In the final analysis, the way these religions have developed and been institutionalized means that these two originators would have found it difficult to identify with them. In the highly bureaucratized and theologically conservative atmosphere that prevails in these religions, Buddha would have found it difficult to be a Buddhist, and Jesus a Christian.

What the contrapuntal method does is to bring various textual worlds together and enable us to picture and, perhaps better yet, envisage an alternative world which may not be accessible if one is confined to one text.

Late Style: Texts and Twilight

Edward Said, in his last days, worked out what he called the "late style," a term he adopted from his mentor, the German philosopher Theodor Adorno.[15] Said was fascinated by the work of artists, composers, and writers which were produced in the final years of their lives. These, in his view, "acquire a new idiom" which he labels the "late style."[16] These works attest to "an apotheosis of artistic creativity and power."[17] This late style is about timelessness. By timelessness, Said means that in art and in life in general what is "appropriate to early life is not appropriate to its later stages, and vice versa."[18] He even cites the words of Ecclesiastes that for everything there is a season and a time.

Working on the idea of lateness in a range of Western canonical artists, Said observes that artists at the twilight of their creative careers register two kinds of response in their work. One is serenity and maturity, and the other is anarchy and anomaly. In the first, lateness is seen as ripeness and the crown of a lifetime achievement. At the end of their artistic life, nearing death, the work of certain artists reflects a sense of mellowness, wisdom, harmony, and resolution, and an attempt to sanitize the rebelliousness of the earlier career. Such a neat ending and tidying up, in Said's view, is an act

of power which these artists like to wield. This control and management of their work is, in some ways, like the Orientalist scholarship
which Said himself helped to expose. But there is the other kind of
response in late work which was directly opposite to what was
achieved earlier and shows discordance and disconnection. It is this
kind of lateness which appealed to Said, the lateness that displays
"intransigence, difficulty and unresolved contradiction."[19] In contrast to the common perception that lateness brings harmony and
serenity, certain writers near the end of their creative period are at
odds with the world and show disagreement and disruptiveness in
their work. When one "would expect serenity and maturity, one
instead finds a bristling, difficult, unyielding – perhaps even
inhuman – challenge."[20] Said's interest was in the writers who "stir
up more anxiety, tamper irrevocably with the possibility of closure,
leave the audience more perplexed and unsettled than before."[21] It
is this type of late style that Said finds "deeply interesting." He
clarifies: "I'd like to explore the experience of late style that involves
a nonharmonious, nonserene tension and above all a sort of deliberately unproductive productiveness, a going against."[22]

There are two New Testament writers whose attitude to the dominant political order of their time could be explained by way of
Said's idea of late style. One is Paul, and the other is John, to whom
the Book of Revelation is ascribed. Both, in their late works, have
changed their position with regard to secular powers and the Roman
empire. One seeks a closure to his earlier resistance by advising
Christians to be loyal citizens of the state; and the other, whose
attitude to the rulers was benign at the most in the earlier stage of
his life, now advocates a headlong clash, encouraging Christian
churches in Asia to resist the ruling power.

Paul's attitude to the state authorities expounded in Romans 13,
a late work, has been an enigma to biblical interpreters. Embarrassed
by Paul's kowtowing to the ruling powers, scholars have come up
with a number of conjectures and reasons to clarify Paul's reactionary position. First, Paul is writing under the conviction that the
parousia is imminent and that the old world order, including that
of the Roman empire, of which he and his contemporaries are part,

is going to go away. Second, all empires are dangerous and evil and Roman imperialism is no exception; it is as a survival strategy that the Christian should exercise caution and vigilance. Third, civil obedience has only a limited value. Freeing oneself from tyranny is a human activity which attempts to do something of which only god is capable. Related to this is the idea that Paul stands within the Jewish tradition that affirms that all authority belongs to god (Isa. 41.1–4, 45.1–3; Dan. 2.21; Prov. 8.15; Sir. 10.4, 17.17; Wis. of Sol. 6.1–31; Enoch 46.5). The implication is that Roman power counts for nothing and that the final sovereignty is with god and not the Roman emperor. Fourth, Paul does not advocate confrontation because resistance could result in installing a rebellious and anarchic government more evil and reactionary than the one it seeks to replace.

While all these explanations are plausible, what if we see Paul's pacific mood in Romans 13 as a sign of late style where he is trying to bring a serene resolution to his life's endeavors? What we see in Romans 13 is a different Paul. It is not the same no-nonsense Paul who earlier was an irritant to the Roman empire, and who wrote fearlessly that his struggle was not against flesh and blood but against authorities and world rulers. Now, a changed Paul is trying to temper the relationship with the authorities. This Paul is different from the one we encounter in Acts. Paul in Luke's portrayal was often hauled before the Roman officials and blamed for resisting the Roman imperial power and going against Roman practices. Two incidents reported in Acts warrant our close attention. One was at Philippi, a Roman colony, where he was accused of advocating customs which were not lawful for Romans to accept or practice (Acts 16.20–21). The other was in Thessalonica, where his opponents brought three charges against him and Silas for undermining Roman power. First, Paul and his companions were causing trouble wherever they went; second, they were disobeying the decrees of Caesar; and third, this violation of the decrees of Caesar was due to their belief in another king – Jesus (Acts 17.6–7). Added to this was the question of Paul's loyalty. Faced with the clash of allegiance between Jesus and Caesar, Paul is presented in Luke as one who was devoted to Jesus, and who took every opportunity to proclaim Jesus as the alternative Lord in place of Caesar. In his own letters, Paul emphatically instructs the Corinthian Christians that any legal disputes and grievances among themselves should be dealt with by themselves rather than by turning to the secular courts. He reminds them that it will be Christians, as god's people, who judge not only the world but also the angels (1 Cor. 6.1–8). He was urging Christians to distance themselves from the values, practices, and habits of their neighbors. It must be said that Paul's anti-Roman stance in his early career did not make him an anti-colonialist seeking to destabilize the Roman empire or replace the kingdom of Caesar with the kingdom of god. His main aim was to undertake a contentious assignment for the sake of his new-found Lord.

In his letter to Romans, Paul's old belligerence and boldness have gone. Instead, in keeping with the late style, we see a reflective Paul writing in a kind of condensed and rarefied abstract style. Normally, the commentators take Chapters 12 and 13 as one narrative continuum. What Paul seems to advocate here is political cooperation and social harmony. His message to the Romans is: "Bless those who persecute you; bless and do not curse them" (Rom. 12.14). Gone is the confrontational tone of his earlier days. His advice – "Live peaceably with all" – sums up Paul's new spirit of reconciliation. This mood of harmoniousness goes even further: "if your enemies are hungry, feed them; if they are thirsty, give them something to drink; for by doing this you will heap burning coals on their heads" (Rom. 12.20). What is clear is that the personal desire for reprisal, and people taking upon themselves the task of rectifying the injustices of the civil authorities, are totally ruled out. Instead, they are encouraged to rely on god's effective intervention and leave it to god to deal with such matters: "Beloved, never avenge yourselves, but leave it to the wrath of God for it is written, 'Vengeance is mine, I will repay says the Lord'" (Rom. 12.19). There is also a warning for those who defy authority: "Whoever resists authority resists what God has appointed." There is no damning of the secular leaders, but Paul pays tribute to them and acknowledges that their power is derived from god: "there is no authority except from God and those authorities that exist have been instituted by God" (Rom. 13.1). These civil rulers have been appointed to perform divine services: "for the authorities are God's servants." Paul provides his readers with a list outlining the marks of good citizenship. His recommended activities include communal affection (12.10), hospitality and reciprocal help (12.13), and ready sympathy (12.15). The analogy Paul employs is the analogy of the body (12.4–6), as a model to reinforce mutual dependence and to discourage any disruptive individualism. His message is that personal needs and aspirations must be put under control. The Letter to the Romans, a late work of Paul's, reflects "a special maturity, a new spirit of reconciliation and serenity" and a "remarkable holiness and sense of resolution."[23]

Reliance on selective memory is another sign of lateness in an author's work. Paul totally forgets that it was the same secular power, the Roman empire, which he himself assures us is the very instrument of god, that was responsible for the death of Jesus whom Paul acknowledges as his Lord and savior. Near the end of his life, Paul is anxious to distance himself from his earlier image as an instigator of civil disobedience. While, in the Book of Acts, Paul in desperation solicited the support of Rome against his Jewish opponents, here, in the Letter to the Romans, in "a spirit of wise resignation,"[24] a mark of lateness, he relies on the same secular authority in order to shield the new Christian community from harm.

His sending back Philemon is another example of Paul's late mellowness. The slave is returned to the owner and to his bondage, thus going against Paul's own gospel of the freedom which he claimed was bought on the cross. In his attempt to please the authorities, Paul's earlier radical theological streak, too, is muted. Now, trying to be an obedient citizen, Paul imparts a new wisdom – love and respect – ideals which are music to the ears of the rulers (13.7–8).

Another kind of lateness is exhibited by the author of the Book of Revelation. Unlike Paul's, it is the kind of lateness which appeals to Said. The coded and symbolic language that the author employs in the Book of Revelation shows how "angry and disturbed" he was. What the author does is to "stir up more anxiety" and "leave the audience more perplexed and unsettled than before."[25]

The Book of Revelation has all the hallmarks of late style. The enigmatic and symbolic nature of the Book has been a puzzle to readers over the years. Its vibrant ambiguous images, its description of calamities, exploitation, and suffering, its war motifs and glorification of martyrdom, have elicited favorable interpretations from a variety of people, ranging from right-wing Christian evangelicals to the marginalized of the world. Unlike the Fourth Gospel, where the author is amiable and affirmative, here he is argumentative and disruptive and there is a "sort of deliberately unproductive productiveness, a going against."[26] It is a type of lateness which signifies not concord and resolution but the sort of contradiction and unsettlement that Said liked to promote. The suggestion of late style in the Book of Revelation depends on the notion that it was written by the author of the Fourth Gospel. Both the content and even the identity of the author have been the subject of wild guesses and conjectures. What is advocated as historical authenticity in the field of the New Testament is at the most an educated guess.

There was strong external attestation for the idea that it was the same author who produced John's Gospel and the Book of Revelation. The early Church fathers like Justin Martyr, Irenaeus, and Tertullian were of the view that both were written by John. It was modern criticism which questioned such a view. Subjecting both texts to literary and historical analysis, historical critics advanced the hypothesis that the two books were written by different persons, and they suggested names such as John Mark or John the Elder as the possible author of the Book of Revelation. The hold of historical criticism is so strong that it has tended to obscure the considerable amount of common vocabulary and the common style and grammar found in the two works. In his study comparing the two books, Swete came to the conclusion that there was a "strong presumption of affinity between the Fourth Gospel and the Apocalypse."[27] What if the author of these two writings was the same and the Book of Revelation was a late work of John? What if the differences between the Fourth Gospel and the Book of the

Revelation were deliberate and intended? What if he was an angry and disturbed old man revisiting issues he previously earlier thought he had resolved? What if the last book in the New Testament is the daring and wild meditation of an elderly seer? What if the Book of Revelation is a late work aimed at producing argument, controversy, and commotion?

Far from achieving a harmonious synthesis, the Book of Revelation is a disruptive response which disregards the apolitical nature of the Fourth Gospel and becomes confrontational, confused, and distressing. The author's views on political rulers and on Christian teachings provide a marked contrast to the gospel and the epistles. In the Fourth Gospel there is little indication as to the author's attitude to the Roman empire, whereas the last book of the New Testament is driven with a stubborn and contradictory passion. In the Fourth Gospel the Roman empire is almost seen as safe. There is an affirmative and a resigned attitude towards the Roman presence, and a feeling of futility in resisting it. In contrast, in the Book of Revelation, there is a categorical censure of the Roman power expressed through the use of oblique images and idioms of apocalyptic thinking. In John's Gospel, the arrest and trial of Jesus is the only narrative where the menacing presence of the Roman power is recounted. As the narrative pans out, one gets the impression that there is recognition and even acknowledgment of Roman rule. Three incidents bear this out. First, to the question put by Pilate, Jesus announces himself as "a king not from this world," thus declaring that his kingship is not a threat to Roman rule. Second, the narrative makes it clear that Pilate himself was not held responsible for Jesus's death and the blame was put squarely on the Jews. Third, the words of the chief priest potentially acknowledge the supremacy of the Roman power: "We have no king but the emperor" (Jn 19.15). In the Book of Revelation, the lateness in the thinking of the author is seen in his unleashing of an onslaught on the political, commercial, and economic tyranny of the Roman empire, though it is not directly mentioned by name. The opposition between the empire and the people is described in the coded binary language of beast–lamb. The harmonious synthesis that is found in the Fourth

Gospel has given way to hostility. For instance, love which is so prominent in the Fourth Gospel is replaced with vengeance and violence in the Book of Revelation. What Said thought about Beethoven's late works could well be said about the Book of Revelation. They remain "unreconciled, uncoopted by a higher synthesis: they do not fit any scheme, and they cannot be reconciled or resolved, since their irresolution and unsynthesized fragmentariness are constitutive, neither ornamental nor symbolic of something else."[28]

One of the marks of the late style is that it does not provide "concessions to ... readers, no summaries, small talk, helpful road signs, or convenient simplifying."[29] The author's symbolic use of words, images, phrases, and numbers baffles the audience. The style of writing in the Fourth Gospel, as Swete observed, "flows along smoothly from the prologue to the end; there is no startling phrase, no defiance of syntax; ... [it] seldom or never offends" the readers, whereas the writer of the Apocalypse is full of "eccentricities," "roughness," and "audacities"[30] which confuse his audience. The lateness of style does not provide neat options or alternatives. It is inhabited by discontinuities and incompleteness. Where, late in his career, Paul persuaded Christians to be reconciled to the Roman empire, the message of the author of the Book of Revelation is to withdraw from the enticements of the empire. John passionately advises Christians in Asia Minor not to be attracted by the market and more importantly not to have upon themselves the mark of the beast – the mark which enables them to buy and sell (Rev. 13.17, 18). He wants them to opt out of the economic order: "Come out of her, my people, so that you do not take part in her sins; and so that you do not share in her plagues" (Rev. 18.4). He does not want them to be part of an exploitative economic system but he does not give a plausible alternative. The writer of the Book of Revelation himself is a figure of lateness, "an untimely, scandalous, even catastrophic commentator on the present."[31]

Another sign of lateness in John's work is his return "to ancient myth or antique forms."[32] His reclamation and use of Jewish apocalyptic materials, and the allusions to the Hebrew scriptures, are the effect of the late style. Such a recovery of ancient material disarms the audience by rendering familiar information as an engaging spectacle and making it relevant rather than concepts fossilized in the past. The lateness of his style is seen in John's contrapuntal reading, which interweaves apocalyptic thinking, prophetic writings, Hebrew scriptural allusions, imperial edicts, Hellenistic magical elements, and the Jesus tradition. In his appropriation of them, John is always critical and ironic, and the resultant discourse is incomprehensible without them.

The late style involves leaving inevitable gaps in the narrative. The author poses questions without providing answers. There are confusions in the narrative which remain without any resolution. For example, the author urges his recipients to oppose the current economic order and urges them to come out of the oppressive system: "the merchants of the earth have grown rich from the power of her luxury," so "come out of her" (Rev. 18.4), but he does not provide Christians in Asia Minor with any alternative economic solutions.

Misappropriation and subversion of language are another mark of late style. The author of the Book of Revelation is often accused of crimes against Greek syntax. His unconventional style has been an irritant to the purists. This grammatically unpolished style, in R.H. Charles's view, is a calculated device that has its own steadiness and regularity of thought and grammatical patterns which are unmatched in any other ancient writings. His mixing of Greek and Hebrew, as Charles has demonstrated, was due to his peculiar style: "while he writes in Greek, he thinks in Hebrew," and this has naturally affected his way of writing.[33] Thinking in the native language and writing in the colonizer's is a mark of postcolonial hybridity. The mangling and violation of the ordinary rules of grammar might "have been a kind of protest against the higher form of Hellenistic culture. It would have been an act of cultural pride of a Jewish Semite. Such acts fit well with the type of message expressed in Revelation ... It is analogous to the refusal of some American blacks to 'talk right.' "[34]

The late style is characterized by a sense of "apartness and exile and anachronism"[35] and a sense of being out of place and time. The author of Revelation himself was an exile. He was on the "island called Patmos because of the word of God and the testimony of Jesus" (Rev. 1.9). The island must have been different from where the author started his life and career. But it is here, in an unfamiliar and often hostile environment, that John's late work takes shape in resentment and in a mutinous mood. The late style is characterized by the author's struggle to create meaning when the world around him seems to be defiant and adverse to any sort of meaningfulness.

In today's religious and political climate, John's call for the ultimate triumph of the exalted, militant Church would be difficult to support. So also the book's overtly misogynist perceptions. In its cry for justice, the book completely overlooks the status of women. Like most of the resistance literature, while castigating the bigger political and economic enemy, the author copies and strengthens the then negative images of women. Quoting Adorno, Said writes: "The maturity of late works does not resemble the kind one finds in fruit. They are ... not round, but furrowed, even ravaged. Devoid of sweetness, bitter and spiny, they do not surrender themselves to mere delectation."[36] This perfectly befits the hermeneutical intentions and content of the Book of Revelation.

Luke: Gloomy News for The Poor and Good News for The Rich

Representation is one of the major rhetorical devices by which colonial ideology exercises its power. Representation is about construction of the "other" and at the same time it is also about how such constructions stereotype the identities of both the colonized and the colonizer in such terms as race, class, and gender, and in religious and sexual categories. This caricaturing is based on the fact that colonizers saw themselves and their cultures as true manifestations of what a human being should be, or how a culture should be.

Colonial caricatures generate two types of representation. One is the misrepresentation of the colonized, and the other is the affirmative presentation of the colonizer. The (mis)representation of the colonized operates in dialectically opposite ways. At one level, there is the demonization which perceives the colonized "other" as mute, inferior, unintelligent, and incapable of any initiative. At another level, there is the eulogization of the colonized for having virtues and dignified traits such as piety and innocence. The affirmative presentation of the colonizer extols and stabilizes the virtues, values, and interests of the dominant classes. The positive portrayals of the West are about not simply marveling at its virtues but also asserting its self-identity and self-importance. More importantly, they are about controlling and dominating the colonized other. What representation does is to slot, umpire, and make assumptions about the other people and turn them into neat and manageable cultural and ethnic objects. It divides the world into us and them, and creates an uneasy and a complicated social hierarchy. Such binary thinking perpetuates certain myths such as the "other" as an undifferentiated category, and more pertinently, it keeps alive the idea that there is a standard against which the "other" can be assessed and absolved.

The rhetoric of representation is central to the understanding of the Parable of the Rich Man and Lazarus (Luke 16.19–31). The parable is a prime example of both categories of stereotyping – misrepresentation and affirmative presentation. The manner in which the poor and the rich are represented both in the text and in the subsequent interpretations illustrates how these representations are governed by the politics of interpretation, theological persuasion, and ideological motives.

First, Lazarus is represented as a mute participant throughout the parable, although he is central to the fate of the Rich Man. At the outset, it appears this parable has two pivotal characters – Lazarus and the Rich Man. As the narrative progresses, Lazarus fades into the background, and it is the Rich Man and his brothers, not Lazarus, who become central to the plot. The story is framed and shaped by the life and fate of the Rich Man and his friends, so much so that Jeremias suggested that the parable should be renamed the "Parable of Six Brothers."[37] Actually, the narrative thrust of the parable makes one wonder whether it should be called "Dialogue between Two Rich Men." When the Rich Man and Abraham enter into a discussion, Lazarus is further pushed back. A closer reading of the parable will reveal that it was essentially an earnest conversation between two wealthy people. While the exchanges go on, Lazarus does not speak a single word, and his silence is potent throughout the parable. The non-speaking and the peripheral role assigned to Lazarus is in keeping with Luke's portrayals of the marginalized. Luke, in popular perception, has been acknowledged as a champion of those who are on the sidelines of society – the poor, widows, women, and the Gentiles. But what is noticeable about this marginalized community in Luke is that there is no self-representation, nor does it offer a counter-narrative. There is a denial of agency to the poor. These peripheral groups hardly voice their opinion. They rarely speak or speak to each other. The prodigal son on his return does not utter a single word of the speech which he so carefully rehearsed. When a reception was organized to celebrate his return, it was the father who pleads with the elder son to be gracious and join the reception. Even on rare occasions when the marginalized speak, they are seen as a nuisance, as in the case of the importunate widow. The marginalized are spoken of, or spoken to, but rarely do they themselves venture to speak. In fact their role is to act as a perfect foil to the Rich Man, the exact role played by Lazarus.

Second, Lazarus, and by extension the poor, is represented as inactive. He not only does not speak but also rarely acts. Nowhere in the parable was Lazarus depicted as taking any initiative of his own. He was motionless throughout. The graphic image of his passive nature is depicted in the scene where the dogs were licking him. There was no attempt on his part to shoo them away. The narrative provides two other illustrations of Lazarus's stationary status. When the request was made to Abraham to send Lazarus so that he could dip the tip of his finger in water and cool the tongue of the Rich Man, Lazarus remained immobile and there was no move on his part to do anything. This same state of non-activity continues when the Rich Man urges Abraham to send Lazarus to warn his brothers.

Third, the parable reinforces the dependency culture of the poor. This comes out subtly in the naming of the main protagonist. While it is customary for the gospel writers to give no names to the poor, and most of the characters in the parable are nameless, the naming of Lazarus is intriguing. His name, Lazarus, means "god is his only help," or "he whom God helps." Giving such a name is another indication that the poor are at the mercy of others and they are entirely dependent on benefactors or on god for relief from their miserable status. Such a state of reliance is compensated and rewarded generously. An illustrative case in point is the Magnificat (Luke 1.46–55). The reversal of the role anticipated in Mary's song is that carried out by the equitable action of god because the poor relied on god for their redemption. The Magnificat is not a diatribe against the wealthy and the strong as it is perceived in popular imagination, but a pledge to rescue those who depend on god's compassion and power for their deliverance.

Fourth, the parable reiterates another stereotypical image of the poor: they are at the beck and call of the master. Lazarus is still at the Rich Man's service. He was asked to dip the tip of his finger in water that could cool the tongue of the Rich Man. Moreover, he was urged to go and warn the brothers of the Rich Man. The poor are expected to carry out the task for the rich without any reward or remuneration. In another parable of Luke, a master had his servant work both in the field and in the house, and yet he received no thanks for what he did because it was expected of the poor (Luke 17.7–9).

While the poor are being misrepresented, the rich and the dominant classes are shown in a positive light. These symbols of affluence are made very clear to the readers at the outset. This was signaled in a number of ways. The name given to the Rich Man, his wealth, his clothes, and his extensive and extravagant meals, confirm his standing in society and his affluence. In the Vulgate version, the Rich Man is called Dives which means wealthy, thus establishing his financial means. The color of the attire he wore is described as purple, a sign that he not only was a well-to-do person but also had some connections with royalty or officialdom. The significance of the purple worn by the Rich Man prompts Bernard Brandon Scott to name the parable as "A Rich Man Clothed in Purple." A purple robe in the Bible is a symbol for royalty. The Median kings wore purple robes (Judges 8.26). The daily feasting that went on in the Rich Man's household was an indication of his lavish and flamboyant living. Abraham himself does not lag behind; the Hebrew scripture records his wealth. In Gen. 13.2, Abraham is described as "rich in live-stock, in silver, and in gold." He was willing to pay an enormous amount (400 shekels) to buy a burial field for his wife Sarah (Gen. 23.12–16). Luke describes Abraham, too, organizing a banquet in the kingdom of god (13.22–30).

Luke's representation of the rich confirms the clannish nature of the wealthy people. The Rich Man in the parable is portrayed as a person who was part of a big family and a person who really cares for them. The Rich Man's main concern continues to be his own family – his five brothers – rather than poor people. The family bond becomes even more evident when he addresses Abraham as "Father." At one stroke, not only does he appeal to the family ties but also he asserts his right to be treated as a member of the family unit. Abraham on his part upholds this family link by calling him "Son." While the rich in Luke are seen as taking care of one another, the poor are shown as fighting among themselves. Whenever banquets are held, the rich invite their "relatives," "brothers," and "friends" (Luke 14.12). The Rich Man pleads for his brothers' future. In contrast, Lazarus is depicted as a person with no family attachment – a solitary figure wallowing in his own misery. More importantly, the poor in Luke are portrayed as uncaring and do not show solidarity among themselves. When the servant was punished for his failure to invest his master's money prudently (Luke 19.22–27), those servants who were praised for their marketing enterprise barely speak on his behalf. In the Parable of the Truthful and Wise Servant (Luke 12.42–46) the servant hits the fellow servants. The servant who alters the account gives the impression that servants left on their own without their masters cannot be trusted.

Biblical commentators, for their part, humanize the rich by providing information which is not in the text. The concern of the Rich

Man for his own brothers when he himself was in torment was, in Alexander Findlay's view, an indication that he was not "altogether inhuman."[38] Another conjecture the commentators come up with is the civilized nature of the Rich Man who did not complain about Lazarus when he was sitting at the palace gate although he looked like a "disgusting object."[39] Montefiore warns his readers that they should not assume that the Rich Man was "specially cruel." The fact that Lazarus was at the Rich Man's gate shows that "he occasionally got something, otherwise he would have taken up his quarters elsewhere."[40] Montefiore further assures his readers that the crumbs that fell from the table looked reasonable and generous. They were not mere morsels but "big bits of bread which were used to clean or dry the hands after the eaters had dipped them, for example, in a dish full of bits of meat and gravy." In those napkinless days, bits of bread were used to wipe the hands and the bits "were then thrown outside the gate or the table."[41] Some commentators exempt the Rich Man from any wrongdoing: "There was no suggestion that he was cruel or insulting to Lazarus, that he exploited him in any way, or took unfair advantage of his poverty."[42]

The exploitative system which produces wealth and poverty hardly figures in the commentaries on Luke. The tendency among the biblical commentators is to reduce the Rich Man's actions to some human frailties and follies. To give some random samples: "sublime carelessness" and "social exclusion that wealth encourages";[43] "self-righteousness"[44] and "perverse and stupid self assurance";[45] "selfish living";[46] "thoughtlessness or carelessness";[47] "heartlessness and cruelty."[48] Whilst the commentators minimize the wealth that led to the Rich Man's predicament, they underplay the poverty of Lazarus. The fact that Lazarus lay at the gates of the Rich Man does not mean that he was paralyzed, but the intention was "to give a realistic description of an Oriental street scene."[49] Lazarus's reward is attributed to some abstract ideas: devotedness and piety,[50] his utter "dependence on God,"[51] his meekness,[52] and he being "a godly man."[53] The bliss Lazarus is now enjoying in heaven is due to the saintly status of the unfortunate: "poor" is almost a synonym for "saint."[54]

Biblical scholars tend to dismiss the parable as having nothing to do with inequalities in society. The parable is not about "class struggle"[55] or "class feeling."[56] Schweizer made it clear in his exegesis that this parable is not about "God's distributive justice."[57] In Jeremias's view, Jesus did "not want to comment on a social problem,"[58] and he went on to ask, "where has Jesus ever suggested that wealth in itself merits hell, and that poverty in itself is rewarded by paradise?"[59] Similarly, Stanley Glen does not subscribe to the view that the Rich Man ended up in perdition for "no other reason than the fact he was rich" or for that matter that Lazarus "ended in glory for no other reason than the fact he was poor." To treat sinfulness and piety in socioeconomic terms would mean introducing a "sociological interpretation"[60] to the Bible. Martin claimed that the parable was hardly a denunciation of all rich and wealthy people. If that were the case, "Abraham would not be presiding at the feast."[61]

While most of the commentators interpret the parable as a warning to the rich, some commentators see it as a warning about the rising power of the poor. McFadyen, who worked in Nagpur, India, during the height of colonialism, cautioned his readers that the Lazaruses of our time would not be satisfied with mere crumbs. They would demand a bigger share: "They have learned that if they knock, if they knock hard enough and persistently enough, the door will gradually open and admit them to some share in the daily banquet."[62] He also warned about opening the British markets to India, China, and Africa in the name of free trade. Such a commercial arrangement, in his view, was "blindness and much myopia."[63]

At a time when post-independent India was trying to engage in state-sponsored development programs based on socialist principles, this parable was used as a warning against communism which was seen as a potential threat to the newly freed state. Wilfred Scopes, who worked in India, reckoned that the parable had a "message for the present social revolution in East Asia," that "excessive wealth and abject poverty ought never to be allowed to exist side by side," which the communists might exploit. His solution to the menacing presence of communism was to make the communist ideal of social justice a part of the biblical tradition. His advice was that Christians must do everything possible to promote social justice, develop new insights, and inculcate responsible action, not for fear of communism but because they "stand in the succession of prophets who were concerned with social justice and followers of him who set forth the truth of the brotherhood of man."[64]

Representation, as I explained earlier, is about producing stereotypes. Stereotypes work on dubious simplifications and preset perceptions. Thus, they have the ability to defame, insult, and isolate the vulnerable and at the same time praise, assuage, and legitimize the authority of the powerful. This parable is a prime example of disparaging the poor and providing succor to the rich. Once the portrayals of the "other" have attained the status of truth, they play a central role in public discourse. In many cases, the "other" becomes the scapegoat for a larger problem in society, and as such slander leads into violent behavior.

Finally, to bring this section to a close, a couple of points. Luke's understanding of the poor looks parochial in this pluralistic world and his solution sounds paternalistic in a world which is becoming more polarized economically. For Luke, the poor meant only Christians. For instance, when there was famine, the community in Antioch decided that each one of them would send as much as possible to help those fellow believers in distress in Judea (Acts 11.27–30). Thomas Schmidt has drawn attention to the fact that during the "world-wide famine" Christians apparently ignored the needs of their non-Christian neighbors but risked the "danger of long distance travel to supply believers in Judea."[65]

Luke's answer to ameliorate poverty is very modest and conservative. His solution to the problem was to encourage alms-giving and mutual assistance. Luke's Jesus is often reported as urging people to give alms within their means, "So give for alms those things that are within (11.41)"; and John the Baptist, too, encourages his listeners to share their possessions, "Whoever has two coats must share with anyone who has none; and whoever has food must do likewise" (3.11).

Luke is rather silent about addressing the causes of poverty. This may be due to two factors. One, Luke's narrative world is populated by people who wield economic power and political influence. It was to this group his gospel was addressed. The group consisted of people from the upper ranks of Roman society, namely the senatorial class – people such as Sergius Paulus, the pro-consul of Cyprus (Acts 13.7), and Manaen, who had been brought up with Herod the Tetrarch (Acts 13.1). Then there was the centurion Cornelius (Acts 10.1ff), the Ethiopian eunuch, and anonymous Greek men and women of high social standing (Acts 17.12). To this powerful elite, one can also add Barnabas, Ananaias, and Sapphira, who were people of property (Acts 4.37, 5.1–11). Lydia the purple cloth seller was wealthy enough to offer hospitality to Paul and his friends (Acts 16.14–15). The two denarii the Good Samaritan left with the innkeeper was not a small amount but a substantial one equal to "three weeks worth of food for one person or about 1% of an ancient Palestinian family's annual budget."[66]

In Luke's Gospel Jesus freely mixes with the rich. He accepts invitations from various classes of rich people like the Pharisee (7.36, 11.37) and the rulers (14.1, 12). The well-to-do women provide for his necessities and those of his disciples out of their own wealth (8.3). He is also associated with the Roman centurion and Jairus in the act of healing (Luke 7.1–7; 8.40–56). Tax collectors were his disciples (Levi 5.27–28) and Zacchaeus, the chief tax collector, was one of his followers (19.1–10). In Mark (10.22–23) and Matthew (Matt. 19.22–23), when the young man goes away, Jesus speaks to the disciples, whereas in Luke Jesus speaks to the rich ruler (18.23–24). Luke's typical citizen is a well-off person. The fact that, in Luke's description of the anointing scene, Jesus's famous words – the poor are always with you – are missing, is a further proof that the poor were not the major concern of Luke's narrative world. As Luke reports, the way the community organized their life "there was not a needy person among them" (Acts 4.32–37; 2.43–47).The Acts do not give any indication of people being poor. The crucial word *ptochos* (poor) does not appear in Luke's second volume. Instead, he uses *endees* to indicate that there were only needy ones, not really poor.

The second reason for not tackling the question of poverty is a reluctance on the part of Luke to assign the blame to the Roman imperial presence. Poverty in Palestine was largely the result of Roman imperial policies which led to the expropriation of farmland, the reorganization of Palestine, and the imposition of heavy taxes; and to this one could add the crop failure which was not the making of the Romans. The reluctance to blame the Romans may be due to the strong imperial presence in the form of Roman emperors (Augustus, Tiberius, and Claudius), governors, prefects, and centurions, and this might have prevented Luke from pointing the finger at the rulers. Luke scarcely comments on the moral and social implications of the imperial rule and has nothing to say about the ethics of the origins of wealth production. What Luke encourages is benevolence on the part of individual Christians. The poor in Luke were taught to believe in charity, whereas today's poor demand justice. What the poor are looking for is not crumbs but a place at the table. What today's underdeveloped countries are looking for is not handouts and helping hands but fair trading relationships. The campaigning groups and those in the field agree that the current international trade rules are not favorable towards poorer countries. In one sense, the Rich Man's comment that the scriptures themselves are not sufficient has an element of truth in it. What is urgently needed is the rectification of these adverse trade regulations which disadvantage the poor nations, and fairer trade arrangements that would benefit the underdeveloped countries more than foreign aid.

The unnamed Argentinian interrogator in a sense echoes what Luke wants to convey. During the 1976 coup in Argentina a number of people were imprisoned and tortured. One of them was a Catholic priest, Orlando Virgilio Yorio. One day his interrogator told him that the priest's reading of Jesus's words were plainly wrong:

> You interpreted Christ's doctrines in too literal a way. Christ spoke of the poor, but when he spoke of the poor in spirit you interpreted this in a literal way and went on to live, literally, with poor people.

In Argentina those who are poor in spirit are the rich and in future you must spend your time helping the rich, who are those who really need spiritual help.[67]

This was exactly what Luke was doing.

Concluding Remarks

These postcolonial reading practices differ from the traditional exegesis in three respects. The traditional exegesis concentrates on minute historical details of the text and its complex linguistic nuances and provides historical explanations that led to its production. What postcolonial biblical criticism does is to combine the best of the above exegetical procedures, but it then goes a further step by placing the texts and their subsequent interpretations in ancient and modern colonial contexts. Second, as a reading practice, postcolonial exegesis deliberately contravenes the neatly defined religious and textual exclusivity of traditional exegesis which confines itself to Hebraic and Hellenistic texts. Postcolonial criticism goes beyond these narrow borders and has a wider hermeneutical base which includes texts which come out of other religious traditions. Such interpretative work is normally dismissed by the mainstream as belonging to comparativists or indologists. While the mainstream confines itself largely to Christian texts, postcolonial biblical criticism perceives its task as seeing connections and disjunctures between texts of various religions. Third, unlike the traditional reading practice, these examples treat exegesis and interpretation as a single and unified process. In other words, the historical and the hermeneutical are one interrelated and continuous activity.

Unlike other critical practices, postcolonial biblical criticism does not envisage its task as rescuing the Bible from its colonial impulses and trying to present it as a counter-imperial document. Some of the liberative practices such as feminist, dalit, environmentalist, and gay and lesbian, while criticizing the Bible for its patriarchal, casteist, anti-nature, sexual-orientation biases, try to make it a suitable and respectable book by unearthing its egalitarian values. These emancipatory practices tend to replace one set of awkward texts with another raft of acceptable texts which support those feminist, dalit, environmentalist, and gay and lesbian causes. The Bible may have emancipatory tendencies in its treatment of certain issues, but it reaffirms dominant norms in other parts elsewhere. For instance, there is opposition to monarchy and at the same time affirmation of monarchical rule and dynasties. Postcolonialism, on the other hand, is not in the business of cleansing the Bible of its colonial tendencies and substituting these with a counter-imperial version. Postcolonialism regards the Bible as a contested and ambiguous book. Postcolonial biblical criticism questions the potential of the Bible to preserve and protect the dominant and also in the process unsettles its position as a primary source for the dominant to strengthen their grip.

The purpose of postcolonial biblical criticism is not to produce another neat exegesis. Such rereading inevitably tends to be apologetic and self-defensive. What it does is to produce historical knowledge, insights, and analysis and to detect biases both in the text and in interpretation in order to help shift the preconceptions of the reader. It encourages readers to look anew and question their preconceived notions both of the Bible and of their own understanding. The hope of postcolonial exegesis is that the ancient text sheds its imperial, mystifying, archaic, and repressive image and realigns itself with postmodern, postcolonial causes.

Notes

1   Benjamin Jowett, "On the Interpretation of Scripture," in *Essays and Reviews*, 6th edn (Longmans, Green, 1861), p. 338.
2   Lord Hauksbank, a character in Salmon Rushdie's *The Enchantress of Florence* (London: Cape, 2008), p. 15.
3   G. Ernest Wright, *The Old Testament against Its Environment* (London: SCM, 1950), p. 42.
4   All citations of the *Mahavastu* are taken from J.J. Jones, ed., *The Mahavastu Volume II* (London: Luzac, 1952).

5   All citations of the *Buddhacarita* are taken from E.H. Johnston, trans., *Asvaghosa's Buddhacarita or Acts of the Buddha* (Delhi: Motilal Banarsidass, 1984).

6   Jerome, *Against Jovinianus*, http://www.newadvent.org/fathers/30091.htm, accessed September 16, 2008.

7   R. Elmar and Kersten Holger Gruber, *The Original Jesus: The Buddhist Sources of Christianity* (Shaftesbury: Element, 1995), p. 239.

8   J.J. Jones, "Foreword," in J.J. Jones, trans., *The Mahavastu Volume I* (London: Luzac, 1949), p. xi.

9   Saul Trinidad, "Christology, Conquista, Colonization," in *Faces of Jesus: Latin American Christologies*, ed. Jose Miguez Bonino (Maryknoll, NY: Orbis, 1983), p. 49.

10 Dassetz Teitaro Suzuki, trans., *The Lankavastra Sutra: A Mahayana Text* (London: Routledge, 1932), p. 125.

11 Edward Conze, ed., *Buddhist Texts through the Ages* (New York: Philosophical Library, 1954), pp. 109–110.

12 Richard S. Cohen, "Shakyamuni: Buddhism's Founder in Ten Acts," in *The Rivers of Paradise: Moses, Buddha, Confucius, Jesus, and Muhammad as Religious Founders*, eds David Noel Freedman and M.J. McClymond (Grand Rapids, MI: Eerdmans, 2001), pp. 133–134.

13 Cohen, "Shakyamuni," p. 133.

14 Bruce J. Malina, "Mother and Son," *Biblical Theology Bulletin* 20, 2 (1990), p. 56.

15 Edward W. Said, *On Late Style* (London: Bloomsbury, 2006).

16 Said, *On Late Style*, p. 6.

17 Said, *On Late Style*, p. 7.

18 Said, *On Late Style*, p. 5.

19 Said, *On Late Style*, p. 7.

20 Said, *On Late Style*, p. 12.

21 Said, *On Late Style*, p. 7.

22 Said, *On Late Style*, p. 7.

23 Said, *On Late Style*, p. 6.

24 Said, *On Late Style*, p. 7.

25 Said, *On Late Style*, p. 7.

26 Edward W. Said, "Thoughts on Late Style," *London Review of Books* (August 5, 2004), 3.

27 Henry Barclay Swete, *The Apocalypse of St John: The Greek Text with Introduction, Notes and Indices* (London: Macmillan, 1922), p. cxxx.

28 Said, *On Late Style*, p. 12.

29 Said, *On Late Style*, p. 23.
30 Swete, *The Apocalypse of St John*, p. cxxix.
31 Said, *On Late Style*, p. 14.
32 Said, *On Late Style*, p. 135.
33 R.H. Charles, *Studies in the Apocalypse: Being Lectures Delivered Before the University of London* (Edinburgh: Clark, 1913), p. 82.
34 Adela Yarbro Collins, *Crisis and Catharsis: The Power of the Apocalypse* (Philadelphia: Westminster, 1984), p. 47.
35 Said, "Thoughts on Late Style," p. 5.
36 Said, *On Late Style*, p. 12.
37 Joachim Jeremias, *The Parables of Jesus*, rev. edn (London: SCM, 1963), p. 186.
38 Alexander J. Findlay, *Jesus and His Parables* (London: Epworth, 1950), p. 88.
39 Oliver Chase Quick, *The Realism of Christ's Parables: Ida Hartley Lectures Delivered at Colne, Lancs, 1930* (London: SCM, 1931), p. 44.
40 C.G. Montefiore, *The Synoptic Gospels: Edited with an Introduction and a Commentary in Two Volumes*, vol. II (London: Macmillan, 1927), p. 539.
41 Montefiore, *The Synoptic Gospels*, p. 538.
42 J.F. McFadyen, *The Message of the Parables* (London: Clark, 1933), p. 174.
43 Quick, *The Realism of Christ's Parables*, p. 44.
44 Johannes Nissen, *Poverty and Mission: New Testament Perspectives on a Contemporary Theme* (Leiden: Interuniversity Institute for Missiological and Ecumenical Research, 1984), p. 79.
45 Eduard Schweizer, *The Good News According to Luke* (Atlanta, GA: Knox, 1984), p. 262.
46 Hugh Martin, *The Parables of the Gospels and Their Meaning for Today* (London: SCM, 1937), p. 185.
47 McFadyen, *The Message of the Parables*, p. 174.
48 Montefiore, *The Synoptic Gospels*, p. 538.
49 Herman Hendrickx, *The Parables of Jesus: Studies in the Synoptic Gospels* (London: Chapman, 1986), p. 200.
50 Nissen, *Poverty and Mission*, p. 79.
51 Thomas E. Schmidt, *Hostility to Wealth in the Synoptic Gospels* (Sheffield: Sheffield Academic, 1987), p. 157.
52 McFadyen, *The Message of the Parables*, p. 176.
53 William Arnot, *The Parables of Our Lord* (London: Nelson, 1865), p. 472.
54 Fred B. Craddock, "Luke," in *Harper's Bible Commentary*, ed. James L. Mays (San Francisco: Harper and Row, 1988), p. 1035.

55 Martin, *The Parables of the Gospels*, p. 186.

56 Martin, *The Parables of the Gospels*, p. 182.

57 Schweizer, *The Good News According to Luke*, p. 262.

58 Jeremias, *The Parables of Jesus*, p. 186.

59 Jeremias, *The Parables of Jesus*, p. 185.

60 Stanley J. Glen, *The Parables of Conflict in Luke* (Philadelphia: Westminster, 1962), p. 72.

61 Martin, *The Parables of the Gospels*, p. 186.

62 McFadyen, *The Message of the Parables*, p. 175.

63 McFadyen, *The Message of the Parables*, p. 175.

64 Wilfred Scopes, *The Parables of Jesus and Their Meaning for the Indian Church Today* (Madras: Christian Literature Society, 1955), p. 135.

65 Schmidt, *Hostility to Wealth*, p. 215.

66 Douglas E. Oakman, "The Buying Power of Two Denarii," *Foundations and Facets Forum* 3, 4 (1987), 33–38 (p. 37).

67 Alberto Manguel, *A History of Reading* (London: Flamingo, 1997), p. 289.

7

Afterword
Postcolonial Biblical Criticism
The Unfinished Journey

Actually, everyday we develop a new theory.[1]

I say to you, friends and fellow revolutionaries, that colonialism is NOT dead.[2]

The debates about postcolonialism center roughly around three things: the fact of colonial and postcolonial reality; the resultant political, historical, and cultural changes; and the scholarly study of the work that emerged out of the colonial encounter.

Does postcolonialism matter? Yes it does. It matters because it routinely repeats that which is worth repeating, as well as that which is in danger of being forgotten and written out. The past is remembered not in the way religious fundamentalists want to remember it. What fundamentalists of all shades want is to simplify narratives and discard any awkward and dissenting voices. This they do by making a particular textual reading representative by winnowing out uncomfortable texts; or by creating an uncomplicated version of history which can serve the political and religious requirements of their narrow cause; or by fixing an imaginative

Exploring Postcolonial Biblical Criticism: History, Method, Practice, First Edition.
R. S. Sugirtharajah.
© 2012 R. S. Sugirtharajah, with the exception of Chapter 3 © 2012 Blackwell Publishing Ltd.
Published 2012 by Blackwell Publishing Ltd.

identity freed from often competing and contradictory identities. When postcolonialism excavates the past, it does exactly the opposite. It brings out inconvenient truths and muddles the narrative by pinpointing its complex nature. It constantly insists that there is no going back to a past which was safer, a text which was secure, and an identity which was pure. Postcolonialism may not redeem past or present suffering, but it persistently reminds us about the causes of the current messiness and uneasiness which have their roots in the past. It also cautions us about how empires both ancient and modern work, and, more importantly, how to guard against the old imperial impulses repeating themselves.

Postcolonialism is also a reminder that one of the forgotten lessons of colonialism is that people of different races and cultures do not ordinarily want to be ruled by an alien power. From the earlier anti-colonial movements to the current Iraqi and Afghan resistance, we are provided with conspicuous examples of this oppositional stance.

The truth about postcolonialism is that it is not really a theory but a way of looking at the production of knowledge of both the past and the present. It enables one to look at the data using certain techniques and practical awareness gained from colonial experience. Theories do not have a fixed status. They are susceptible to changes caused by new questions and the internal debates generated among the practitioners. Sometimes, novelty wears off and energy and enthusiasm fade. But theories do matter. As Terry Eagleton wrote in his *After Theory*, as a reasonable means of systematic reflection "on our guiding assumptions it remains as indispensable as ever."[3] What matters is the search for truth and justice. What is important is whether the commitment lasts. Liberation theology lost its nerve when it shifted from being a theology of liberation to being *about* a theology of liberation.

Continuing Colonial Intentions

The question persists: why do we need postcolonialism in the twenty-first century – a post-imperial century in which old-style colonialism has largely disappeared? In other words, does postcolonialism have any purchase? There are four factors which lead me to think that postcolonialism will continue to be a potent weapon: (a) if a nation thinks that it is superior to others and the "other," and that those others should be converted to a "better" way of life; (b) if there is market there to be exploited; (c) if sacred texts sanction physical and spiritual conquest; and (d) if scholarship, both secular and biblical, continues to display marks of colonial impulses and Orientalism.

The rhetoric of empire has hardly vanished from the discourse and its tone and content have hardly changed. The vocabulary associated with nineteenth-century empire is now being churned out with renewed force. The standard colonial rhetoric involves highlighting the suffering of the people under a despot; portraying the ruler as an arrogant and corrupt leader who does not know his own people; and painting a picture of the people as hapless victims incapable of any political action of their own. Having set the tone, the master/colonizer then invades the country in order to alleviate the suffering and bring democracy, liberty, and peace. The Iraq invasion has all the hallmarks of colonial rhetoric. Kamil Mahdi, an Iraqi political exile, has shown in an article in *The Guardian* how Tony Blair, the former British prime minister, invoked colonial rhetoric to invade Iraq.[4] In this post-imperial age, there are calls for liberal intervention. Even before 9/11, and before Bush and Blair had their messianic vision of the new world order, the conservative historian Norman Stone was calling for an "enlightened re-imperialism." What he meant was that, just as in the nineteenth century, the "civilized states" should be given an international mandate to "intervene in the maintenance of order" in Africa.[5] Jonathan Powell, who was Tony Blair's chief of staff, argued that the British government could attack a country even it had not posed any threat to the UK but threatened British interests, provided that the war was winnable and a satisfactory post-war government could be set up.[6] Similar sentiments were expressed by the former British foreign secretary David Miliband who claimed that despite the mistakes made in the Iraq and Afghan Wars, the UK had a moral duty to "intervene –

sometimes militarily – to help to spread democracy throughout the world."[7] Terms such as neo-colonialism and informal colonialism were used as a way of describing the unbalanced relationships between the former colonizers and the formerly colonized.

Geographical occupation may be a thing of the past, but newer forms of control and subjugation continue to mark the relationship between old Western powers and their former colonies. The conventions, customs, manners, and frame of mind which nourished the old empires are now being reintroduced – with the free market, international financial agencies, and non-governmental organizations taking the place of armies, administrators, and missionaries. The old territorial empire may have gone but the principles of enticing and controlling go on. The West after the collapse of communism is prompting the rest of the world to share its values. These values come in a variety of forms from political ideas to consumer goods. Have a close look at these words: "Hence, too, a liking sprang up for our style of dress, and the 'toga' became fashionable. Step by step they were led to things which dispose to vice, the lounge, the bath, the elegant banquet. All this, in their ignorance, they called civilization, when it was part of their servitude."[8] These were the words of Tacitus about the Roman occupation of Britain in the first century. The message is that the old imperial trick of enticing the "other" goes on under different guises. Instead of Roman banquets we have now McDonald's; baths are replaced by theme parks, and togas by Armani suits.

Furthermore, we often forget that there is an internal form of colonialism where the linguistic, religious, and casteist majority within those nations tries to exert power and control over minority communities. The Hindutuva ideals propagated by some fundamentalist Hindus in India whereby other religious groups should come under the saffron flag, and the Sinhala Buddhists' ethnonationalism preached by the Sinhalese in Sri Lanka, are examples of such internal colonialism. The reality is that our world will never be post-imperial.

One of the cleverest tricks of modern imperialism is to convince the public that it is engaged in doing good to the people. Jawaharlal

Nehru detected this at the height of colonialism. He was writing when the British occupied Iraq under the mandate of the League of Nations. In his *Glimpses of World History,* written to his daughter Indira from various British prisons, he shows not only how history has an uncanny knack of repeating itself but also how euphemistic and liberative language is used as a vehicle to shape tyrannical and reactionary political ideals:

> The novel feature of the modern type of imperialism is its attempt to hide its terrorism and exploitation behind pious phrases about "trusteeship" and the "good of the masses" and "the training of the backward peoples in self-government" and the like. They shoot and kill and destroy only for the good of the people shot down. This hypocrisy may be perhaps a sign of advance, for hypocrisy is a tribute to virtue, and it shows that the truth is not liked, and is therefore wrapped up in these comforting and deluding phrases, and thus hidden away. But somehow this sanctimonious hypocrisy seems far worse than the brutal truth.[9]

Those who marvel at C.S. Lewis's fantasy novels often forget something he wrote which has relevance for today:

> Of all tyrannies, a tyranny sincerely exercised for the good of its victims may be the most oppressive. It may be better to live under robber barons than under omnipotent moral busybodies. The robber baron's cruelty may sometimes sleep, his cupidity may at some point be satiated; but those who torment us for our own good will torment us without end for they do so with the approval of their conscience. They may be more likely to go to heaven yet at the same time likelier to make a hell of earth.[10]

Postcolonial criticism will continue to have purchase as long as the Bible contains three potent elements which spur people and nations to embark upon colonial adventure. The ideas enshrined in the Bible – conquest, conversion, and election – are a heady mixture which has the potential to turn innocent, cultured, and erudite men, yes mainly men, into violent predators. The Bible contains verses such as "Every place whereon the soles of your feet shall tread shall be yours: from the wilderness and Lebanon, from the river, the river Euphrates, even unto the uttermost sea shall your coast be. There shall no man be able to stand before you: [for] the LORD your God shall lay the fear of you and the dread of you upon all the land that ye shall tread upon, as he hath said unto you" (Deut. 11.24, 25) – statements which fuel the imagination of nations as if these words were spoken for them to enact. Along with the words of conquest enshrined in the pages of the Bible is the idea that the heathen must hear the gospel. Conversion which is a divine act is appropriated as a god-given mission to turn the people of the world to Christianity. Conversion with its all good intentions is essentially a colonizing act. Making a people conform to one set of beliefs and practices because they are superior to the other is a form of colonialism. Added to this is the idea of the chosen race. Verses like "Thou art an holy people unto the Lord thy God and the Lord hath chosen thee to be a peculiar people unto himself, above all the nations that are upon the earth" (Deut. 14.2) endow their role in history with an imagined importance. As long as such notions are enshrined in the Bible, colonialism will continue.

The idea of chosen people is not confined to Christians only. The *Mahavamsa*, the sixth-century Sinhalese chronicle, encourages the notion that Sinhalese Buddhists are a chosen people with the special mission to preserve Buddhism in the island. One of those who made use of the Jewish notion of election was the Buddhist reviver Anagarika Dharmapala. Kitsiri Malalgoda, who studied the growth of Buddhism in Sri Lanka, notices how the nationalists read into *The Mahavamsa* something like the Hebrew scripture's idea of an elect nation: "Rather as the Old Testament [built] up the concept of Israel as a specially chosen people, so did the *Mahavamsa* build up the special destiny of the Sinhalese people and the island of Sri Lanka in relation to Buddhism."[11] The call for an Islamic caliphate transcending nation-states, supported by vague Koranic references, Islamic jurisprudence, and history by some Islamic groups, is another indication that control and conquest are not confined to one particular religion. Colonizing, as the epigraph in Chapter 2 claimed, is not simply a Bible thing.

Postcolonialism will need to play a vigilant role as long as secular and biblical scholarship continue to espouse colonial and Oriental tendencies. This can happen in two ways. The first is when nationalists and mainstream politicians want to rehabilitate empire for political and propaganda purposes. Michael Gove, the Education Secretary of the newly formed Coalition government of the United Kingdom, has appealed to pro-empire historians like Niall Ferguson and Andrew Roberts to rewrite the history curriculum for schools. The idea is to celebrate the empire as an "exemplary force for good."[12] Such curriculum rewriting, in keeping with the political preferences of the Secretary of State to praise Western domination and overlook the cultural, environmental, and economic sufferings caused to the subjugated, will keep the postcolonial critics busy. Similarly the classic marks of Orientalism which continue to appear in the work of biblical scholars, examples of which we saw in Chapter 4, will keep the practitioners of postcolonial criticism attentive and watchful.

Future Tense: Moving between the Vernacular and the Cosmopolitan

What should be our next move? What I am going to say may not be particularly original, but it is worth saying. We need to engage simultaneously in two dialectically opposite exercises. One is to raid the vernacular archives or, as Din, a politically radical character in Tash Aw's novel, would have put it, to explore "non-standard sources" which are outside the current Western interpretative interest, such as "folk stories, local mythology, or ancient manuscripts written on palm leaves."[13] Such a task is not to reify the indigenous literature but to identify both the resistance and the collusive narratives embedded in them. The other is to engage in wider cosmopolitan issues. In other words, what I propose is to foster what I call a Third Hermeneutics, which engages with both indigenous and cosmopolitan agendas.

We need to change our textual focus from hermeneutical works in English to interpretations that come out of, to use a phrase from Homi Bhabha, "other sites of meanings." Much of our interpretative practice has concentrated on interpretative works written in English. There were reasons for this. They were easy to access and the market and the academy were in thrall to the exotic nature of this stuff. Some of us exploited it and introduced issues and ideas which were not part of the mainstream agenda. We need now to listen to voices and perspectives which emerge outside Western publishing houses and universities, and which do not accord with academic expectations. I am referring to the writings which emerge out of vernacular traditions.

I recently came across examples in Tamil history where the Bible was appropriated by those on the margins. One was the folk Bible[14] and the other a dramatized version of Jesus's last days performed during Easter week.[15] This particular drama is called Sepulchre Dance Drama. The origins of these narratives, especially the Sepulchre Dance Drama, go back to the Portuguese colonial days in the north-western part of Sri Lanka. True to folk tradition, these retellings of the Biblical stories do not have a single author but evolved over time. These were the people's response to the missionaries' versions of the Bible. They deserve a close reading and full attention. This may have to wait for a later day. For the current purpose, let me highlight a few things. Ongoing through these folk versions, it is clear that they are not a lazy imitation of the canonical version of the Bible. They introduce dramatic situations and twists to the biblical stories. For a start, the gospels are virtually silent about Jesus's infant life. These Tamils, who were raised on the childhood stories of Krishna and Rama, embellish the texts with stories about Jesus's infancy which incorporate elements from Tamil culture. There are two scenes which illustrate this indigenizing process. One is the smearing of the tongue of the newborn with mashed rice, juggery, and asafoetida – a local ritual. The Tamil Folk Bible includes a scene in which Jesus's parents perform this ritual. The other scene is of the infant Jesus feeding his parents broth. Broth feeding is one of the fundamental duties of a son to his parents. By inserting these rituals which are peculiar to Tamils, not only was the cultural and geographical gulf between Palestine and the Tamil country bridged, but also Jesus the Semite was turned into a Dravidian. Another example of indigenization has to do with the animals and birds which occupy Tamil Noah's ark. All of these are native to Tamil country. The folk Easter narrative has an interesting end to the story of Caiphas, which is not found in the gospel narratives. Caiphas is seen as responsible for Jesus's death and as such, according to native justice, he should not go unpunished. The play ends with Caiphas being taken to hell to reap his karma.

There are comparable examples of so many untold and unexamined stories in other language traditions that we need to recover. For example, there must be a number of responses of both resistance and compliance hidden away in Church archives and magazines concerning how Korean Christians responded to the Japanese occupation. Mobilizing the practices and experiences of the vernacular tradition for hermeneutical possibilities is not to reify or trumpet, but is to reinvestigate and juxtapose with the mainstream story to demonstrate that there is another version worth hearing.

While engaging with unexplored and unexamined indigenous literature, we need at the same time to widen our hermeneutical horizons and interests to include metropolitan issues. Being part of one's own national or regional world is not enough. This is what some Western academics would like us to be in. It has been drilled into our heads by them that we ought to write what is familiar to us and what we know best. This way, our work can be isolated and pigeonholed. Whether we like it or not, the West has entered our history and has become an integral part of it. More disturbingly, the Western discourse is seen as universal, whereas ours is dubbed local. One way to break through this impasse is to confront and clarify the Western universalist pretensions with Asian, African, and Latin American experiences and practices. A character in Nam Le's short story encapsulates what I am trying to convey: "You could *totally* exploit the Vietnamese thing. But *instead*, you chose to write about lesbian vampires and Colombian assassins and Hiroshima orphans – and New York painters with haemorrhoids."[16] One can, as the character says, take advantage of the "Vietnamese thing" or the "Indian thing" or the "Chinese thing," but by involving and interacting with the Western discourse we can puncture its totalizing claims and lead to new energies and forms. The hermeneutical task is not only to embrace the richness and the ugliness of the indigenous tradition but also to interact with the potential proffered and the problems posed by metropolitan values.

Two concluding thoughts. The constant challenge a postcolonial critic faces is how to maintain marginal status. How to be on the edge. How to remain an outsider. There is danger awaiting those who are located in the academies. Universities are increasingly becoming collaborators with corporate capitalism rather than being its critics. Our knowledge production is being managed to suit the demands of the market. What is happening now is, to use Terry Eagleton's phrase, the "managerialization" of mind. The university wants to know the economic impact of our outputs, but knowledge is more than economic benefits. It is about raising awkward questions, upsetting received ideas, and challenging power. The dilemma of the outsider is poignantly captured by Virginia Woolf: "I thought how unpleasant it is to be locked out; and I thought how it is worse, perhaps, to be locked in."[17]

What postcolonial biblical criticism has done is to treat texts no longer as moral or spiritual reservoirs, but as a system of codes which interpreters must disentangle in order to reveal the hidden power relations and ideologies lurking in supposedly innocent narratives. Texts were analyzed not to seek spiritual nourishment but to reveal the reactionary and hegemonic values encoded in them – though there may be spiritual nourishment in that. Until now, postcolonial biblical critics have been faithfully heeding their version of the famous words of the former American president John Kennedy: ask not what the text can do for you, but what you can do for the text. We have been doing extraordinary things with the texts. Brilliant textual analysis itself, though, is not enough. We are not going to overcome the social deprivation or the marginalization by simply decoding texts. Poverty, war, suicide bombings, caste killings, racial discriminations, and sexual harassments are not imaginary constructs which will disappear if properly deconstructed.

I should like to bring this volume to a close with a quotation from an interview Amitav Ghosh gave on the occasion of the publication of his novel *Sea of Poppies*. This in a way encapsulates what I am trying to achieve here:

> The present incarnation of Empire is in fact uncannily like the old one, with its island prisons, its ... jails, its "cantonments," and ... its ... good intentions. This is why we can't turn away saying "who cares?" ... There is not much we can do about the past, but it is certainly within our power to withhold the assent it demands from us in the present day – not in order to seek retribution for what happened, but, as Gandhi famously said, to make sure that it does not happen again.[18]

Notes

1 Asya Kazanci, a character in Elif Shafak, *The Bastard of Istanbul* (London: Viking, 2007), p. 181.
2 Part of a fiery speech made by Din, a politically radicalized character in Tash Aw's novel, *Map of the Invisible World* (London: Fourth Estate, 2009), p. 153.
3 Terry Eagleton, *After Theory* (London: Allen Lane, 2003), p. 2.
4 Kamil Mahdi, "Iraqis Will Not Be Pawns in Bush and Blair's War Game," *The Guardian* (February 25, 2003), 20.
5 Norman Stone, "Why the Empire Must Strike Back," *The Observer* (August 18, 1996), 22.
6 Jonathan Powell, "Why the West Should Not Fear to Intervene," *The Observer* (November 18, 2007), 34.
7 David Miliband, "UK Has Moral Duty to Intervene," *The Guardian* (February 2, 2008), 1.
8 Tacitus, *The Agricola and Germany of Tacitus*, trans. Alfred John Church and William Jackson Brodribb (London: Macmillan, 1808), p. 19.
9 Jawaharlal Nehru, *Glimpses of World History* (New Delhi: Jawaharlal Nehru Memorial Fund, 1982 (1935)), pp. 773–774.

10   C.S. Lewis, *God in the Dock: Essays on Theology and Ethics*, ed. Walter Hooper (Grand Rapids, MI: Eerdmans, 1970), p. 292.

11   Kitsiri Malalgoda, *Buddhism in Sinhalese Society 1750–1900: A Study of Religious Revival and Change* (Berkeley, CA: University of California Press, 1976), p. 22. The quote is B.H. Farmer, *Ceylon: A Divided Nation* (London: Oxford University Press, 1963), p. 8.

12   Seumas Milne, "This Attempt to Rehabilitate Empire Is a Recipe for Conflict," *The Guardian* (June 10, 2010), 31.

13   Aw, *Map of the Invisible World*, p. 23.

14   A. Sivasubramanian, *Kristhavamum Thamil sulalyum* (Madras: Vamsi, 2007), especially Chapter 1.

15   A. Sivasubramanian, *Vasahappa: Dance Drama* (Palyamkottai: Folklore Resources and Research Centre, 2007).

16   Nam Le, *The Boat* (Edinburgh: Canongate, 2009), p. 10 (italics in original).

17   Virginia Woolf, *A Room of One's Own* (Harmondsworth: Penguin, 1945), pp. 25–26.

18   Amitav Ghosh, "Confronting the Past," an interview with Priyamvada Gopal, *The Hindu Literary Review*, online, June 1, 2008.

References

Abdel-Malek, Anouar. "Orientalism in Crisis," *Diogenes* 44 (Winter 1963), 103–140.

Alatas, Syed Hussein. *The Myth of the Lazy Native: A Study of the Image of the Malays, Filipinos and Javanese from the 16th to the 20th Century and Its Function in the Ideology of Colonial Capitalism.* London: Cass, 1977.

Arnot, William. *The Parables of Our Lord.* London: Nelson, 1865.

Aschroft, Bill, Griffiths, Gareth, and Tiffin, Helen. *The Post-Colonial Studies Reader*, 2nd edn. London: Routledge, 2006.

Avalos, Hector. "*The Gospel of Lucas Gavilán* as Postcolonial Biblical Exegesis," *Semeia* 75 (1996), 87–105.

Avalos, Hector. *The End of Biblical Studies.* Amherst, MA: Prometheus, 2007.

Aw, Tash. *Map of the Invisible World.* London: Fourth Estate, 2009.

Baly, Denis. *The Geography of the Bible: A Study in Historical Geography.* London: Lutterworth, 1957.

Berquist, J.L. "Postcolonialism and Imperial Motives for Canonization," *Semeia* 75 (1996), 15–35.

Exploring Postcolonial Biblical Criticism: History, Method, Practice, First Edition.
R. S. Sugirtharajah.
© 2012 R. S. Sugirtharajah, with the exception of Chapter 3 © 2012 Blackwell Publishing Ltd.
Published 2012 by Blackwell Publishing Ltd.

188

Bhabha, Homi K. *The Location of Culture*. London: Routledge, 1994.

Birch, S., ed. *Records of the Past: Being English Translations of the Assyrian and Egyptian Monuments*, vol. 1. London: Bagster, 1873.

Bird, J.G. "The Letter to the Ephesians," in *A Postcolonial Commentary on the New Testament Writings*, eds F.F. Segovia and R.S. Sugirtharajah. London: Clark, 2007. 265–280.

Blaiklock, E.M. *The Acts of the Apostles: An Historical Commentary*. London: Tyndale, 1959.

Boehmer, Elleke and Morton, Stephen, eds. *Terror and the Postcolonial*. Oxford: Wiley-Blackwell, 2010.

Boer, R. "Remembering Babylon: Postcolonialism and Australian Biblical Studies," in *The Postcolonial Bible*, ed. R.S. Sugirtharajah. Sheffield: Sheffield Academic, 1998. 24–48.

Boer, R. "Marx, Postcolonialism, and the Bible," in *Postcolonial Biblical Criticism: Interdisciplinary Intersections*, eds S.D. Moore and F.F. Segovia. London: Clark, 2005. 166–183.

Boer, R. "Resistance versus Accommodation: What to Do with Romans 13," in *Postcolonial Interventions: Essays in Honor of R.S. Sugirtharajah*, ed. T.-s.B. Liew. Sheffield: Sheffield Phoenix, 2009. 109–122.

Borges, Jorge Luis. *Fictions*. London: Penguin, 1998.

Bradbury, Ray. *Fahrenheit 451*. New York: Ballantine, 1953.

Broadbent, R. "Writing a Bestseller in Biblical Studies or All Washed Up on Dover Beach? *Voices from the Margin* and the Future of (British) Biblical Studies," in *Still at the Margins: Biblical Scholarship Fifteen Years after*Voices from the Margin, ed. R.S. Sugirtharajah. London: Clark, 2008. 139–150.

Broadbent, R. "One Step Beyond or One Step Too Far? Towards a Postcolonial Future for European Biblical and Theological Scholarship," in *Postcolonial Interventions: Essays in Honor of R.S. Sugirtharajah*, ed. T.-s.B. Liew. Sheffield: Sheffield Phoenix, 2009. 296–309.

Carroll, Robert P. "Cultural Encroachment and Biblical Translation: Observations on Elements of Violence, Race and Class in the Production of Bibles in Translation," *Semeia* 76 (1996): 39–68.

Carter, W. *Matthew and the Margins: A Sociopolitical and Religious Reading*. Maryknoll, NY: Orbis, 2000.

Carter, W. "The Gospel of Matthew," in *A Postcolonial Commentary on the New Testament Writings*, eds F.F. Segovia and R.S. Sugirtharajah. London: Clark, 2007. 69–104.

References

Charles, R.H. *Studies in the Apocalypse: Being Lectures Delivered before the University of London*. Edinburgh: Clark, 1913.

Chen, Kuan-Hsing. *Asia as Method: Toward Deimperialization*. Durham, NC: Duke University Press, 2010.

Chia, "On Naming the Subject: Postcolonial Reading of Daniel 1," in *The Postcolonial Biblical Reader*, ed. R.S. Sugirtharajah. Oxford: Blackwell, 2006. 171–185.

Cohen, Richard S. "Shakyamuni: Buddhism's Founder in Ten Acts," *The Rivers of Paradise: Moses, Buddha, Confucius, Jesus, and Muhammad as Religious Founders*, eds David Noel Freedman and M.J. McClymond. Grand Rapids, MI: Eerdmans, 2001. 121–232.

Collins, Adela Yarbro. *Crisis and Catharsis: The Power of the Apocalypse*. Philadelphia: Westminster, 1984.

Columbus, Christopher. *The Book of Prophecies Vol. III*, trans. Blair Sullivan, ed. Roberto Rusconi. Berkeley, CA: University of California Press, 1997.

Connor, K.R. "'Everybody Talking about Heaven Ain't Going There': The Biblical Call for Justice and the Postcolonial Response of the Spirituals," *Semeia* 75 (1996), 107–128.

Conze, Edward, ed. *Buddhist Texts through the Ages*. New York: Philosophical Library, 1954.

Coomaraswamy, Ananda K. *The Dance of Shiva: Fourteen Indian Essays*. New Delhi: Munshiram Manoharlal, 1970.

Craddock, Fred B. "Luke," in *Harper's Bible Commentary*, ed. James L. Mays. San Francisco: Harper and Row, 1988. 1010–1043.

Crossley, James G. *Jesus in an Age of Terror: Scholarly Projects for a New American Century*. London: Equinox, 2008.

Crossley, James G. "Jesus and the Jew since 1967," in *Jesus Beyond Nationalism: Constructing the Historical Jesus in a Period of Cultural Complexity*, eds W. Blanton, James G. Crossley, and Halvor Moxnes. London: Equinox, 2009. 119–137.

Daniell, David. *The Bible in English: Its History and Influence*. New Haven: Yale University Press, 2003.

Davids, Rhys T.W. *Lectures on the Origin and Growth of Religion, as Illustrated by Some Points in the History of Indian Buddhism: The Hibbert Lectures 1881*. London: Williams and Norgate, 1891.

Davids, Rhys T.W. *Buddhism: Being a Sketch of the Life and Teachings of Gautama, the Buddha*. London: Society for Promoting Christian Knowledge, 1910.

190

Donaldson, L.E. "Postcolonialism and Biblical Reading: An Introduction," *Semeia* 75 (1996), 1–14.

Donaldson, L.E. "The Sign of Orpah: Reading Ruth through Native Eyes," in *The Postcolonial Biblical Reader*, ed. R.S. Sugirtharajah. Oxford: Blackwell, 2006. 159–170.

Dube, M.W. "Reading for Decolonization (John 4: 1–42)," *Semeia* 75 (1996), 37–59.

Dube, M.W. "Savior of the World but Not of This World: A Post-Colonial Reading of Spatial Construction in John," in *The Postcolonial Bible*, ed. R.S. Sugirtharajah. Sheffield: Sheffield Academic, 1998. 118–135.

Dube, M.W. "Rahab Says Hello to Judith: A Decolonizing Feminist Reading," in *The Postcolonial Biblical Reader*, ed. R.S. Sugirtharajah. Oxford: Blackwell, 2006. 142–158.

Eagleton, Terry. *After Theory*. London: Allen Lane, 2003.

Edwards, Justin D. *Postcolonial Literature: A Reader's Guide to Essential Criticism*. Basingstoke: Palgrave Macmillan, 2008.

Elliott, John H. *What is Social-Scientific Criticism?* Minneapolis: Fortress, 1993.

Elmar, R. and Gruber, Kersten Holger. *The Original Jesus: The Buddhist Sources of Christianity*. Shaftesbury: Element, 1995.

Featherstone, Simon. *Postcolonial Cultures*. Edinburgh: Edinburgh University Press, 2005.

Findlay, Alexander J. *Jesus and His Parables*. London: Epworth, 1950.

Forsdick, Charles. "The French Empire," in *The Routledge Companion to Postcolonial Studies*, ed. John McLeod. London: Routledge, 2007. 32–45.

Fraser, Robert. *Book History through Postcolonial Eyes: Re-writing the Script*. London: Routledge, 2008.

Gilroy, Paul. *After Empire: Melancholia or Convivial Culture?* Abingdon: Routledge, 2004.

Glen, Stanley J. *The Parables of Conflict in Luke*. Philadelphia: Westminster, 1962.

Goff, Barbara, ed. *Classics and Colonialism*. London: Duckworth, 2005.

Goff, Barbara. "Introduction," in *Classics and Colonialism*, ed. Barbara Goff. London: Duckworth, 2005. 1–24.

Gupta, Akhil. *Postcolonial Developments: Agriculture in the Making of India*. Durham, NC: Duke University Press, 1998.

Hakluyt, Richard. *Discourse of Western Planting*, eds David B. Quinn and Alison M. Quinn. London: Hakluyt Society, 1993.

References

Hardt, Michael and Negri, Antonio. *Empire*. Cambridge: Harvard University Press, 2000.

Hardy, Spence R. *The Sacred Books of the Buddhists Compared with History and Modern Science*. Colombo: Wesleyan Mission Press, 1863.

Harrison, Nicholas. *Postcolonial Criticism, History, Theory and the Work of Fiction*. Cambridge: Polity, 2003.

Hendrickx, Herman. *The Parables of Jesus: Studies in the Synoptic Gospels*. London: Chapman, 1986.

Hirai, Kinza Rigue M. "The Real Position of Japan toward Christianity," in *The World's Parliament of Religions: An Illustrated and Popular History of the World's First Parliament of Religions Held in Chicago in Connection with the Columbian Exposition of 1893*, vol. I, ed. John Henry Barrows. Chicago: Parliament, 1893. 444–450.

hooks, bell. *Teaching to Transgress: Education as the Practice of Freedom*. New York: Routledge, 1994.

Hooper, J.S.M. *The Bible in India with a Chapter on Ceylon*. London: Oxford University Press, 1938.

Horrell, David G. "Introduction," *Journal for the Study of the New Testament* 27, 3 (2005), 251–255.

Horsley, R.A. *Paul and Empire: Religion and Power in Roman Imperial Society*. Harrisburg, PA: Trinity, 1997.

Horsley, R.A. "Renewal Movements and Resistance to Empire in Ancient Judea," in *The Postcolonial Biblical Reader*, ed. R.S. Sugirtharajah. Oxford: Blackwell, 2006. 69–77.

Israel, H. "Cutchery Tamil versus Pure Tamil: Contesting Language Use in the Translated Bible in the Early-Nineteenth-Century Protestant Tamil Community," in *The Postcolonial Biblical Reader*, ed. R.S. Sugirtharajah. Oxford: Blackwell, 2006. 269–283.

Jenkins, Simon. "Democracy Is Ill Served by Its Self-Appointed Guardians," *The Guardian* (March 5, 2008), 35.

Jeremias, Joachim. *The Parables of Jesus*, rev. edn. London: SCM, 1963.

Jobling, D. "Very Limited Ideological Options: Marxism and Biblical Studies in Postcolonial Scenes," in *Postcolonial Biblical Criticism: Interdisciplinary Intersections*, eds S.D. Moore and F.F. Segovia. London: Clark, 2005. 184–201.

Johnston, E.H., ed. *Asvaghosa's Buddhacarita or Acts of the Buddha*. Delhi: Motilal Banarsidass, 1984.

Jones, J.J., ed. *The Mahavastu Volume I*. London: Luzac, 1949.

Jones, J.J., ed. *The Mahavastu Volume II*. London: Luzac, 1952.

Jowett, Benjamin. "On the Interpretation of Scripture," in *Essays and Reviews*, 6th edn. Longmans, Green, 1861. 330–433.

Kelber, W.H. "Roman Imperialism and Christian Scribality," in *The Postcolonial Biblical Reader*, ed. R.S. Sugirtharajah. Oxford: Blackwell, 2006. 96–111.

Kim, U.Y. *Decolonizing Josiah: Toward a Postcolonial Reading of the Deuteronomistic History*. Sheffield: Sheffield Phoenix, 2005.

King, K.L. "Canonization and Marginalization: Mary of Magdala," in *The Postcolonial Biblical Reader*, ed. R.S. Sugirtharajah. Oxford: Blackwell, 2006. 284–290.

King, Richard C., ed. *Post-Colonial America*. Urbana, IL: University of Illinois Press, 2000.

Koschorke, Klaus, Ludwig, Frieder, and Delgado, Mariano, eds. *A History of Christianity in Asia, Africa, and Latin America 1450–1990: A Documentary Source Book*. Grand Rapids, MI: Eerdmans, 2007.

Kwok, Pui-lan. "Making the Connections: Postcolonial Studies and Feminist Biblical Interpretation," in *The Postcolonial Biblical Reader*, ed. R.S. Sugirtharajah. Oxford: Blackwell, 2006. 45–63.

Lapham, Henry A. *The Bible as Missionary Handbook*. Cambridge: Heffer, 1925.

Le, Nam. *The Boat*. Edinburgh: Canongate, 2009.

Lewis, C.S. *God in the Dock: Essays on Theology and Ethics*, ed. Walter Hooper. Grand Rapids, MI: Eerdmans, 1970.

Liew, T.-s.B. "Tyranny, Boundary, and Might: Colonial Mimicry in Mark's Gospel," in *The Postcolonial Biblical Reader*, ed. R.S. Sugirtharajah. Oxford: Blackwell, 2006. 206–223.

Liew, T.-s.B. "The Gospel of Mark," in *A Postcolonial Commentary on the New Testament Writings*, eds F.F. Segovia and R.S. Sugirtharajah. London: Clark, 2007. 105–132.

Life in the United Kingdom: A Journey to Citizenship. Norwich: Stationery Office, 2004.

Loomba, Ania, Kaul, Suvir, and Bunzl, Matti, eds. *Postcolonial Studies and Beyond*. Durham, NC: Duke University Press, 2005.

Mahdi, Kamil. "Iraqis Will Not Be Pawns in Bush and Blair's War Game," *The Guardian* (February 25, 2003), 20.

Malalgoda, Kitsiri. *Buddhism in Sinhalese Society 1750–1900: A Study of Religious Revival and Change*. Berkeley, CA: University of California Press, 1976.

Malina, Bruce J. "Mother and Son," *Biblical Theology Bulletin* 20, 2 (1990), 54–64.

References

Malina, Bruce J. *Windows on the World of Jesus: Time Travel to Ancient Judea.* Louisville, KY: Westminster/Knox, 1993.

Manguel, Alberto. *A History of Reading.* London: Flamingo, 1997.

Martin, Hugh. *The Parables of the Gospels and Their Meaning for Today.* London: SCM, 1937.

Mbuwayesango, D.R. "How Local Divine Powers Were Suppressed: A Case of Mwari of the Shona," in *The Postcolonial Biblical Reader*, ed. R.S. Sugirtharajah. Oxford: Blackwell, 2006. 259–268.

Mbuwayesango, D.R. "Canaanite Women and Israelite Women in Deuteronomy: The Intersection of Sexism and Imperialism," in *Postcolonial Interventions: Essays in Honor of R.S. Sugirtharajah*, ed. T.-s.B. Liew. Sheffield: Sheffield Phoenix, 2009. 45–57.

McLeod, John, ed. *The Routledge Companion to Postcolonial Studies.* London: Routledge, 2007.

McLeod, John. "Introduction," in *The Routledge Companion to Postcolonial Studies*, ed. John McLeod. London: Routledge, 2007. 1–18.

McFadyen, J.F. *The Message of the Parables.* London: Clark, 1933.

Miliband, David. "UK Has Moral Duty to Intervene," *The Guardian* (February 12, 2008), 1.

Milne, Seumas. "This Attempt to Rehabilitate Empire is a Recipe for Conflict," *The Guardian* (June 10, 2010), 31.

Montefiore, C.G. *The Synoptic Gospels: Edited with an Introduction and a Commentary in Two Volumes*, vol. II. London: Macmillan, 1927.

Moore, S.D. *Empire and Apocalypse: Postcolonialism and the New Testament.* Sheffield: Sheffield Phoenix, 2006.

Moore, S.D. "Mark and Empire: 'Zealot' and 'Postcolonial' Readings," in *The Postcolonial Biblical Reader*, ed. R.S. Sugirtharajah. Oxford: Blackwell, 2006. 193–205.

Moxnes, Halvor, Blanton, Ward, and Crossley, James G. "Introduction," in *Jesus Beyond Nationalism: Constructing the Historical Jesus in a Period of Cultural Complexity.* London: Equinox, 2009. 1–7.

Mozoomdar, Protop Chunder. "The World's Religious Debt to Asia," in *The World's Parliament of Religions: An Illustrated and Popular History of the World's First Parliament of Religions Held in Chicago in Connection with the Columbian Exposition of 1893*, vol. II, ed. John Henry Barrows. Chicago: Parliament, 1893. 1083–1092.

Mozoomdar, Protop Chunder. "The Brahmo-Somaj," in *The World's Parliament of Religions: An Illustrated and Popular History of the World's First Parliament of Religions Held in Chicago in Connection with the Columbian*

Exposition of 1893, vol. I, ed. John Henry Barrows. Chicago: Parliament, 1893. 345–351.

Müller, Max F. *Chips from a German Workshop*, vol. IV. London: Longmans, Green, 1875.

Müller, Max F. "Preface to *The Sacred Books of the East*," in *The Sacred Books of the East Translated by Various Oriental Scholars*, ed. Max F. Müller. Oxford: Clarendon, 1879. ix–xxxviii.

Müller, Max F. *Physical Religion: The Gifford Lectures Delivered before the University of Glasgow 1890*. London: Longmans, Green, 1891.

Müller, Max F. "The Parliament of Religions: Chicago 1893," in *Collected Works of the Right Hon. F. Max Müller XVIII, II, Essays on the Science of Religion*. London: Longmans, Green, 1901. 324–341.

Nagarkar, B.B. "The Work of Social Reform in India," in *The World's Parliament of Religions: An Illustrated and Popular History of the World's First Parliament of Religions Held in Chicago in Connection with the Columbian Exposition of 1893*, vol. I, ed. John Henry Barrows. Chicago: Parliament, 1893. 767–779.

Nehru, Jawaharlal. *Glimpses of World History*. New Delhi: Jawaharlal Nehru Memorial Fund, 1982 (1935).

Niebuhr, Reinhold. *The Irony of American History*, with a new introduction by Andrew J. Bacevich. Chicago: Chicago University Press, 2008.

Nissen, Johannes. *Poverty and Mission: New Testament Perspectives on a Contemporary Theme*. Leiden: Interuniversity Institute for Missiological and Ecumenical Research, 1984.

Oakman, Douglas E. "The Buying Power of Two Denarii," *Foundations and Facets Forum* 3, 4 (1987), 33–38.

Okakura, Tenshin. *The Awakening of Japan*. London: Murray, 1905.

Panikkar, K.M. *Asian and Western Dominance: A Survey of the Vasco Da Gama Epoch of Asian History 1498–1945*. London: Allen and Unwin, 1959.

Phythian-Adams, W.J. "The Geography of the Holy Land," in *A New Commentary on the Holy Scripture Including the Apocrypha*, eds Charles Gore, Henry Leighton Goude, and Alfred Guillaume. London: SPCK, 1928. 634–646.

Pilch, John J. *The Cultural World of Jesus: Sunday by Sunday, Cycle B*. Collegeville, PA: Liturgical Press, 1994.

Pilch, John J. *The Cultural World of Jesus: Sunday by Sunday, Cycle A*. Collegeville, PA: Liturgical Press, 1995.

Pilch, John J. *The Cultural World of Jesus: Sunday by Sunday, Cycle C*. Collegeville, PA: Liturgical Press, 1997.

References

Pinto, Shiromi. *Trussed*. London: Serpent Tail, 2006.

Powell, Allan Mark. *What is Narrative Criticism?* Minneapolis: Fortress, 1990.

Powell, Jonathan. "Why the West Should Not Fear to Intervene," *The Observer* (November 18, 2007), 34.

Prior, M. *The Bible and Colonialism: A Moral Critique*. Sheffield: Sheffield Academic, 1997.

Quayson, Ato. *Postcolonialism: Theory, Practice or Process?* Cambridge: Polity, 2000.

Quick, Oliver Chase. *The Realism of Christ's Parables: Ida Hartley Lectures Delivered at Colne, Lancs, 1930*. London: SCM, 1931.

Ringe, S.H. "The Letter of James," in *A Postcolonial Commentary on the New Testament Writings*, eds F.F. Segovia and R.S. Sugirtharajah, London: Clark, 2007. 369–379.

Roy, Rammohun. *The English Works of Raja Rammohun Roy*, ed. Jogendra Chunder Ghose. New Delhi: Cosmo, 1906.

Rule, William Harris. *Oriental Records: Monumental Confirmatory of the Old Testament Scriptures*. London: Bagster, 1877.

Rushdie, Salman. *The Enchantress of Florence*. London: Cape, 2008.

Said, Edward W. *Orientalism*. London: Penguin, 1978.

Said, Edward W. *Culture and Imperialism*. London: Chatto & Windus, 1993.

Said, Edward W. "Orientalism and After," in *A Critical Sense: Interviews with Intellectuals*, ed. Peter Osborne. London: Routledge, 1996. 65–86.

Said, Edward W. "Edward Said in Conversation with Neeladri Bhattachrya, Suvir Kaul and Ania Loomba," *Interventions* 1, 1 (1998), 81–96.

Said, Edward W. *Power, Politics, and Culture: Interviews with Edward Said*, ed. with introduction by Gauri Viswanathan. New York: Pantheon, 2001.

Said, Edward W. *Orientalism*. London: Penguin, 2003.

Said, Edward W. *Humanism and Democratic Criticism*. New York: Columbia University Press, 2004.

Said, Edward W. "Thoughts on Late Style," *London Review of Books* (August 5, 2004), 3–7.

Said, Edward W. *On Late Style*. London: Bloomsbury, 2006.

Schmidt, Thomas E. *Hostility to Wealth in the Synoptic Gospels*. Sheffield: Sheffield Academic, 1987.

Schueller, Johar Malini. *U.S. Orientalisms: Race, Nation and Gender in Literature 1790–1890*. Ann Arbor, MI: University of Michigan Press, 1997.

Schweizer, Eduard. *The Good News According to Luke*. Atlanta, GA: Knox, 1984.

Scopes, Wilfred. *The Parables of Jesus and Their Meaning for the Indian Church Today*. Madras: Christian Literature Society, 1955.

Segovia, F.F. "Biblical Criticism and Postcolonial Studies: Toward a Postcolonial Optic," in *The Postcolonial Bible*, ed. R.S. Sugirtharajah. Sheffield: Sheffield Academic, 1998. 49–65.

Segovia, F.F. "Mapping the Postcolonial Optic in Biblical Criticism: Meaning and Scope," in *Postcolonial Biblical Criticism: Interdisciplinary Intersections*, eds S.D. Moore and F.F. Segovia. London: Clark, 2005. 23–78.

Sen, Amartya. *The Argumentative Indian: Writings on Indian History, Culture and Identity*. London: Allen Lane, 2005.

Sen, Keshub Chunder. *Keshub Chunder Sen's Lectures in India* (London: Cassell, 1901).

Sen, Keshub Chunder. *Keshub Chunder Sen's Lectures in India* (London: Cassell, 1904).

Sen, Keshub Chunder. *Keshub Chunder Sen in England: Diaries, Sermons, Addresses and Epistles*, reprint 1980 (Calcutta: Writers Workshop, 1871).

Shafak, Elif. *The Bastard of Istanbul*. London: Viking, 2007.

Sivasubramanian, A. *Kristhavamum Thamil sulalyum*. Madras: Vamsi, 2007.

Sivasubramanian, A. *Vasahappa: Dance Drama*. Palyamkottai: Folklore Resources and Research Centre, 2007.

Smith, George. *The Conversion of India: From Pantaenaus to the Present Time* A.D. *193–1893*. London: Murray, 1893.

Smith, George Adam. *The Historical Geography of the Holy Land Especially in Relation to the History of Israel and of the Early Church*. London: Hodder and Stoughton, 1909.

Soelle, Dorothee and Schottroff, Luise. *Jesus of Nazareth* (London: SPCK, 2002).

Spindler, H.R. "Indian Studies of the Gospel of John: Puzzling Contextualization," *Exchange* 27, 1 (1980), 1–54.

Spivak, Chakravorty Gayatri. *In the Other Worlds: Essays in Cultural Politics*. New York: Routledge, 1988.

Spivak, Chakravorty Gayatri. *The Postcolonial Critic: Interviews, Strategies, Dialogues*, ed. Sarah Harasym. New York: Routledge, 1990.

Spivak, Chakravorty Gayatri. *A Critique of Postcolonial Reason: Toward a History of the Vanishing Past*. Cambridge: Harvard University Press, 1999.

Spivak, Chakravorty Gayatri. *Death of a Discipline*. New York: Columbia University Press, 2003.

Spivak, Chakravorty Gayatri. *Other Asias*. Malden, MA: Blackwell, 2008.

Stone, Norman. "Why the Empire Must Strike Back," *The Observer* (August 18, 1996), 22.

Strandenaes, Thor. "Anonymous Bible Translators: Native Literati and the Translation of the Bible into Chinese 1807–1907," in *Sowing the Word: The Cultural Impact of the British and Foreign Bible Society 1804–2004*, eds Stephen Batalden, Kathleen Cann, and John Dean. Sheffield: Sheffield Phoenix, 2004. 121–148.

Sugirtharajah, R.S. "From Orientalist to Post-colonial: Notes on Reading Practices," *Asia Journal of Theology* 10, 1 (April 1996), 20–27.

Sugirtharajah, R.S. *Asian Biblical Hermeneutics and Postcolonialism: Contesting the Interpretations*. Maryknoll, NY: Orbis, 1998.

Sugirtharajah, R.S. "A Postcolonial Exploration of Collusion and Construction in Biblical Interpretation," in *The Postcolonial Bible*, ed. R.S. Sugirtharajah. Sheffield: Sheffield Academic, 1998. 91–116.

Sugirtharajah, R.S. *The Bible and the Third World: Precolonial, Colonial and Postcolonial Encounters*. Cambridge: Cambridge University Press, 2001.

Sugirtharajah, R.S. *Postcolonial Criticism and Biblical Interpretation*. Oxford: Oxford University Press, 2002.

Sugirtharajah, R.S., ed. *The Postcolonial Biblical Reader*. Oxford: Blackwell, 2006.

Suzuki, Daisetz Teitaro, trans. *The Lankavatra Sutra: A Mahayana Text*. London: Routledge, 1932.

Swami Vivekananda. "Hinduism," in *The World's Parliament of Religions: An Illustrated and Popular History of the World's First Parliament of Religions Held in Chicago in Connection with the Columbian Exposition of 1893*, vol. I, ed. John Henry Barrows. Chicago: Parliament, 1863. 128–129, 968–978.

Swete, Henry Barclay. *The Apocalypse of St John: The Greek Text with Introduction, Notes and Indices*. London: Macmillan, 1922.

Syjuco, Miguel. *Ilustrado*. New York: Farrar, Straus and Giroux, 2010.

Tacitus. *The Agricola and Germany of Tacitus*, trans. Alfred John Church and William Jackson Brodribb. London: Macmillan, 1808.

Tamez, E. "The Hermeneutical Leap of Today," *Semeia* 75 (1996), 203–205.

Taylor, Clair. "The Spanish and Portuguese Empires," in *The Routledge Companion to Postcolonial Studies*, ed. John McLeod. London: Routledge, 2007. 46–58.

Tennent, James Emerson. *Christianity in Ceylon: Introduction and Progress under the Portuguese, the Dutch, the British, and American Missions: With an Historical Sketch of the Brahmanical and Buddhist Superstitions*. London: Murray, 1850.

Tharoor, Shashi. *The Great Indian Novel*. New Delhi: Penguin, 1989.

Tibawi, A.L. *English Speaking Orientalists: A Critique of Their Approach to Islam and Arab Nationalism*. London: Luzac, 1964.

Tiffin, Helen and Huggan, Graham. *Postcolonial Ecocriticism: Literature, Animals, Environment*. London: Routledge, 2010.

Trautmann, Thomas R., ed. *The Madras School of Orientalism: Producing Knowledge in Colonial South India*. New Delhi: Oxford University Press, 2009.

Trinidad, Saul. "Christology, Conquista, Colonization," in *Faces of Jesus: Latin American Christologies*, ed. José Míguez Bonino. Maryknoll, NY: Orbis, 1983. 49–65.

Vidal, John. "The Great Green Land Grab," *The Guardian G2* (February 13, 2008), 6–9.

Viswanathan, Gauri. "Introduction," in *Power, Politics, and Culture: Interviews with Edward Said*, ed. Gauri Viswanathan. New York: Pantheon, 2001. xi–xxi.

West, G.O. "What Difference Does Postcolonial Biblical Criticism Make? Reflections from a (South) African Perspective," in *Postcolonial Interventions: Essays in Honor of R.S. Sugirtharajah*, ed. T.-s.B. Liew. Sheffield: Sheffield Phoenix, 2009. 256–273.

Whitelam, K.W. *The Invention of Ancient Israel: The Silencing of Palestinian History*. London: Routledge, 1996.

Williams, Raymond. *Culture and Society*. London: Hogarth, 1993.

Wintour, Patrick. "Miliband: UK Has Moral Duty to Intervene," *The Guardian* (February 12, 2008), 1.

Woolf, Virginia. *A Room of One's Own*. Harmondsworth: Penguin, 1945.

Wright, G. Ernest. *The Old Testament against Its Environment*. London: SCM, 1950.

Wright, G. Ernest. "The Old Testament: A Bulwark of the Church against Paganism," *Occasional Bulletin from the Missionary Research Library* 14, 4 (1963), 1–10.

References

Young, Robert J.C. *Postcolonialism: An Historical Introduction.* Oxford: Blackwell, 2001.

Zerbe, G. and Orevillo-Montenegro, M. "The Letter to the Colossians," in *A Postcolonial Commentary on the New Testament Writings,* eds F.F. Segovia and R.S. Sugirtharajah. London: Clark, 2007. 294–303.

Index of Scriptural References

Acts
Acts, 73
2.43–7, 169
4.32–7, 169
4.37, 169
5.1–11, 169
10.1, 169
11.27–30, 168
13.1, 169
13.7, 169
16:13–40, 106
16.14–15, 169
16.20–1, 154
17.6–7, 154
17.12, 169

1 Corinthians
1 Corinthians, 73
6.1–8, 155
7.29, 65
7.31, 65

Colossians
1.13–20, 82
2.8–34, 82

Daniel
1, 58, 64
2.21, 154

Deuteronomy
Deuteronomy, 85
11.24, 25, 181
14.2, 181

Ecclesiastes
Ecclesiastes, 152

Enoch
46.5, 154

Ephesians
Ephesians, 85
6.12, 39

Exploring Postcolonial Biblical Criticism: History, Method, Practice, First Edition.
R. S. Sugirtharajah.
© 2012 R. S. Sugirtharajah, with the exception of Chapter 3 © 2012 Blackwell Publishing Ltd.
Published 2012 by Blackwell Publishing Ltd.

Index of Names and Subjects

Exploring Postcolonial Biblical Criticism: History, Method, Practice, First Edition.
R. S. Sugirtharajah.
© 2012 R. S. Sugirtharajah, with the exception of Chapter 3 © 2012 Blackwell Publishing Ltd.
Published 2012 by Blackwell Publishing Ltd.

Index of Names and Subjects

Index of Names and Subjects